Sociology of the

Series Editors
Katherine Appleford
Kingston University London
London, UK

Anna Goulding
University of Newcastle
Newcastle, UK

Dave O'Brien
University of Edinburgh
Edinburgh, UK

Mark Taylor
University of Sheffield
Sheffield, UK

This series brings together academic work which considers the production and consumption of the arts, the social value of the arts, and analyses and critiques the impact and role of cultural policy and arts management. By exploring the ways in which the arts are produced and consumed, the series offers further understandings of social inequalities, power relationships and opportunities for social resistance and agency. It highlights the important relationship between individual, social and political attitudes, and offers significant insights into the ways in which the arts are developing and changing. Moreover, in a globalised society, the nature of arts production, consumption and policy making is increasingly cosmopolitan, and arts are an important means for building social networks, challenging political regimes, and reaffirming and subverting social values across the globe.

More information about this series at
http://www.palgrave.com/gp/series/15469

Victoria Durrer • Raphaela Henze
Editors

Managing Culture

Reflecting On Exchange In Global Times

Editors
Victoria Durrer
Queen's University Belfast
Belfast, UK

Raphaela Henze
Heilbronn University
Künzelsau, Germany

ISSN 2569-1414   ISSN 2569-1406   (electronic)
Sociology of the Arts
ISBN 978-3-030-24648-8   ISBN 978-3-030-24646-4   (eBook)
https://doi.org/10.1007/978-3-030-24646-4

This Palgrave Macmillan imprint is published by the registered company Springer Nature Switzerland AG.
The registered company address is: Gewerbestrasse 11, 6330 Cham, Switzerland

Acknowledgements

We would like to thank the Arts and Humanities Research Council in the United Kingdom. This publication has been made possible through their funding of our international research network, *Brokering Intercultural Exchange: Interrogating the Role of Arts and Cultural Management* (www. managingculture.net), in addition to support from the Würth Foundation. We also thank the many researchers, practitioners, and policymakers who took part in our seminars so far. Without them, these contents would not have been possible.

Praise for *Managing Culture*

"This important book focuses on a relatively neglected aspect of cultural policy: the training, methods, practices, and agenda-setting by cultural managers Equally important is the exchange among managers, communities and institutions and the encounter of values and perspectives on their practice. Indeed, the book itself is a product—and future direction—of such an exchange, an ongoing one that can be followed and joined online."

—George Yúdice, *Professor of Latin American Studies, and of Modern Languages and Literatures at the University of Miami, USA*

"The Enlightenment claim for the universal nature of European culture looks ever more fragile in a globalising world with changing power dynamics. This valuable book questions the critical assumptions underlying the systems of thought and practice in contemporary artistic production, highlighting especially the mutual reinforcement of dominant approaches in education and management. A bracing, vital read for anyone concerned with cultural management, which helps distinguish habit and self-interest from what might be of real and lasting value."

—Francois Matarasso, *Community artist and writer*

Contents

Notes on Contributors

Hilary S. Carty is Director of the Clore Leadership Programme and an experienced lecturer, consultant, facilitator and coach, specialising in leadership development, management and organisational change. A published Visiting Professor/Lecturer, Hilary's work in arts and cultural development has been recognised with the award of Honorary Doctorates from leading universities in the UK.

Milena Dragićević-Šešić is Professor and Head of the UNESCO Chair in Studies of Interculturalism, Art and Cultural Management, and Mediation in the Balkans at the University of Arts in Belgrade. She is also the director of the Research Institute of the Faculty of Dramatic Arts and Guest Lecturer at numerous world universities. She has published 16 books and 150 essays in 17 languages and received the Ordre des Palmes académiques in 2002.

Victoria Durrer is Senior Lecturer in Arts Management and Cultural Policy, Queen's University Belfast, UK, and the co-founder of Brokering Intercultural Exchange, an AHRC-funded research network on arts and cultural management, and the all-island research network, Cultural Policy Observatory, Ireland. She is a co-editor of the *Routledge Handbook of Global Cultural Policy*.

Carla Figueira is Director of the MA in Cultural Policy, Relations and Diplomacy and of the MA in Tourism and Cultural Policy at the Institute for Creative and Cultural Entrepreneurship, Goldsmiths, University of London, UK. Before becoming an academic, she was an arts manager at the Department of Culture of the Municipality of Lisbon, Portugal.

Aimee Fullman is Director of the Arts Management Program at George Mason University, USA. She has worked as a researcher, policy adviser, programme manager and deputy director for such notable institutions as the British Council, National Endowment for the Arts, Americans for the Arts, UNESCO, Institute of International Education, American Voices and the Foundation Center.

Lisa Gaupp is Research Associate at Leuphana University of Lueneburg, Germany, and co-editor of *Diversity and Otherness between Standards and Life-Worlds: A Transcultural Approach*. She was a fellow of the German National Academic Foundation, lived in the USA, Haiti, Guatemala and Spain, and was Executive Manager of the 2009 Hannover International Violin Competition.

Raphaela Henze is Professor of Arts Management at Heilbronn University in Germany and Co-Investigator of the Arts & Humanities Research Council funded, international and transdisciplinary network Brokering Intercultural Exchange (www.managingculture.net). Prior to joining Heilbronn University, Henze worked in several senior management positions in universities, ministries and non-profit organisations. Her main research focus is on the impacts of globalisation and internationalisation on arts management and arts management education as well as on the role of arts and culture in times of rising populism. She has published widely on these topics and has been a speaker at numerous international conferences.

Javier J. Hernández-Acosta is Assistant Professor and Director of the Business Department at Universidad del Sagrado Corazón in Puerto Rico. He is the founder of Inversión Cultural, a non-profit organisation that supports creative industries and author of the book *Emprendimiento*

Creativo. He is also a musician, creative entrepreneur and board member of multiple cultural organisations.

Ruhi Jhunjhunwala is a Cultural Manager from India. She has worked primarily in the performing arts sector and specialises in festival management and international collaborations. She was the festival manager of the Attakkalari India Biennial, a contemporary movement arts festival in Bangalore, before moving to London to study MA in Performance and Culture Studies at Goldsmiths, University of London.

Shu-Shiun Ku is Assistant Professor in the Department of Cultural and Creative Industries at the National Pingtung University, Taiwan. She was the CEO of the 2017 National Cultural Congress and Culture White Paper project. Previously, she had worked in the media sector and a government institution in Taiwan.

Jerry C. Y. Liu is Professor and Director of Graduate School of Arts Management and Cultural Policy at the National Taiwan University of Arts. He is the President of Taiwan Association of Cultural Policy Studies. Liu is the author of *ReOrient: An East Asian Approach on Cultural Policy and Cultural Governance* (2018, in Chinese).

Nina Mihaljinac is Assistant Professor of Cultural Management and Cultural Policy at the Faculty of Dramatic Arts and UNESCO Chair in Cultural Management in Cultural Policy at the University of Arts in Belgrade. She is also a guest lecturer at the Université Lumière Lyon 2.

Melissa Nisbett is Senior Lecturer in the Department of Culture, Media and Creative Industries at King's College London. Her research explores the relationship between culture and power, and she has published widely on a range of topics including cultural policy, cultural diplomacy, soft power, cultural tourism and cultural relations.

Kayla Rush is an anthropologist of art, music and performance. She teaches sociology at Clark State Community College in Springfield, Ohio, and is General Editor of the *Irish Journal of Anthropology*. She is co-editor of a forthcoming special issue of *Liminalities*, titled *Performance and Politics, Power and Protest.*

J. P. Singh is Professor of International Commerce and Policy at the Schar School of Policy and Government, George Mason University. Singh has authored six scholarly books, edited four books and published nearly 100 scholarly articles. He has worked with international organisations such as UNESCO, the World Bank and World Trade Organization.

Maruška Svašek is Reader in Anthropology in the School of History and Anthropology, Queen's University Belfast. Major publications include *Anthropology, Art and Cultural Production* (2007), *Moving Subjects, Moving Objects: Transnationalism, Cultural Production and Emotions* (2012), and (with Birgit Meyer) *Creativity in Transition. Politics and Aesthetics of Cultural Production Across the Globe* (2016).

Amy Walker is Cultural Manager and Consultant specialising in supporting the professional development of artists and international exchange initiatives. Previous positions include Executive Director of Highlight Arts, an Edinburgh-based arts organisation that programmes international events and festivals, and Deputy Director of Gasworks and Triangle Network, a global network of grass-roots arts organisations.

Abbreviations

2017 NCCWP	2017 National Cultural Congress and Culture White Paper
AAAE	Association of Arts Administration Educators
ALIA	The Asian League of Institutes of the Arts
ANCER	Asia Pacific Network for Cultural Education Research
CCA	Council for Cultural Affairs
CEP	Community Empowerment Project
CP	Cultural Policy
CSSTA	Cross-Strait Service Trade Agreement
Cultural Renewal	Preparatory Office for the Cultural Renewal Foundation
DPP	Democratic Progressive Party
ECF	European Cultural Foundation
ELIA	European League of Institutes of the Arts
ENCATC	European Network on Cultural Management and Policy
EU	European Union
EUNIC	European Union National Institutes for Culture
GDP	Gross Domestic Product
HDR	Human Development Report
HE	Higher education
HR	Human resources
ICP	Institute of Puerto Rican Culture (Spanish)
IDB	International Development Bank
IPCC	Intergovernmental Panel on Climate Change

IR	International relations
KMT	Kuomintang
LTD	Limited
MA	Master
MDG	Millennium development goals
MENA	Middle East North Africa
MOC	Ministry of Culture
NCP	National Cultural Policy
NEA	National Endowment for the Arts
NGO	Non-governmental Organization
NTUA	National Taiwan University of Arts
PRC	People's Republic of China
PRSP	Poverty Reduction Strategy Papers
ROC	Republic of China
SDG	United Nations Sustainable Development Goals
SIDA	Swedish International Development Cooperation Agency
SMART	Strategic Management in the Arts for Theatre
TAM	Training assistance missions
TAPCS	Taiwan Association of Cultural Policy Studies
ToT	Training for trainers
UK	United Kingdom
UN	United Nations
UNCTAD	United Nations Conference on Trade and Development
UNDP	United Nations Development Programme
UNESCO	United Nations Educational, Scientific and Cultural Organization
US	United States
USA	United States of America
WDR	World Development Report

List of Figures

List of Tables

1

Introduction

Victoria Durrer and Raphaela Henze

While not a new phenomenon, globalisation and internationalisation have facilitated new means for "crossovers between cultures." (Bennett, 2001, p. 19). While globalisation refers to the process of increasing social, economic and political international exchange and interdependency, internationalisation is understood as:

> specific policies and programmes undertaken by governments [and] academic systems [and] institutions, and even individual departments that cope with or exploit globalisation (Altbach, 2004, p. 6).

Both facilitate new forms of exchange between individuals and groups across cultures and between and within nations. The exchange of cultural

V. Durrer (✉)
Queen's University Belfast, Belfast, UK
e-mail: v.durrer@qub.ac.uk

R. Henze
Heilbronn University, Künzelsau, Germany
e-mail: raphaela.henze@hs-heilbronn.de

© The Author(s) 2020
V. Durrer, R. Henze (eds.), *Managing Culture*, Sociology of the Arts,
https://doi.org/10.1007/978-3-030-24646-4_1

values, ideas, and knowledge this brings can lead to forms of 'cultural colonialism' and inequality. Such exchanges can equally offer new, creative and alternative cultural experiences (Cowan, 2002, p. 6; Dewey & Wyszomirski, 2004).

Much literature has explored these ideas in relation to culture more broadly (Mishra, 2017) and heritage and museums (Bennett, 1995; Clifford, 1997; MacDonald, 1998; Gray, 2015) as well as popular or commercial and broadcast arts (Miller, 2007; Singh, 2011). This collection explores these ideas within the field of arts and cultural management.[1] In 'managing' creative and aesthetic expressions, as symbolic expressions of culture (Hall, 1997), the contributions here largely focus on the fine visual and performing arts (theatre, dance and music). As Ebewo and Sirayi (2009) explain,

> culture plays such a fundamental role in shaping the personality of an individual in society and the character of the world that due attention must be given to the management of its organisations and institutions. (p. 281)

Yet despite important art historical research (see Brockington, 2009), Isar (2012) rightly points out that research has largely neglected fuller consideration of how cultural workers are active agents who "transmit", guard, and exchange "ideas, values and practices [within] global economic change" (pp. 2–3), thus influencing the politics of representation on a global scale.

Consideration of socialisation processes existing in arts and cultural management practice but also in education and training are critical to this discussion. These processes include the exchange between 'cultures' that take place in the devising, development, delivery and staging of artistic and cultural projects and productions. They also include examination of teaching and learning experiences concerning that practice. In fact, the growing professionalisation of arts and cultural management practice through the standardisation and legitimation that education and training now provide on an international scale plays as important a role in representation as the practice of management itself (see Shome, 2009). To date, the role of either and their integration as social practices in the politics of representation, has yet to be fully interrogated.

What research does exist is siloed and disconnected. It focuses on particular cultural forms or is isolated in different academic disciplines or in arts and cultural management practice handbooks and readers. Further, while there has been some research on the personal experiences of exchange within practice (Rösler, 2015; Rowntree, Neal, & Fenton, 2010), there has been virtually none regarding education. Practitioners, researchers and educators have thus lacked opportunity to question how the field's dominant ideologies and their own actions impact on global exchange (Henze, 2017). This limitation has so far stilted critical discourse on the subject (DeVereaux, 2009). It has also narrowed the potential for understanding the field's impact on cultural understanding and rights on a societal level.

Chapters in this collection address this gap. Contributions consider the institutions, organisations, groups and individuals who coordinate and lead the protection, marketing, mediation and financial organisation of creative and aesthetic expressions. They also consider the experiences of those involved in, and in receipt of, education and training. Ways in which 'crossovers' are explored in this context include:

1. project activities between individuals, institutions and/or organisations working or residing in different countries and the experience of those involved in them; and
2. teaching and learning within higher education as well as training activities led by cultural institutions.

Consequently, the contributions presented see 'exchange' as interaction between individuals, communities (of identity and of practice), institutions, and/or nations with different (and perhaps similar) values and perspectives.

Culture

In thinking about 'culture', we approach the term in three ways. First, in the anthropological sense of culture as a whole 'way of life', such as language, habits and common traditions (Williams, 1989, p. 6). Such aspects are 'ordinary'. That is, they are commonly known, understood and shared amongst a group of people in ways that shape collective identity and the common reasons and processes for how and why groups come to conduct life in specific social, political and economic ways (NicCraith, 2003)—cultural logics, as it were.

Secondly, it is an approach to understanding culture "in the context of artistic output" (Paquette & Beauregard, 2018, p. 19). These are the symbolic forms of representation through which we produce, reproduce, circulate and interpret meaning (Hall, 1997, p. 3). Meaning here refers to "ideas, knowledge, values and beliefs" (Hesmondhalgh & Saha, 2013, p. 188). Often times, artistic output is used to mark "differences and similarities in taste and status within [and among] social groups" (Miller & Yúdice, 2002, p. 1). Paquette and Beauregard (2018, p. 19) refer to this marking as the 'aesthetic register', which has resonance in the anthropological sense of culture. They explain

> Much in the same way that culture in the aesthetic register is understood as a question of taste, so do the elements of culture-as-a-way-of-life—that is to say the language, customs, etc., that go into a culture—represent tastes and choices—albeit "unconscious canons of choice" (Benedict, 1934[2005], pp. 47–48) that have gradually evolved and come into being [over time]. (p. 19)

How this comes into being, relates in part to our final interpretation of culture: the culture of a field—arts and cultural management. As a field, those engaging in arts and cultural management come to share (and possibly contest) knowledge, habits, traditions, language and values, which are in turn informed by, and informing of, the forms of culture discussed above (Paquette & Redaelli, 2015; Bourdieu, 1993). Knowledge in the field is shaped through the work of practitioners and consultants and by academic researchers from diverse disciplines (anthropology, cultural policy, cultural studies, sociology, management and political science). Education and training, organisational cultures, recruitment practices, and personal, social as well as professional relationships are some of the ways in which people come to learn and/or question these forms of knowledge, traditions, language and values (Brim & Wheeler, 1966).

To elaborate, the decisions taken and avoided in showcasing particular artists and in framing their work both physically and conceptually through marketing materials and exhibition and staging choices are part of a process of meaning making and representation (in the anthropological sense of culture). Studies investigating reception of work and evidencing social and economic impact of that experience equally plays a part. The establishment of education and training has particularly come to 'professionalise' and legitimise these practices, in ways that were once largely established from learning-in-practice or learning through work or career development (Suteu, 2006). As 'signifying practices', together these processes contribute to the setting of "the rules, norms and conventions by which social life is ordered and governed" (Hall, 1997, p 4).

Management and Culture

In further exploring the notion of 'managing culture' presented in this collection, it has been useful to draw on the work of the late Zygmunt Bauman (2004), which provides deft explication of the relationship of one to the other. Taking a historical and sociological approach, his work reminds us of the chronology of things, as it were, where the emergence of the term 'management' predated that of 'culture'. In doing so, he detailed the nature of power and control that is deeply embedded within each term. He (Bauman 2004) explained,

> Deep in the heart of the 'culture' concept lies the premonition or tacit acceptance of an unequal, asymmetrical social relation—the split between acting and bearing the impact of action, between the managers and the managed, the knowing and the ignorant, the refined and the crude. (p. 64)

Forms of regulation that exist between but also within nations are particularly implicated in the management of culture. As Singh (2018) explores this in detail elsewhere, it will not be repeated in full here. Of relevance to our discussion on arts and cultural management, he explains that regulation historically took the form of royal patronage, particularly within Europe, though not without its international reach and impact

(Keblusek & Noldus, 2011). This form was altered by industrialisation and the eventual growth of urbanisation, a rising middle class and the 'knowledge economy'. The growth of certain cultural industries, particularly in relation to commercial and broadcast arts, helped shape thinking about regulation as a form of 'public interest'; for instance, safeguarding access as well as ensuring market availability, increasing cultural democracy and preventing (or propagating) state propaganda (Singh, 2018).

Australia, the Republic of Ireland, Canada, the United Kingdom and the United States of America now see forms of regulation by way of an Arts Council model. Therein, the funding of arts and cultural activity is determined by an expert panel of arts and cultural 'peers' and arguably independent from government influence (and at varying degrees due to the nature of the cultural logics and public policies in those nations) (Upchurch, 2016; Durrer, 2018). Other nations, like China, take very different approaches. International bodies, such as the United Nations Educational Scientific and Cultural Organisation (UNESCO) and the European Union's (EU) Commission on Culture, have also come to play in the process of regulation over time (Singh, 2018; Dâmaso, 2018). For instance, the EU's Commission on Culture regulates, in some sense, cultural exchanges between (and in some cases beyond) European nations through Culture Cooperation funds, with goals of bringing nations together to celebrate a sense of shared 'European' identity and support transnational and international exchange and mobility.

Management also takes the form of administrative practices that can challenge or "reinforce historically and institutionally established aesthetic, [geopolitical and social] hierarchies" and ways of doing business (Negus, 2002, p. 512). Theories of practice demonstrate that ordinary, workplace experiences in addition to the ways in which people relate to and view one another can become habitual (Barnes, 2001). Described above in relation to arts and cultural management, the discourse in the field tends to focus on tactics and techniques in strategic planning, fundraising and marketing, for instance, rather than questioning why practitioners, organisations and institutions are engaged in such work and in those ways (DeVereaux, 2009). Yet arts and cultural management research shows that when in an unfamiliar situation, environment or circumstance, administrative routines and habits may be challenged and altered as a result (Durrer, 2017). Part of understanding the management of culture is understanding the negotiation that takes place between these broader forms of regulation and the everyday practices of management. This process is both personal and social.

Rights

Acknowledging the contested and paradoxical, yet inevitability of the relationship of management to culture and particularly within the neo-liberal project, Bauman's (2004) analysis shows us that 'voice', agency and rights (Freire, 1970; Hall, 1997; Chakravorty Spivak, 1988), are equally embedded in these terms: specifically, who, what and how particular 'cultural voices' are represented and how that is managed. In doing so, he positioned 'managers' and 'culture creators'—without fully defining who they might be—in a rivalry. He explained that while managers and culture creators have a shared goal: "to make the world different from what it is at the moment and/or from what it is likely to turn into if left alone" (2004, p. 65), they may disagree

> about the direction which…intervention should take. More often than not their strife is about who is to be in charge; to whom belongs, or ought to be given, the right to decide the direction, and to select the tools with which its pursuit is monitored as well as the measures by which its progress is assessed. (p. 65)

Educator and philosopher, Paolo Freire (1970) refers to cultural voice as the ability of people to name their world. Internationally, this may be most recognised as preservation and respect for cultural diversity and the right to 'choose cultural expressions' as a broader, human right, detailed within *UNESCO'S Universal Declaration on Cultural Diversity* (2002) and its subsequent *Convention* (UNESCO, 2005, Convention 3). Work by Yúdice (2009) and Bennett (2001) illustrate the varying colonial and postcolonial readings that may be made of these terms. This history makes navigating these terms on a global stage and within particular practices like arts and cultural management, difficult (Henze, this volume). The scope of who and what is included and excluded in this 'navigation' becomes even more problematic when considering that many policies and practices in relation to arts and cultural management are dominated by a 'cultural elite' existing in small, exclusive and self-legitimising networks of influence (Griffiths, Miles, & Savage, 2008). International exchanges may expand these networks, but it remains to be seen how inclusive they may actually be.

In fact, while attempting to promote difference and foster intercultural understanding, or the ability to know, accept, value and empathise with alternative perspectives and perceptions of the world (Marginson & Sawir, 2011), particular 'voices' and ideologies may dominate. 'Voices' and ideologies are disseminated by way of global corporations, but also through education, philosophy, religion, advertising and art (Singh, 2018, p. 89; Miller & Yúdice, 2002, p. 7) as well as arts and cultural management. These disciplines create representations that may foster anxieties, as much as a sense of familiarity and fellowship. Anxieties relate to fears of "foreign influences... refugees, terrorists, Chinese or Indian capital and products of religious ideas", Hollywood and Americanisation (Singh, 2018, p. 89). They also concern the merging, homogenising or even "loss of an identity" (Singh, 2018, p. 89). Further, they are experienced and exhibited individually, collectively and politically.

Ultimately, the employment and intention of terms, like 'cultural voice' and 'cultural diversity' in policy documents and declarations (see also the *United Nations Declaration on Human Rights*) are only *frameworks* of value. They are a means by which "groups and individuals can struggle to defend their preferences and ways of life" (Yúdice, 2009, p. 120). However such principles are "accepted" or not, established or not, realised or not, through social practices (Yúdice, 2009, p. 133). Arts and cultural management plays a key role in this regard. As a 'signifying practice' (Hall, 1997), the field of arts and cultural management, and the players within, determine what comes into representation, for whom, in what ways and to what extent. They read and interpret certain cultural expressions, thus granting, taking or shaping (particular) 'cultural voices'.

Contents

With these points in mind, we return to Bauman's (2004) positioning of 'management' and 'culture'. While we agree there is contestation in the management of culture, this volume seeks to raise two key points, oft-neglected in broader discussions on the topic, and particularly within forms of global exchange. First, while inherently mindful of the growing globalisation of culture over time, Bauman's reading (and not surprisingly) is highly influenced by Global North Western,[2] theories (e.g., Arendt, Adorno, Horkheimer) or 'knowledge regimes' (Liu, 2016, p. 2). As such, it is particularly related to a Global North Western interpretation of modernity, which at

> a basic level…is an expression of a society's sculpting of a 'good life' through methods, techniques and processes that the society sees as appropriate for the betterment of itself and the development of its population. (Shome, 2012, p. 202)

With growing emphasis on the relationship of artistic output—and the management of it—to fostering economic growth, a sense of identity, social cohesion, sustainable development, and peace and reconciliation on and across the global stage (Durrer, 2018), culture, in all our uses employed here, is particularly tied to this understanding of modernity. There is an assumption that globalisation has assisted in "spreading" modernity "from the West into 'backward' parts of the world" (Shome, 2012, p. 199; Featherstone, 1996). While we do not purport to say this is what Bauman (2004) meant, we highlight that narrow views on management as a notion of 'betterment' and the relationship of culture to that, neglects the unique cultural logics or values, ideologies and structures of particular nations, communities and peoples (Featherstone, 1996; Shome, 2012). Shome (2012) points out that the interpretation of 'betterment' may vary depending upon these differing cultural logics. Within arts and cultural management, Liu (2016) illustrates this point through application of Confucian, Buddhist and Taoist views and the traditional Chinese conception of nature to critique the growing managerialist approach to 'measuring' the economic, social, political, personal and aesthetic value of arts and cultural activities. The assumptions both Liu and Shome question are deeply ingrained and play out in the exchange activities that take place in the field of arts and cultural management. The contributors to this volume address the lack of exploration of these issues existing to date.

Second, while conceptually astute in implicating tradition, routine and habit as key aspects of how management is enacted and altered, Bauman's (2004) point neglects empirical analysis of the personal nature of the practice and how the personal is informing of the social nature of practice. The process of globalisation is "bound together in increasing webs of interdependencies and power balances" (Featherstone, 1995, pp. 12–13; Isar, 2012). While not necessarily equal, it is no longer possible to reduce an analysis of global exchange to a dichotomous discussion of 'the west and the rest' or of central and peripheral nations' (Featherstone, 1995). The role of individuals and their social interaction through exchange activities are thus crucial here to understanding how arts and cultural management as a field may reinforce particular values as well as promote new ones (Lidichi, 1997, p 205). As argued by Durrer (2017)

> individuals' associations and interactions with one another are as significant in establishing or challenging routines and habits as an individual's own skills and knowledge. (p27; see also Warde, 2014)

Contributors to this volume address this issue. In all of the forms discussed above, culture is not a stable, but rather a "fluid concept…a set of ideas reactions, expectations [in constant flux] as people and groups themselves change" (Watson, 1997, p. 8 from Nicrath, p. 2). The recognition of agency and influence of arts and cultural managers is important here. The authors take into account that the significance of this agency differs within different national and international contexts. Still, having a sense of

> when and how…routines, habits and codes [of practice, hierarchy and rules] are broken or maintained—by who, in what way ways, and with what consequences (Negus, 2002, p. 511)

can reveal how social and cultural hierarchies are manifest, challenged and upheld.

The chapters herein explore these ideas. The collection is divided into four sections: *conditions, practice, education* and *future directions.* Before detailing the discussions, we make a few acknowledgements. First, each contributor tackled the issues posed above from their own vantage points. These viewpoints are shaped by different national and local contexts, but also disciplines: arts and cultural management, anthropology, cultural and cultural policy studies, sociology and international relations and based in personalised practice, education and academic experiences. Mindful of the richness of these differing contexts, we did not all always agree on chosen terminology and language or their meaning. As such, each author takes as a starting point clarification of key terms which may be under debate. This illustrates the breadth of how the questions we pose collectively, may be approached individually.

Secondly, the opportunity to bring together these diverse viewpoints has been made possible through the Arts and Humanities Research Council (AHRC, UK), which funded our international and interdisciplinary research network, *Brokering Intercultural Exchange: Interrogating the Role of Arts and Cultural Management,* in 2016. While some point out the non-binding character of networks, we have experienced the opposite. Networks, particularly in the arts and cultural sector area, are an important resource and platform for providing the space for critical reflection (Cvjeticanin, 2011; Laaksonen, 2016; Henze, 2018). In initially establishing *Brokering Intercultural Exchange,* we started as a small and pre-formed group of 20, largely European, practitioners and researchers who were interested in exploring and questioning intercultural exchanges, particularly how and why they take place in arts and cultural management practice and education. We expected the group's work to come to a close, once the lifecycle of the grant was completed in 2018. Instead, the network grew, having brought together approximately 125 scholars, Ph.D. students, practitioners, policy-makers as well as artists from 25 countries across the globe for intensive workshops and discussions. In fact, individuals requested that it remain active, with continued annual events supported by the Würth Foundation and the generosity of colleagues we have met along the way. Work remains available and ongoing at www.managingculture.net with literature lists, podcasts, presentations and articles as well as continued gatherings, kept small to facilitate greater debate and discussion.

We take this opportunity to acknowledge the many individuals who took part in all these activities so far. While obviously not all participants could contribute pieces, we hope they will feel that their voices and ideas are here heard. Still, we know that voices are still missing in this collection. As a result, the orientation of some of these contributions is perhaps influenced by a Global North Western perspective (Shome, 2009) as is, undoubtedly, the shape of this volume. This absence does not, however, diminish the capacity of this collection to highlight how difference and power take shape within global exchange. Rather, it raises the importance of 'hidden voices' more strongly (Henze & Durrer, 2018). What is clear to us now, is that while we may be starting from different places and coming from different vantage points, there is a growing, though not self-important, recognition of our individual and professional place in how perceptions and realities of cultural rights are shaped through global exchange. This book reflects that recognition.

Conditions

The collection begins with discussions by Singh, Henze and Rush on broader issues that we have learned are shared across the experiences of arts and cultural management as a field. Singh focuses on two increasingly apparent dichotomies: a protectionism that is fostering greater support of national cultures alongside an encouragement of the recognition, inclusion and acceptance of cultural diversity and voice (Hall, 1997). The swing to the right in many European countries and the rise of populist parties in many different parts of the world make it ever more apparent that arts and cultural managers have a role to play in how cultures are represented within the context of globalisation.

These circumstances set the frame for debating the responsibilities and the role of managers as Henze does in her contribution about power mechanisms inherent in our (knowledge) systems, particularly focusing on the language we use in (international) arts and cultural management practice. She raises concerns about the ethnocentrism of our frames of reference and the marginalisation of discourses particularly from the Global South. An anthropologist, Rush also refers to language particularly in relation to 'value'. Taking influence from her discipline of study, she describes how differing, yet connected understandings of 'value' in arts and cultural management may foster a 'cracked art world'. She explores how this conceptualisation of 'value' may provide new mechanisms for debate and discussion for cultural exchanges in arts and cultural management.

Practice

Studies on arts and cultural management practice (Henze, 2017; Mandel & Allmanritter, 2016) indicate that the personality and goals of individual arts and cultural managers are significant influencers over national and institutional regulations, structures or procedures regarding how (and why) arts and cultural management is practised internationally. The role of arts and cultural management in representation can be evidenced in the practice of individual arts and cultural managers, individuals who "produce and mobilise culture" and are actors who determine what "particular cultural forms gain... in autonomy and prestige" (Featherstone, 1995, p. 3). A number of chapters address this point. Svasek's chapter speaks particularly to the role of arts managers as "re-writers" of art history not only in the establishment of arts centres but also in the works they select for display.

In considering European performing arts festivals, Gaupp focuses on the role of the 'festival curator', understood as a cultural broker, cultural intermediary as well as a gatekeeper who is embedded in a complex field of 'the curatorial'. As postcolonial critique, the chapter shows how curatorial practice is deeply influenced by power relations and conventions, as well as network structures and processes. She illustrates how such practices can, by selecting and promoting certain non-European artists, foster a 'canon of diversity' within a frame of paternalism.

Jhunjhunwala and Walker refer to this paternalism when reflecting on their experiences in numerous international and intercultural arts projects particularly in India and the UK. Their contribution acknowledges the "vital role" arts and cultural managers play "in ensuring that assumptions and stereotypes are not institutionalised." Debates on structure and agency are at play in their contribution, which implicitly calls for greater reflexivity in practice while also recognising the role of funders in facilitating this process.

Education

While separated within the volume in order to allow for a more focused analysis on their unique attributes and circumstances, the areas of practice and education are inextricably linked. Together, they make up the philosophical foundations that have developed the discipline, with practitioners often involved in the formation and teaching of higher educational and training courses. This consideration is set by Durrer who provides a snapshot of internationalisation in arts and cultural management education. With a particular focus on higher education, she demonstrates that there exists very little critical examination of programme development, curriculum design, and teaching and learning practices that have emerged alongside or even resulted from internationalisation. Durrer raises ethical concerns for educators working within this context and suggests ways to facilitate greater reflexivity in teaching and learning practice.

Looking at training initiatives led by international cultural institutes, Dragićević-Šešić and Mihaljinac refer to the geopolitical influence that shapes how arts and cultural management practice is legitimised. Their empirical study in Middle Eastern and North African countries (MENA) reveals how international arts and cultural "exchanges still largely flow from economic and former colonial powers". Done in culturally unaware and patronising ways, they may result in carrying through and reinforcing cultural inequalities existing at a global scale. Nisbett's empirical study of international student experience in a cultural industries programme in a United Kingdom university makes real the concerns that Durrer voices. By highlighting the challenges as well as tensions that internationalisation brings to the classroom, her contribution critically reflects on the vague but widespread assumption that international diversity will ipso facto enhance student learning experiences and facilitate intercultural understanding.

The conventions established through practice, and how they are disseminated or challenged through practitioners-as-teachers within arts and cultural management education is explored by Carty, a practitioner-educator herself. Her personal reflection on teaching as a 'culturally diverse' practitioner indicates some of the more widespread implications that such teaching has for how we, as a society, approach, relate to and understand ourselves and others. She reflects on her position, which uncomfortably situates her simultaneously as 'representative' of professional practice as well as an entire race, something equally reflected on in practice by Jhunjhunwala and Walker. Her contribution illustrates the inequalities historically and socially embedded in our higher education institutes and the discipline of arts and cultural management (Ahmed, 2012; Kilomba, 2013; Bennett, 1995) and how these may be navigated in the classroom.

Future Directions

This concluding section of the book addresses key concerns moving forward, specifically cultural rights and the environment. While all chapters point out challenges and ways forward, Hernández-Acosta presents an ideological slant on how we might view the agency and social role of arts and cultural managers and the profession more broadly. Ku and Liu think about these ideas in policymaking practice. Considering cultural rights, Ku and Liu test its potentials and limits through the co-governing and co-managing process of a cultural policy project, 2017 National Cultural Congress and Culture White Paper' (2017 NCCWP) in Taiwan. The authors suggest that the co-designed democratic mechanism, together with the empowering strategies, and co-governing/co-management strategies adopted there are the key to facilitate people's cultural rights in that context. Taking the lessons learned from this specific location more broadly, they argue that everyday contacts between various cultural groups will benefit public participation in cultural affairs and strengthen peoples' cultural rights.

Finally, the collection closes with consideration of the relationship of arts and cultural management to an issue that is shared on a global scale: The Earth's current ecological crisis. Figueira and Fullman reflect on the need to rethink cultural relations and exchange in order to meaningfully engage in creating solutions for this crisis within the interdisciplinary context of the Critical Zone. From this perspective, they examine relevant theory and practical aspects of international relations, arts and cultural management, and cultural policy to explore the possibilities and limitations of each of these areas of study in addressing sustainability during the Anthropocene era. Cultural relations and exchange are advocated for as critical contributions towards adapting to climate change alongside the underutilised potential of the arts and humanities. Bringing practice and education back together, cultural engagement within higher education, through arts and cultural management programmes, is then positioned as a significant leverage point intervention to change systems in order to achieve a sustainable cosmopolitan and inclusive human society.

The chapters presented use different methodologies and approaches but they all address issues that are of utmost importance in our transforming societies. As research by Henze (2017) has shown, internationalisation and globalisation cannot be avoided by arts and cultural managers regardless of where they are based or what kind of policies prevail in their respective countries. These chapters open up not only a scholarly debate on issues of exchange, but hopefully also a debate that has an impact on how we continue to work jointly, fairly and without paternalism on pressing issues of our time. We hope to find ways to bring together more voices from parts of the world thus far marginalised in our discourses. We are convinced that a knowledge base that is not limited to Western narratives will benefit the entire discipline. Having said this, it becomes apparent that still a lot of challenging as well as highly interesting work lies ahead. We are looking forward to continuing to contribute to this work through the *Brokering Intercultural Exchange* network and highly encourage our readers to join this discussion.

Notes

1. The discipline itself is varyingly referred to as 'arts management', 'arts administration', 'cultural administration' or 'cultural management', depending upon the national context. In an effort to represent this variety in as brief a way as possible, we have employed the term 'arts and cultural management' throughout the book. In some instances, authors refer specifically to 'arts management'.
2. While acknowledging that referring to the uniqueness of different nations and peoples in this fashion is reductive to an extent, for the sake of clarity of our broader argument, we refer to the Global North West as encompassing North America, Europe and Australasia.

References

Ahmed, S. (2012). *On being included: Racism and diversity in institutional life*. Durham, NC: Duke University Press.

Altbach, P. (2004). Globalisation and the university: Myths and realities in an unequal world. *Tertiary Education Management, 10*(1), 3–25.

Barnes, B. (2001). Practice as collective action. In T. Schatzki, K. Knorr-Cetina, & E. von Savigny (Eds.), *The practice turn in contemporary theory* (pp. 17–28). Abingdon: Routledge.

Bauman, Z. (2004). Culture and management. *Parallax, 10*(2), 63–72.

Benedict, R. (1934 [2005]). *Patterns of culture*. New York: Mariner Books.

Bennett, T. (1995). *The birth of the museum: History, theory, politics*. Abingdon: Routledge.

Bennett, T. (2001). *Differing diversities: Transversal study on the theme of cultural policy and cultural diversity*. Brussels: Council of Europe.

Bourdieu, P. (1993). *The field of cultural production*. Cambridge, UK: Polity Press.

Brim, O., & Wheeler, S. (1966). *Socialisation after childhood: Two essays*. New York: John Wiley & Sons.

Brockington, G. (2009). *Internationalism and the arts in Britain and Europe at the Fin de Siècle* (No. 4). Oxford: Peter Lang.

Clifford, J. (1997). *Museums as contact zones*. Cambridge, MA: Harvard University Press.

Cowan, T. (2002). *Creative destruction: How globalisation is changing the world's cultures*. Princeton, NJ: Princeton University Press.

Cvjeticanin, B. (2011). Networks: The evolving aspects of culture in the 21st century. *Cluturelink.org*. Retrieved October 6, 2016, from http://www.culturelink.org/publics/joint/clinkconf/Cvjeticanin_Networks.pdF

Dâmaso, M. (2018). The art collection of the United Nations: Origins, institutional framework and ongoing tensions. In V. Durrer, T. Miller, & D. O'Brien (Eds.), *The Routledge handbook of global cultural policy* (pp. 215–232). Abingdon: Routledge.

DeVereaux, C. (2009). Practice versus a discourse of practice in cultural management. *The Journal of Arts Management, Law, and Society, 39*(1), 65–72.

Dewey, P. & Wyszomirski, M. (2004). International issues in cultural policy and administration: A conceptual framework for higher education. *International Conference on Cultural Policy Research*, Montreal, Quebec. Retrieved March 22, 2016, from http://neumann.hec.ca/iccpr/PDF_Texts/Dewey_Wyszomirski.Pdf

Durrer, V. (2017). 'Let's see who's being creative out there': Lessons from the 'Creative Citizens' programme in Northern Ireland. *Journal of Arts & Communities, 9*(1), 15–37.

Durrer, V. (2018). The relationship between cultural policy and arts management. In V. Durrer, T. Miller, & D. O'Brien (Eds.), *The Routledge handbook of global cultural policy* (pp. 64–86). Abingdon: Routledge.

Ebewo, P., & Sirayi, M. (2009). The concept of arts/cultural management: A critical reflection. *The Journal of Arts Management, Law, and Society, 38*(4), 281–295.

Featherstone, M. (1995). *Undoing culture: Globalisation, postmodernism and identity*. London: Sage.

Featherstone, M. (1996). Localism, globalism, and cultural identity. In R. Wilson & W. Dissanayake (Eds.), *Global/local: Cultural production and the transnational imaginary* (pp. 46–77). Durham, NC and London: Duke University Press.

Freire, P. (1970). *Pedagogy of the oppressed*. New York: Continuum.

Gray, C. (2015). *The politics of museums*. Basingstoke: Palgrave Macmillan.

Griffiths, D., Miles, A., & Savage, M. (2008). The end of the English cultural elite? *The Sociological Review, 56*(1), 187–209.

Hall, S. (1997). Introduction. In S. Hall (Ed.), *Representation: Cultural representations and signifying practices* (pp. 1–11). London: Sage.

Henze, R. (this volume). More than just lost in translation: The ethnocentrism of our frames of reference and the underestimated potential of multilingualism. In V. Durrer & R. Henze (Eds.), *Managing culture: Reflecting on exchange in our global times* (pp. 51–80). Basingstoke: Palgrave Macmillan.

Henze, R. (2017). *Introduction to international arts management.* Weisbaden: Springer VS Verlag.

Henze, R. (2018). Eurocentrism in European arts management. In M. Dragisevic Sesic & J. Vickery (Eds.), *Cultural policy and populism* (pp. 31–43). Cultural Policy Yearbook, Istanbul Bilgi University. Istanbul: İletişim.

Henze, R., & Durrer, V. (2018). Reflecting on brokering exchange, Special issue: Cultural inequalities. *Arts Management Quarterly, (129)*, 3. Retrieved April 15, 2019, from https://www.artsmanagement.net/dlf/5680ecf0035b86 4c3a10f90c6c2502ab,1.pdf

Hesmondhalgh, D., & Saha, A. (2013). Race, ethnicity, and cultural production. *Popular Communication, 11*(3), 179–195.

Isar, Y. (2012). Shifting economic power: New horizons for cultural exchange in our multi-polar world. Salzburg Global Seminar, White Paper Theme 2, Salzburg, Vol. 8, Session 490. Retrieved October 10, 2016, from https://www.salzburgglobal.org/fileadmin/user_upload/Documents/2010-2019/2012/490/whitepaper3_490.pdf

Keblusek, M., & Noldus, B. V. (2011). *Double agents: Cultural and political brokerage in early modern Europe.* The Netherlands: Brill.

Kilomba, G. (2013). *Plantation memories: Episodes of everyday racism.* Münster: Unrast Verlag.

Laaksonen, A. (2016). D'Art Report 49 international culture networks. *Media. ifacca.org.* Retrieved September 14, 2016, from http://media.ifacca.org/files/DArt49_International_Culture_Networks.pdf

Lidichi, H. (1997). The poetics and politics of exhibiting other cultures. In S. Hall (Ed.), *Representation: Cultural representations and signifying practices* (pp. 151–222). London: Sage Publications.

Liu, J. C. Y. (2016). The ecology of culture and values: Implications for cultural policy and governance. *ENCATC Scholars*, 6, np. Retrieved April 15, 2019, from http://blogs.encatc.org/encatcscholar/?p=1592

Macdonald, S. (Ed.). (1998). *The politics of display: Museums, science, culture.* London and New York: Routledge.

Mandel, B. & Allmanritter, V. (2016). Internationalisation in the professional field of arts management—Effects, challenges, future goals and tasks for arts and cultural managers in international contexts. In F. Imperiale & M. Vecco (Eds.), *Cultural management education in risk societies—Towards a paradigm and policy shift?!, ENCATC Conference Proceedings* (pp. 262–276). Brussels: ENCATC. Retrieved February 8, 2019, from https://www.encatc.org/media/1487-encatc_ac_book_2016.pdf

Marginson, S., & Sawir, E. (2011). *Ideas for intercultural education*. Basingstoke: Palgrave Macmillan.

Miller, T. (2007). *Cultural citizenship cosmopolitanism, consumerism, and television in a neoliberal age*. Philadelphia: Temple University Press.

Miller, T., & Yúdice, G. (2002). Introduction: The history and theory of cultural policy. In T. Miller & G. Yúdice (Eds.), *Cultural policy* (pp. 1–34). London: Sage Publications.

Mishra, P. (2017). *Age of anger. A history of the present*. Milton Keynes: Penguin Random House.

Negus, K. (2002). The work of cultural intermediaries and the enduring distance between production and consumption. *Cultural Studies, 16*(4), 501–515.

NicCraith, M. (2003). *Culture and identity politics in Northern Ireland*. Basingstoke: Palgrave Macmillan.

Paquette, J., & Beauregard, D. (2018). Cultural policy in political science research. In V. Durrer, T. Miller, & D. O'Brien (Eds.), *The Routledge handbook of global cultural policy* (pp. 19–32). Abingdon: Routledge.

Paquette, J., & Redaelli, E. (2015). *Arts management and cultural policy research*. Basingstoke: Palgrave Macmillan.

Rösler, B. (2015). The case of Asialink's arts residency program: Towards a critical cosmopolitan approach to cultural diplomacy. *International Journal of Cultural Policy, 21*(4), 463–477.

Rowntree, J., Neal, L., & Fenton, R. (2010). *International cultural leadership: Reflections, competencies and interviews*. London: Cultural Leadership Programme. Retrieved February 11, 2016, from http://creativeconomy.britishcouncil.org/media/uploads/files/International_Cultural_Leadership_report.pdf

Shome, R. (2009). Post-colonial reflections on the 'internationalization' of cultural studies. *Cultural Studies, 23*(5–6), 694–719.

Shome, R. (2012). Asian modernities: Culture, politics and media. *Global Media and Communication, 8*(3), 199–214.

Singh, J. (2011). *Globalized arts: The entertainment economy and cultural identity*. New York: Columbia University Press.

Singh, J. (2018). Regulating cultural goods and identities across borders. In V. Durrer, T. Miller, & D. O'Brien (Eds.), *The Routledge handbook of global cultural policy* (pp. 89–101). Abingdon: Routledge.

Spivak, G. C. (1988). Can the subaltern speak? In C. Nelson & L. Grossber (Eds.), *Marxism and the integration of culture* (pp. 271–313). Urbana: University of Illinois Press.

Suteu, C. (2006). *Another brick in the wall: A critical review of cultural management education in Europe*. Amsterdam: Boekmanstudies.

UNESCO. (2002). Universal declaration on cultural diversity. Paris: UNESCO. Retrieved April 15, 2019, from http://unesdoc.unesco.org/images/0018/00 1803/180303m.pdf

UNESCO. (2005). Convention on the protection and promotion of the diversity of cultural expression. Paris: UNESCO. Retrieved April 15, 2019, from http://portal.unesco.org/en/ev.php-URL_ID=31038&URL_DO=DO_TOPIC&URL_SECTION=201.html

Upchurch, A. (2016). *The origins of the arts council movement: Philanthropy and policy*. London: Palgrave Macmillan.

Warde, A. (2014). After taste: Culture, consumption and theories of practice. *Journal of Consumer Culture, 14*(3), 279–303.

Watson, J. (1997). *Golden arches east: McDonald's in East Asia*. Stanford: Stanford University Press.

Williams, R. (1989). *Resources of hope: Culture, democracy, socialism*. London: Verso.

Yúdice, G. (2009). Cultural diversity and cultural rights. Human rights in Latin American and Iberian cultures. *Hispanic Issues On Line, 5*(1), 110–137. Retrieved April 15, 2019, from https://conservancy.umn.edu/bitstream/handle/11299/182848/hiol_05_08_yudice_cultural_diversity_and_cultural_rights_0.pdf?sequence=1

Part I

Conditions

2

Culture and International Development: Managing Participatory Voices and Value Chains in the Arts

J. P. Singh

Introduction

The cultural turn in international development can be traced back to the 1980s. Culture—whether understood as collective ways of life in the anthropological sense, or symbolic representations in the artistic sense—would seem central to development efforts. Development interventions are intrinsically cultural in being largely passed through or aimed at collective formations be they nation-states or local societies. However, the study of culture is a relatively new entrant in the lexicon of international development. In hindsight, this is surprising.

The absence of cultural ideas from development thought becomes understandable when exhuming the rather technocratic and overly economistic models that informed the efforts of post-war institutions of development such as the World Bank or the bilateral aid agencies. While situated in a particular development context, that of European 'modern-

J. P. Singh (✉)
George Mason University, Fairfax, VA, USA
e-mail: Jsingh19@gmu.edu

V. Durrer, R. Henze (eds.), *Managing Culture*, Sociology of the Arts,
https://doi.org/10.1007/978-3-030-24646-4_2

25

ization' and notions of progress, the lessons were universalized into 'ahistoric' formulas that could be applied anywhere. Critiques from social scientist and the rise of participatory development practices have now brought culture to the fore of development.

This essay analyses two important aspects of culture and international development:

1. Notions of human well-being that are fundamental to both involving people in development efforts and in thinking of how they may participate in improving their lives. The chapter distinguishes between the ability of cultural expressions to allow people to 'name their world' (cultural voice and identity) versus affordances—the ability of cultural expressions to allow people to do things they were unable to do before.
2. *Cultural infrastructures*: Cultural expressions require sustainable infrastructures that allow for cultural creation, production, distribution, archiving—the value chain of cultural expressions. A permissible social and political environment is important throughout the value chain as is proper training and access to finance and technologies.

Taking both factors together, the chapter emphasizes cultural processes that sustain cultural production rather than the product itself. The world of art often privileges, in policy and ideas, final products over the infrastructures that may or may not be able to sustain such products in the long run. The ecology of culture and development, however, includes notions of human well-being and the value chain that must be brought together. The process model in this chapter looks beneath the 'end-product' of an artistic production to examine the ways that culture sustains development. The anthropological 'ways of life' understanding of culture informs the artistic 'symbolic representations' aspect of culture.

The essay is divided into three parts: (1) a survey of the literature on culture and development, (2) human well-being and culture, and (3) a cultural infrastructure and value chain perspective with empirical examples. The review is interdisciplinary drawing from anthropology, cultural studies, economics, post-colonial history and literatures, international relations, political science, and sociology.

Bringing Back Culture

International development efforts in the post-World War II era fashioned a narrative from a specific European experience, and both its assumptions and its transferability were eventually called into question from anthropologists and sociologists. Arturo Escobar (1995) writes that abstract representations constitute reality, and the development narrative 'created' a historical reality that policymakers and academics believed. In hindsight, the cultural folly of the early development gestalt is easy to see. The local context of societies and cultures was missing in the development models that sought to improve their condition.

This section examines cultural policies in post-colonial states and the ways that international and national efforts opened up participatory spaces.

Cultural Policies

The newly independent post-colonial governments lacked the legitimacy, resources, and imagination to play an effective role in cultural policy making. The policy and elite consensus around economic development emphasized agricultural and industrial development, and cultural policy had little role to play in these efforts that became known as modernization policies. If anything, while the colonial era movements often evoked cultural history and heritage for solidarity, the post-colonial state viewed culture more or less as traditional.

The post-colonial state inherited the legitimacy attached to being at the forefront of modernization efforts in the developing world, but its primary resources were directed toward agriculture and industry. As such, the consensus among cultural policy specialists is that cultural products received "a comparatively low priority, when pitted against the needs of a developing economy, a backward industry" (Vatsayan, 1972). In states such as China and Cuba, headed in the communist direction, a focus on culture was also seen as decadent and bourgeois.

With respect to cultural organizations or infrastructures such as production studios and museums, government agencies were ill-equipped to deal with cultural heritage, promotion, or exchanges. Very few developing countries singled out culture or creative industries for prioritization, with the exception of a few state-sponsored programs here and there and impetus given to cultural tourism in a few places. Rudolph's (1983, p. 12) summary of cultural policies in India could be taken to apply to many other parts of the developing world: "Government's reluctance to respect the autonomy of cultural organizations created to promote the values and interests of the arts (and history) is in part a reflection of its paternalism". The state used its pulpit to speak about modernization and the value of the nation-state but, being resource constrained, it was not instrumental in putting any heft behind implementing policies to help the existing cultural sectors.

Culture and Development

Culture is a process. The cultural turn in development has meant examining complex and subtle changes in ways of life and their representations as they influence development. On the latter, the desired goals of development interventions were 'outputs' such as per capita income, rate of industrialization or agricultural productivity. The cultural turn reflects a more bottom-up participatory effort in development.

Table 2.1 is a preliminary survey of the literature on culture and development. The grand view of culture and development posits the West as civilized and developed while the developing world is cast as uncivilized and inferior, in some accounts, or in opposition to the West in others. The grand view includes a clash of civilizations. Occasional controversies in the world of art that evoke the grand view include those holding a canonical view of Eurocentric art. A slightly less grand view, not shown in Table 2.1, still identifies each culture with 'core values' and posits cultures as somewhat distinct from each other but does away with the grandness of one culture being inferior or superior. However, this view also remains problematic because of its essentialism and staticity. The social science, anthropological, and cultural studies views of culture are discussed in detail later, but they allow for learning, hybridity, possibilities,

Table 2.1 Three views of culture and development and a possible hybridity

	Grand view	Social science/anthropology	→ Hybrid view ←	Cultural studies
Theme/s	'Us' versus 'Them'	Culture as a way of life: adaptation and efficiency	Cultural adaptation and hierarchies	Culture ('way of life') but an arena for power struggles
Notes on identity	Identity fixed through time	Cultural hybridity manifests in various ways: Cultural studies scholars especially pay attention to the way power hierarchies are reproduced through hybridity.		
Notes on human action/agency	Humans are rational and instrumental	Agency embedded in social circumstances	Structures/agency	Agency/resistance/structure
View of art	Backward versus progressive art	Arts reflect society	Art can bring about marginal change	Art reflects power structures including ideology
Possibility of development interventions	Infuse positive cultural outlook	Situate development interventions in social/cultural understandings	Intervention and participation	Limited by current power structures
Intellectual antecedents	Pericles, Weber	North (1994)	Freire (2000/1970)	Said (1978)
Current practice/practitioners	Harrison and Huntington (2002)	Rao and Walton (2004)	Participatory Action Research	Escobar (1995)

and constraints for human agency, and resisting or challenging cultural hierarchies.

The Rise of Participatory Development

Narratives are not only contested but they also respond to each other. The persistent counter-narrative to ideas shaped and implemented from international organizations was that they were not in touch with grassroots contexts and participation. The instrumental imaginary of the post-war international development is often characterized as monologic. Participatory narratives are therefore presented as inherently emancipatory in allowing populations voice and freedom.

Another way to engage participation is to situate development, ideationally, within the broader context of culture of everyday life in an anthropological sense. Institutional economics, with its focus on evolutionary rules governing human behavior hints at culture but does not engage it explicitly. North (1994, p. 364) writes:

> It is culture that provides the key to path dependence—a term used to describe the powerful influence of the past on the present and future.

Nevertheless, the language of culture is difficult to construct in political economy without the slippery slope of attributing everything unexplained attributed to cultural factors. An important publication from the World Bank (Rao & Walton, 2004), reflecting the build-up of initiatives in other UN agencies described below, brought together interdisciplinary practitioners to conceptualize a development agenda rooted in cultural practices. The volume speaks to understanding preferences, incentives, and behaviors as rooted in cultural practices. However, the broader reaches of the World Bank have not responded to including cultural variables.

The Role of the United Nations and its Specialized Agencies

Historically, UNESCO with its World Heritage program had begun to explicitly promote the idea of cultural policies but the links to development, in the form of alleviation of poverty and deprivation, had not been made. The 1982 World Conference on Cultural Policies, or Mondiacult, held in Mexico City tried to forge this link through an anthropological focus on culture. In 1987, Javier Peréz de Cuéllar, Secretary General of the UN, responded to pressures from the Group of 77 (G-77) developing countries to declare 1988–1997 as the Decade for Culture and Development. The idea of a World Commission on Culture and Development originated from this decade.

In 1993, UN Secretary General Boutros Boutros-Ghali and UNESCO Director-General Federico Mayor created the World Commission on Culture and Development. Former Un Secretary General Javier Peréz de Cuéllar was appointed its President. The Commission presented its report *Our Creative Diversity* to both the UN General Assembly and the UNESCO General Conference in 1995 (Peréz de Cuéllar, 1995). The central lesson of the report is aptly summarized in the oft-quoted first sentence of the report's Executive Summary: "Development divorced from its human or cultural context is growth without a soul" (p. 15).

The World Commission on Culture and Development was responding to various past historical and ideational developments in its report (Arizpe, 2004). *Our Creative Diversity* from the World Commission on Culture and Development (1995) reflects the dual impetus to bring culture into debates on economic development, while being starkly aware that culture must be understood in a liberating sense of an ethic that allows for diversity, pluralism, and freedom. It also considered Samuel Huntington's (1993) provocative thesis on clash of civilization, which posited that the differences between the Judeo-Christian and Islamic-Confucian civilization were irreconcilable and thus an endemic source of conflict. *Our Creative Diversity*, instead, argued that cultural diversity should lead and not thwart endeavors of peaceful coexistence in recognizing that diversity is the basis of interaction and cultural syntheses.

Our Creative Diversity adopted ideas from the United Nations Development Programme's (UNDP) Human Development Reports (HDRs) and argued for development as entitlement to a dignified way of life. It also called for increasing the participation of women and young people, and public and private organizations at all levels of governance to mobilize people for culture and development. The 1998 Stockholm Intergovernmental Conference on Cultural Policies for Sustainable Development marked the end of the World Decade for Cultural Development and followed the work of the World Commission on Culture and Development. The Stockholm conference expanded efforts to galvanize financial and human resources in support of such efforts. A direct result of the *Our Creative Diversity* report was the publication of World Culture Reports (1998, 2000) from UNESCO. In conclusion, though, the agenda for culture and development did not move forward much even as UNESCO has continued to produce reports that highlight its importance (UNESCO, 2009). A mix of resource constraints, lack of clear incentives, and the dominance of other cultural issues within UNESCO are the likely causes. The culture and development narrative was, for example, overshadowed by the debates on cultural diversity, mostly about entertainment/cultural industries at UNESCO (Singh, 2011a, 2011b).

Dialogic Communication and Participatory Action Research (PAR)

The concept of dialogic communication, as a pedagogy of development, dates back to the Brazilian educator and activist Paulo Freire who locates its origins in consciousness awakening—a form of learning and knowing in which the subjects understand their historical circumstances and are able to name the world and themselves within it, thus finding a cultural voice. This is the necessary condition for the oppressed to see their circumstances "as a limiting situation they can transform" (Freire, 2000/1970, p. 49). The next step is dialogic communication, the sufficient condition, which entails problem solving informed by multiple or dialectical perspectives. The latter allow the actors to examine their life situation from multiple perspectives and indulge in problem solving.

Latin American writers responded to Freire in the tradition of development praxis that came to be known as Participatory Action Research

(PAR). It provided not just a critique of modernization theory but also, more recently, of market-based systems in general. However, participation does not necessarily lead to consciousness awakening unless subjects are able to name their world, challenge or question existing power relations, and then articulate action (the A in PAR) aimed toward transformation. PAR scholarship seldom meets all these criteria.

Participation and Global Development Efforts

Central elements of dialogic communication are often missing from development projects that claim to be participatory. At a macro level, the Poverty Reduction Strategy Papers (PRSPs) that the World Bank and the International Monetary Fund introduced in 1999 as a precondition for debt-relief asked for broad participation from communities, stakeholders, and policymakers. In practice, however, PRSPs yielded mixed results; not only is such broad participation impossible to implement, but it also ignores existing power relations (Mansuri & Rao, 2013; Gaynor, 2010). Mansuri and Rao (2013), World Bank economists themselves, are also skeptical of types of participation that are 'induced' from states or powerholders, rather than outcomes of 'organic' civil society or social movement processes. A widely used manual at the World Bank on participatory methods (Rietbergen-McCracken & Narayan, 1998), presents experts who engage people at the grassroots utilizing various participatory techniques. However, in most of these methods, the emphasis is on engagement, rather than questioning the ways in which the experts acquired the codes and representations with which they wish to foster engagement.

Accounts of participatory development often provide a glossy view of these efforts in which societal actors work alongside those in authority with a great degree of harmony. This is an idealized model; participation can also involve conflict. Table 2.2 is illustrative. Along another dimension, societal or political structures may not allow society agency or freedom to participate or these structures may be internalized and constrain societal actors from exercising agency. For example, in a deeply patriarchal society, women may lack political rights, but they may also internalize this repression.

Table 2.2 Cultures of participation and development

	Structured/Hierarchical	Agentic/Horizontal
Consensual (state-dominated)	Stakeholder Discourse Literature: United Nations, International Organizations, Governments Examples: Creative economy (UNCTAD/WIPO) Government-led initiatives	Network Consensual Discourse Literature: transnational and national societal networks Examples: Global Production & Consumption Networks
Conflictual (societal pressures)	Performative Mobilization Discourse Literature: advocacy and performance strategies Examples: social movements' use of ICTs and social media; community theater & performance	Oppositional Discourse Literature: critical theory, organizational behavior Examples: Community radio, community arts productions

Source: Modified for culture and development from Singh, J. P., and Mikkel Flyverbom. "Representing participation in ICT4D projects." *Telecommunications Policy* 40, no. 7 (2016). P. 693

Human Well-Being and Cultural Voice

The development narrative has shifted over time, alongside ideas of participatory development, towards embracing a cultural dimension. The latest iteration of this narrative speaks to subjective well-being of people parallel to an approach that offers the maximum number of possibilities in life (agency) along with dignity and lack of discrimination (Alkire, 2002; Hojman & Miranda, 2018). Participatory practices are important to this cultural shift because they emphasize inclusion and allow people, in the words of Freire, to name their world and articulate their cultural voice (Freire, 2000/1970).

Towards Human Development

The paradigmatic shift in development thought came from the UNDP, through an approach known as human development associated closely with the work of economists Amartya Sen and Mahbub Ul Haq. Amartya

Sen's work (2000) on entitlements and development as freedom sought to go beyond earnings and growth to ask what sort of life people are entitled to in various societies. For example, high per capita incomes in various countries may not instruct us on the roles and freedoms that women might avail in strongly patriarchal societies.

The UNDP was created in 1965 through a synthesis of several development agencies. UNDP and the World Bank are often compared as offering different visions of development. Just as ideas of human development challenged the approach rooted in economic growth, UNDP also countered the World Bank's flagship annual publication, the World Development Report (WDR), published since 1978, with an annual HDR that started to be published in 1990. The HDR began publishing a Human Development Index, which took into account income growth and social entitlements such as education and life expectancy.

The focus on human beings themselves, rather than as part of some output ratio, had precedents. UNDP thus succeeded in making these narratives institutional concerns during a period when international development narratives were settling into a dominant framework that came from the World Bank. In fact, UNDP helped to encourage similar initiatives within the Bank including participatory development. The two agencies have also collaborated on various projects together.

The human development approach has its limitations. UNDP as an agency may be as inaccessible as the World Bank to grassroots development practitioners, including NGOs, and even human development appears as a set of 'technical assistance' programme designed in New York. While UNDP briefly turned towards community-led initiatives in the late 1990s, its connections to the epistemic communities in academia are stronger than knowledge generated at the community level (Murphy, 2006, pp. 347–349).

Beyond UNDP, there are human initiatives that are well defined and even institutionalized. However, many of them are broadly philosophical, and neither of the communities from below nor elite bureaucrats or policymakers know how to engage with them. One such approach is the characterization of poverty as a human rights violation. This approach, advocated by political theorist Thomas Pogge (2007) was briefly deliberated at UNESCO. Pogge argued that just as racism and slavery revealed societal prejudices, so does the continuation of poverty. The human rights approach was adopted in UNESCO in 2001 and related to UNESCO's mandate to remove the structural causes of violence (Singh, 2011b). Nevertheless, within five years the initiative had died with resistance from member-states and the inability to spell out its feasibility (McNeill & Asunción, 2009, pp. 125–128).

The difficulties with institutionalizing and propagating human rights or broadly cultural approaches to development notwithstanding, the idea that development initiatives must have resonance with people's daily lives, is now firmly entrenched. The latest iteration of human development is subjective well-being that builds upon Amartya Sen's approach to development as freedom and capabilities to pursue several alternatives and a life of dignity. Hojman and Miranda (2018, p. 1) develop indictors of subjective well-being that include human agency and dignity:

> Human agency refers to the capability of an individual to control her destiny and make choices to fulfill goals set autonomously. Human dignity is associated with the absence of feelings of shame and humiliation, and is ultimately related to social inclusion.

Their empirical tests, based on a household survey conducted in Chile, show that subjective well-being is related to life satisfaction and higher income. Hajnal and Miranda's tests for agency and dignity stand over and above other psychological personality variables, for which they control and that may be related to notions of well-being.

Cultural Voice and Agency

The notion of human agency and dignity provides a connection with anthropological and social science studies that attend to participation in cultural activities. Cultural expressions make visible the possibilities for their life and, in doing so, they speak to the absence or presence of shame and dignity. However, the possibilities and agency that cultural expressions afford must be weighed against the social hierarchies within which they are embedded and which they help to maintain. As Abu-Lughod

(1986) reminds us in the context of Bedouin poetry, they provide a way of maintaining social hierarchies and exclusion, while also being a vehicle for changing these practices from within and suggesting further possibilities.

Cultural expressions are vehicles for group identity and are often symbols of dignity and identity for groups. Mbaquanga music in South Africa provided a way for people to not only assert a Zulu identity in the post-apartheid multi-ethnic South African society but also to negotiate tradition and modernity (Meintjes, 2003). Similarly, folk theater in India has long called attention to social issues and has also been instrumentalized to raise consciousness about developmental strategies ranging from healthcare to agricultural practices (Srampickal, 1994).

The literature on cultural participation and development ascribes multiple values beyond economic to understanding their importance (Throsby, 2001). These can range from the economic value of cultural activities but also include historic, religious, intrinsic values of arts to communities. Throsby (2001) and Hutter and Throsby (2008) describe the various types of cultural value as follows:

- *Aesthetic value*: or properties of beauty or art shared in a culture
- *Spiritual value*: or value to a religious group
- *Social value*: expressed in terms of identity and location
- *Historical value*: reflecting cultures through time
- *Symbolic value*: as purveyor of representational meaning
- *Authenticity value*: accruing to the original work

These multivalent notions of value provide both a vocabulary and caution for connecting arts with participation and empowerment. Matarasso (1997, p. 88) notes that "participation in the arts has the capacity, in partnership with other initiatives, to tackle serious social problems and the disempowerment which results from them". However, Matarasso goes on to articulate the existential condition of the arts in any society: While arts can be empowering, they are also often devalued in social and educational policy. The ever-present debates internationally on arts funding are an example.

Arts and the Limits to Empowerment

A broader existential concern with arts and social empowerment also arises from the possibilities of agency and voice described above. If arts provide a way for societies to name their world, then they can also limit the possibilities of naming this world in different ways. The not so metaphorical handcuffs have been brought globally to incarcerate cultural producers who dared to question deeply situated cultural meanings even when they might be oppressive.

Cultural sensitivity also brings us to the limits of these cultural possibilities. Political and social freedoms are important for cultural expressions to question the existing understandings that may be oppressive. While the internal vocabulary of cultures may allow for this questioning, it may equally allow for the quashing of these expressions and sanction anything from verbal harassment to bodily violence against the cultural producers.

In summary, there are two possibilities for cultural expressions to question existing development limitations and possibilities. The anthropological and sociological possibility lies in working within the frameworks of practice to situate the new understandings. However, political economists have also called attention to political pluralism and lack of restrictions on human rights in general as incentives toward the production of new cultural expressions:

> Our discussion also points out at the relevance of the State—through education and social policies that affect segregation and stigmatization—in shaping the cultural boundaries that make dignity and equal respect more or less likely to prevail in a given society. (Hojman & Miranda, 2018, p. 10)

In providing a space for cultural expressions, both cultural sensitivity and state-backed political freedoms are important.

A Value Chain Perspective

A cultural infrastructure is necessary to move from cultural participation to sustainable human well-being. Arts practices, no matter how embedded in communities, cannot survive without adequate support extending from political and social space to create art, financial rewards for cultural production, and adequate exhibition and distribution networks. We have traced the context of cultural voices in the developing world at various levels and multiple arts but they all face the problem of an inadequate cultural infrastructure. Pierre Sauvé (2006, p. 6) notes:

> For most developing countries, structural difficulties represent daunting obstacles to cultural production and diffusion. This ranges from factors as diverse as the paucity of disposable income to spend on non-essential consumption, literacy, problem of secure and reliable access to electricity, particularly in rural areas, the low availability of consumer equipment (TVs, DVD players) as well as a general dearth of producers, broadcasters and distributors facilities.

This section briefly documents a few key challenges for the developing world through various stages of cultural production. The supply and demand of creative products entails a value chain as depicted in Fig. 2.1. Developing countries encounter difficulties with all aspects of the value or production chain though, depending on the type of activity, the barriers to entry in particular stages may vary. UNCTAD (2008, p. 44) notes, for example, that in Africa the "value chain is simple (primary inputs combined to produce outputs sold directly to consumers)." Despite the presence of well-known musicians all over sub-Africa, only seven African countries have an established live-performance industry, with venues and equipment. These are Congo, Democratic Republic of Congo, Tanzania, Kenya, South African, Mali, and Senegal. The renowned Senegalese musician Youssou N'Dour, associated with the Wolof polyrhythmic Mbalax-style, has set up his own performance establishment (Thiosanne) and a recording studio (Xippi) in Dakar. However, only South Africa and

Fig. 2.1 Analytical model of the 'cultural production chain' or 'culture cycle'. (Source: Adapted from UNESCO Institute for Statistics. *The 2009 UNESCO Framework for Cultural Statistics: Draft.* December 2007, p. 24)

Zimbabwe possess a well-established recording industry. Nearly 100 percent of music in Africa is pirated and it is thus hard for musicians to earn royalties from local sales. In contrast, Latin America, which accounts for 5 percent of the world music sales, "has an established live music practice, a local and national broadcasting system, a domestic recording industry and in some instances access to international markets" (Cunningham, Ryan, Keane, & Ordonez, 2008, p. 5).

While value chain is presented here in a linear way for illustrative purposes, in practice, the value chain may not only be non-linear but each of the processes illustrated below may occur and reoccur and may be connected to all other parts of the value chain. For example, the lack of exhibition spaces may guide a playwright in the kind of theater she may write. Therefore, another way of imagining the value chain below may be to view each stage as a spoke in a wheel with all parts connected to each other.

The following two cases illustrate in narrative form, a few challenges to value chains in various developing country context:

Case 1: African Book Publishing and Film Production

Cultural infrastructures in Africa reveal a patchwork of support and project-based, rather than sustainable, financing. The example of book production is typical of the challenges. Nearly 98 percent of the books in circulation in Sub-Saharan Africa are textbooks. There were few avenues for literary works although several publishing and distribution network since the late 1980s have helped Pan African Writers' Association (PAWA), African Publishers Network (APNET), Pan African Booksellers Association (PABA), and African Books Collective (ABC) (Nyamnjoh, 2008). The problems of book publishing reflect that of other forms of cultural production. Brickhill (2010) notes that a great deal of artistic production in Africa rests on "cyclical project funding" even when there is infrastructural capacity for training and the development of the arts. Despite these obstacles, African traditions of story-telling have resonated through various artistic practices and cross-overs: Ngũgĩ wa Thiong'o started off writing in English but then turned to his native Gikuyu;

Ousmane Sembène switched from fiction to film to make the point that African story-telling was well suited for multimedia and aural traditions rather than printed texts.

In contrast to book publishing, African filmmaking traditions, while instructive for lack of infrastructural capacity, also feature recent developments that bridge this gap. Burkina Faso, home of the biennial film festival FESPACO, provides an interesting case. Its film industry generally produced two-three films per year since 1971 and was completely dependent on foreign funding (Hoefert de Turégano, 2008). The latter created an elite set of filmmakers but not a general capacity for film production. Meanwhile film distribution remained concentrated with either a French or a US firm. Digital technology has had a two-pronged effect: first, the number of cinemas declined from 50 in 2001 to 19 in 2004 as film viewing moved indoors, but at the same time, new technologies offer filmmakers cost-effective opportunities that they lacked earlier. Famous directors such as Gaston Kabare, Dany Kouyate, Pierre Yomeago and Regina Fanto Nacro have created their own studios. Meanwhile, the government has provided incentives for film from including regional distribution incentives and tightening its copyright laws. However, Hoefert de Turégano (2008, p. 126) summation of Burkina Faso's film industry is equally apt for other similar countries:

> Burkina has a rich film culture, it has a budding local production scene, it is grappling with the problems of distribution and exhibition, it is not neglecting the importance of film education and training, it has the best African film festival in the world, and it has a government that is working to create a structured, legal context for the film and audiovisual sector, in sum, many factors working in its favour. Whether these advantages can be translated into economic success remains to be seen.

A counterpoint comes from South Africa. Lacking finance, South African cinema has been tied up with foreign investors through the government's National Film and Video Foundation, which has an aggressive film development program. Award-winning films such as *Yesterday* (2004), *Hotel Rwanda* (2004), *Tsotsi* (2005), *Beauty* (2011) and *The Wound* (2017) speak to this success. The National Film and Video

Foundation (NFVF) also condemned threats of violence that surrounded the depiction of closeted homosexuality among Xhosa men in *The Wound* and helped the film's producers register their concerns with South Africa Human Rights Commission and the Commission for Gender Equality.

Securing financing and marketing for South African films are NFVF's key objectives and highlight a networked approach in which public and private and domestic and international agencies play a role. The *Indaba Charter* adopted by NFVF and film stakeholders in South Africa in 2005 was clear in mobilizing a network approach and breaking the 'dependency syndrome', which overzealously relies on the government. NFVF has also raised the profile of its films through some high-profile participation moves at international film festivals such as Cannes and Berlin, where it regularly partners with Trade and Investment South Africa (TISA), the semi-autonomous investment promotion vehicle. NFVF also backs South Africa's objective to provide leadership for African cinema in general. South Africa now hosts the Pan African Federation of Filmmakers (FEPACI) responsible for the FESPACO film festival in Ougadougou. As noted earlier, FESPACO was a French-run show for Francophone cinema; the locus of shift to South Africa is significant. West African film industry professionals have long accepted, yet bemoaned French funding and control of their fledgling film industry. They are sceptic of South African moves but equally fatigued from pulling at the patronage strings of French agencies.

Case 2: Jamaican Reggae

Jamaican Reggae stands out as a success story of cultural voice, participation, and production. "Persistently neglected by state and society", Jamaican Reggae provided dignity to the creole "patois speaking Black sub-altern classes" (Paul, 2010, p. 124). The Reggae sound arose through communities and their cultural infrastructures: the "neighborhood sound system" and dancehalls (p. 128). It was then distributed through small labels such as Studio One and Island Records that catered to legends such as Bob Marley and Jimmy Cliff. Nevertheless, the global sales of Reggae have not benefitted Jamaica or its economy, even when the record labels are owned by Jamaican migrants. The business model of Jamaican Reggae was not incentivized towards generating value added at various stages of production (Reis & Davis, 2008). For example, until recently overseas firms controlled up to 14 percent of the Jamaican Reggae royalty deals. The overall result is that despite Reggae's success, Jamaica was not among the top eight recorded music producers in Latin America at the turn of the century. These were: Brazil, Argentina, Central America, Colombia, Paraguay, Uruguay, and Mexico (p. 194).

Conclusion

How are the arts relevant and sustainable in people's lives? Who decides? These two questions not only inform the ecology of culture and international development practices but also their long-term survival. Locating participatory cultural practices is the first step towards making arts sustainable and vibrant. The next steps entail policy incentives and strategy.

Supporting arts value chains at a macro level historically meant either providing economic incentives governing production through property rights (rules guaranteeing tangible and intangible rewards), or direct subsidies and payments to the arts (Caves, 2002; Throsby, 2001; Vogel, 2007). Thinking of property rights and payments in a value chain context needs some calibration at a micro level. Table 2.3 provides a preliminary list of the kinds of incentives and rewards that may be useful at each level of the value chain and lists a few examples of these worldwide. These include openness and guarantees for creative expression, materials incentives for production, networks and exhibition spaces for distribution, and intellectual property rights protections.

There is no single type of incentive or reward that will inform all aspects of the value chain. Fortunately, policies informing all aspects of the value chain are also not necessary. If an arts sector exists, then it probably contains some minimum levels of support at each aspect of the value chain. As seen above, the Jamaican reggae industry drew upon community infrastructure and local record labels in ways that African music has not been able to do. On the other hand, Jamaican musicians have lacked control over international distribution rights.

Table 2.3 Cultural value chain and policy instruments

Creative value chain and target	Policy objectives and instruments	Examples and exemplars
Creative imagination	1. Tolerance and freedom 2. Embedding arts in existing cultural practices 3. Creative flows and hybridity 4. Preserving arts in conflict 5. Security of life for artists	1. Creative cities (Florida, 2002) 2. Openness to commerce (Cowen, 2006) 3. Laws governing freedom of expression; grants and institutions encouraging creative expressions
Production	1. Existence of creative industry infrastructures and talent 2. Security of property rights governing creative production 3. Subsidies to cover revenue deficits and increasing costs of arts (Baumol's cost disease)	1. Creative Britain (DCMS, 1998) 2. Tax incentives for philanthropy and charitable donations (O'Hare, Feld, & Shuster, 1983) 3. Emphasis in most national creative industry plans (UNCTAD, 2008)
Distribution	1. Encouraging arts festivals 2. Access to distribution networks through institutional support 3. Subsidies or grants for creating or accessing distribution networks	1. Rationalizing demand and supply (Frey, 2003); inclusion & expressions (Snowball, 2005) 2. Creating arts/creative product distribution agencies such as South Africa's National Film and Video Foundation
Exhibition	1. State and market incentives for creating exhibition spaces 2. Cultural tourism policies for exhibiting heritage	1. State-led cultural policies (UNESCO, 2009) 2. Tourism campaigns worldwide (OECD, 2009)
Archiving and preservation	1. Copyrights laws 2. Creative commons 3. Creation of physical and digital archives	1. International and national copyright an intellectual property legislations (Watal, 2001) 2. Creativecommons.org 3. National museums (Garcia Canclini, 1995)

Adapted from J.P. Singh. *Globalized Arts: The Entertainment Economy and Cultural Identity*. New York: Columbia University Press. 2011, Chapter 7

An art strategy in a given context would then entail examining the value chain for support where it is most needed. There are also three transversal categories for support that cut across the entire value chain.

- Training and education in the arts
- Availability of finance
- Information infrastructures including websites and telephony

The idea of a value chain is suggested here both as a formal and an intuitive methodology. In a formal sense, a sustainable cultural infrastructure implies taking stock of the inputs required at every stage of production and either qualitatively or quantitatively describing areas of strength and improvement. In an intuitive sense, it implies that even the most informal cultural productions entail a value chain. For example, street theater may seem a perfectly viable practice in a particular setting, but locating missing elements—training for actors, exhibition spaces—can help to locate room for improvement.

Another way to strategize a methodology for support entails understanding the key actors involved in arts production. While governments may play a role in sustaining the arts, often civil society, arts organizations and businesses are far more active in the arts sectors. A case can be made for especially encouraging sustainable business practices due to the existential state of arts funding worldwide. Table 2.4 provides a list of examples of how key actors can be mobilized toward arts production in diverse contexts. It is simplified here for pedagogical reasons—usually any arts sector will feature a variety of actors. Along with incentives noted in Table 2.3, there are many options and strategies toward working with key actors.

A final point now about intervention: While arts must be culturally sustainable, this does not mean that support from outside the culture is undesirable. Only a view of the arts that presents culture as insular and isolated would not see arts as constantly evolving and syncretic. This provides a rationale for intervention, in connecting one form or art with another. However, a far greater reason exists for external intervention. This means that to the extent that development interventions are culturally sensitive, they can both encourage and question existing practices,

Table 2.4 Arts sectors and chief actors involved

Arts sector	Chief actors involved	Notable outcomes
Book publishing in Africa	Publishing and distribution collectives	Networks promoting African writing—Pan African Writers Association (PAWA), African Publishers Network (APNET), Pan African Book Sellers Association (PABA), African Books Collective (ABC)
Fine arts and design	Government-led	Support for arts clusters in China, participatory cultural policy making (CODECU—Puerto Rico), IT and design innovation hubs (several countries)
Creative industries	Firm-led global production networks	Cinema (China, India, South Africa), telenovelas (Latin America), female singers (Lebanon, Egypt)
Arts and technology	Global prosumers (producers and consumers)	Social media, DIY, Nollywood, International Youth Culture (Balinese reggae, death metal, etc.)

albeit through dialogic relationship with actors who are involved at each stage of the arts production.

A culturally sensitive approach to development advocates understanding, not condemnation. It entails locating possibilities and alternatives within cultural frameworks to allow for agency and dignity. Further, in connecting culturally sensitive interventions with cultural infrastructures, we make development interventions even more sustainable in the long run.

References

Abu-Lughod, L. (1986). *Veiled sentiments: Honor and poetry in a Bedouin society.* Berkeley, CA: University of California Press.

Alkire, S. (2002). Dimensions of human development. *World Development, 30*(2), 181–205.

Arizpe, L. (2004). The intellectual history of culture and development institutions. In V. Rao & M. Walton (Eds.), *Culture and public action.* Stanford, CA: Stanford University Press.

Brickhill, P. (2010). The 'creator' as entrepreneur: An African perspective. In H. Anheier & Y. R. Isar (Eds.), *The cultural expressions, creativity and innovation* (The Cultures and Globalization Series 2). Los Angeles, CA: Sage.

Caves, R. (2002). *Creative industries: Contracts between art and commerce.* Cambridge, MA: Harvard University Press.

Cowen, T. (2006). *Good and plenty: The creative successes of American arts funding.* Princeton, NJ: Princeton University Press.

Cunningham, S., Ryan, M. D., Keane, M., & Ordonez, D. (2008). Financing creative industries in developing countries. In D. Barrowclough & Z. Kozul-Wright (Eds.), *Creative industries and developing countries: Voice, choice and economic growth.* London: Routledge.

DCMS. (1998). *Creative industries mapping document.* London: Department of Culture, Media and Sport, United Kingdom.

Escobar, A. (1995). *Encountering development: The making and unmaking of the third world.* Princeton, NJ: Princeton University Press.

Florida, R. (2002). *The rise of the creative class.* New York: Basic Books.

Freire, P. (2000/1970). *Pedagogy of the oppressed.* New York: Continuum.

Frey, B. (2003). Festivals. In R. Towse (Ed.), *A handbook of cultural economics.* Cheltenham, UK: Edward Elgar.

Garcia Canclini, N. (1995). *Hybrid cultures: Strategies for entering and leaving modernity.* Minneapolis, MN: University of Minnesota Press.

Gaynor, N. (2010). *Transforming participation? The politics of development in Malawi and Ireland.* Houndmills: Palgrave Macmillan.

Harrison, L. E., & Huntington, S. (Eds.). (2002). *Culture matters: How values shape human progress.* New York: Basic Books.

Hoefert de Turégano, T. (2008). Film culture and industry in Burkina Faso. In D. Barrowclough & Z. Kozul-Wright (Eds.), *Creative industries and developing countries: Voice, choice and economic growth.* London: Routledge.

Hojman, D. A., & Miranda, A. (2018). Agency, human dignity, and subjective well-being. *World Development, 101,* 1–15.

Huntington, S. P. (1993, Summer). The clash of civilizations? *Foreign Affairs, 72*(3), 22–49.

Hutter, M., & Throsby, D. (Eds.). (2008). *Beyond price: Value in culture, economics and the arts.* Cambridge: Cambridge University Press.

Mansuri, G., & Rao, V. (2013). *Localizing development: Does participation work?* A World Bank Policy Research Report. Washington, DC: The World Bank.

Matarasso, F. (1997). *Use or ornament? The social impact of participation in the arts.* Bournes Green: Comedia.

McNeill, D., & Asunción, L. S. (2009). *Global poverty, ethics and human rights: The role of multilateral organizations*. London: Routledge.

Meintjes, L. (2003). *Sound of Africa: Making music Zulu in a South African studio*. Durham, NC: Duke University Press.

Murphy, C. (2006). *The United Nations development programme: A better way?* Cambridge: Cambridge University Press.

North, D. C. (June 1994). Economic performance through time. *The American Economic Review, 84*(3), 359–368.

Nyamnjoh, F. B. (2008). Globalization and the cultural economy: Africa. In H. Anheier & Y. R. Isar (Eds.), *The cultural economy* (The Cultures and Globalization Series 2). Los Angeles, CA: Sage.

OECD. (2009). *The impact of culture on tourism*. Paris: Organization of Economic Co-operation and Development.

O'Hare, M., Feld, A. L., & Shuster, J. M. (1983). *Patrons despite themselves: Taxpayers and arts policy*. New York: New York University Press.

Paul, A. (2010). The turn of the native: Vernacular creativity in the Caribbean. In H. Anheier & Y. R. Isar (Eds.), *The cultural expressions, creativity and innovation* (The Cultures and Globalization Series 3). Los Angeles, CA: Sage.

Peréz de Cuéllar, J. (1995). *Our creative diversity: Report of the World Commission on Culture and Development*. Paris: UNESCO Publishing. Retrieved March 31, 2019, from unesdoc.UNESCO.org/images/0010/001055/105586e.pdf

Pogge, T. (Ed.). (2007). *Freedom from poverty as a human right: Who owes what to the poor*. Paris: UNESCO Publishing.

Rao, V., & Walton, M. (Eds.). (2004). *Culture and public action*. Stanford, CA: Stanford University Press.

Reis, A. C. F., & Davis, A. (2008). Impact and responses in Latin America and the Caribbean. In H. Anheier & Y. R. Isar (Eds.), *The cultural economy* (The Cultures and Globalization Series 2). Los Angeles, CA: Sage.

Rietbergen-McCracken, J., & Narayan, D. (1998). *Participation and social assessment: Tools and techniques*. Washington, DC: The World Bank.

Rudolph, L. I. (Spring 1983). Establishing a Niche for cultural policy: An introduction. *Pacific Affairs, 56*(1), 5–14.

Said, E. W. (1978). *Orientalism*. New York: Vintage Books.

Sauvé, P. (2006). Introduction. In *Trends in audiovisual market: Regional perspectives from the South*. Paris: UNESCO.

Sen, A. (2000). *Development as freedom*. New York: Anchor Books.

Singh, J. P. (2011a). *Globalized arts: The entertainment economy and cultural identity*. New York: Columbia University Press.

Singh, J. P. (2011b). *United Nations Educational Scientific and Cultural Organization: Creating norms for a complex world*. London: Routledge.

Snowball, J. D. (2005). Art for the masses? Justification for the public support of the arts in developing countries—Two arts festivals in South Africa. *Journal of Cultural Economics, 29*(2), 107–125.

Srampickal, J. (1994). *Voice to the voiceless: The power of people's theatre in India*. New Delhi: Manohar.

Throsby, D. (2001). *Culture and economics*. Cambridge: Cambridge University Press.

UNCTAD. (2008). *The creative economy report: The challenge of assessing the creative economy*. United Nations. UNCTAD/DITC/2008/2.

UNESCO. (1998). *World Culture Report 1998: Culture, creativity and markets*. Paris: UNESCO Publishing.

UNESCO. (2000). *World Culture Report 2000: Cultural diversity, conflict and pluralism*. Paris: UNESCO Publishing.

UNESCO. (2009, October). *UNESCO World Report: Investing in cultural diversity and intercultural dialogue*. Retrieved September 2, 2019, from http://portal.unesco.org/en/ev.php-URL_ID=46731&URL_DO=DO_TOPIC&URL_SECTION=201.html

UNESCO Institute for Statistics. (2007, December). *The 2009 UNESCO Framework for Cultural Statistics: Draft*.

Vatsayan, K. M. (1972). *Some aspects of cultural policies in India*. Paris: UNESCO Press.

Vogel, H. L. (2007). *Entertainment industry economics: A guide for financial analysis* (7th ed.). Cambridge: Cambridge University Press.

Watal, J. (2001). *Intellectual property rights in the WTO and developing world*. The Hague: Kluwer Law International.

World Commission on Culture and Development. (1995). *Our creative diversity*. Paris: UNESCO Publishing.

3

More Than Just Lost in Translation: The Ethnocentrism of Our Frames of Reference and the Underestimated Potential of Multilingualism

Raphaela Henze

Introduction

Several authors have stressed the importance of language skills for arts managers (Mandel, 2016; Henze, 2017a, 2018a). Many arts management programmes outside the Anglophone world offer additional language classes, the primary focus being English. Only two programmes in German-speaking countries require knowledge of a second foreign language apart from English. While a need for a common language is understandable, it should be clear to all involved that the dominance of the English language not only perpetuates inequalities (Jacobsen, 2015, 2018; Henze, 2018a) but also helps to foster a kind of monoculture in the discipline, with Western narratives and epistemologies being particularly dominant. What results is a marginalisation of narratives, especially from the Global South, and a potentially dangerous epistemicide to which researchers and practitioners are both accomplices, even if they are not fully aware (Hall & Tandon, 2017).

R. Henze (✉)
Heilbronn University, Künzelsau, Germany
e-mail: raphaela.henze@hs-heilbronn.de

V. Durrer, R. Henze (eds.), *Managing Culture*, Sociology of the Arts,
https://doi.org/10.1007/978-3-030-24646-4_3

This chapter analyses responses from 25 arts management researchers and practitioners from 25 countries who were asked to define some of the terms most prevalent in current professional debates. Their responses are analysed in order to determine the differences that exist in our understanding of specific terms and concepts. In doing so, the chapter approaches the issue of language in arts management from several different perspectives. It acknowledges the importance of language skills for addressing international and intercultural challenges. It also recognises our responsibility as arts managers for the protection of languages as collective representative systems and traditions, as well as manifestations of creativity and the diversity of the human mind. Furthermore, the text notes that our constant struggle to be as precise and 'politically correct' as possible has resulted in an increase in new terminology, specifically in our discourses on participation, which may actually confuse the concept altogether.

Language Skills

Research by Henze (2017a) raised awareness of the fact that the work of arts managers is increasingly international, even if it is not necessarily conducted transnationally. Of a sample size of 237, 42% of arts management practitioners in German-speaking countries declared their work to be international. Of the arts managers from 43 further countries ($n = 115$), more than 60% declared the same (Henze, 2017a). It is therefore not surprising that the vast majority of these arts managers ranked language skills as highly important for the profession. However, the languages practitioners' considered key was not limited to English. Some even raised concerns regarding the "tendency towards a linguistic mono-culture (everything in English or pseudo-English)" (Henze, 2017a, p. 79). German arts managers particularly mentioned Arabic dialects as important in their communication to new audiences. Its significance can partly be explained by the influx of people from Arab regions to Germany and other EU countries, particularly during the last few years.

Due to globalisation and migration, language skills apart from English are more and more important in intercultural work. Language is widely known as being more than just a transmitter of knowledge. Intercultural work that takes the issue of languages seriously, therefore goes even beyond transferring information and content to new audiences. One's engagement with a non-native language assists in developing awareness, understanding, and empathy with other cultures (Rösler, 2015; Rowntree et al., 2011), which is a necessity for arts managers engaging in intercultural work within societies in transformation (Henze, 2018a).

In international arts management research, we limit ourselves mostly to English, which is the lingua franca for publications and conferences. Funding for translations in arts management research is rare and the responsibility of the respective researcher. It is important to note that this applies to texts that are to be translated into English, but equally important is the translation of texts into other languages and dialects in order to allow for more mutual and multi-directional exchange. Several of those voices that are yet to be heard still find it difficult to build up an international knowledge base due to their lack of expertise in English and unfamiliarity with concepts and narratives (Zheng, 2019).

Apart from overcoming the ethnocentrism of our English-language dominated frame of reference, that—according to Jacobsen—privileges the norms and values of the Anglophone world (Jacobsen, 2018), the arts management discipline, and arts managers as such, have even greater responsibilities concerning languages. Languages are collective memoirs of traditions and cultures and the expression of the human mind and as such they represent the essence of our work. While the desire for common ground in international publications, networks as well as study programmes is understandable and perhaps inevitable, it is also dangerous in how it may exclude important research, narratives, and epistemologies, particularly from the 'Global South'. Limiting ourselves to mainly Western narratives means that much of the content we teach and publish might not necessarily be transferable to different contexts. Furthermore, this dominance equally deprives those originating from Western narratives of the chance to learn new methodologies and approaches (Durrer, this volume). One example is the interpretation and practice of what are coined as 'cultural agents' in South America, a role model developed in parallel to the more 'westernised' notion of the arts manager (Hernández-Acosta, 2013, this volume). A more nuanced understanding of how the role and responsibilities of those in the profession are defined outside the well-explored Western hemisphere could have an impact on our work in rapidly transforming societies. In these times of ongoing and increasing globalisation, solutions for the challenges that most 'Western' societies face will most likely not be found in the West alone (Henze, 2017b, 2018c).

When examining the literature used in most arts management publications as well as study programmes, we—apart from a few well-known exceptions—rarely find contributions from South American, African, Asian, or Arab authors (Abbas & Erni, 2005; Shohat & Stam, 2005; Gutiérrez, Grant, & Colbert, 2016). The question "Why is my curriculum so white?", which was already raised years ago by several US-American and British students, and which refers to the fact that

> university knowledge systems in nearly every part of the world are derivations of the Western canon, the knowledge system created some 500 to 550 years ago in Europe by white male scientist, (Hall & Tandon, 2017, p. 7)

is therefore still enormously relevant. It is the responsibility of arts management researchers to address this by reaching out to colleagues that have long been absent from our discourses. This is not an easy task, as is, to a certain extent, proven by this book project. Making an invitation to debate issues of exclusion and (in)equality does not in and of itself redraw or rebalance lines of power (Durrer & Henze, 2018, p. 3).

Languages as Collective Memoirs and the Importance of Multilingualism

That using a particular language comes with a particular mind-set has been eloquently expressed recently by the French sociologist Francois Jullien (2018, p. 55). Jullien explains that, if we only speak one language, we will lose the ability to reciprocally reflect on our languages, facilitating greater standardisation of thought and practice. Consequently, our thinking will become stereotyped. This danger is becoming increasingly serious when taking into consideration how many languages are disappearing. According to pessimistic estimates by the *Society for Endangered Languages*, up to 90% of the 6500 languages still spoken today will die out within this century (Dittwald et al., 2007). Sometimes minority languages are stigmatised and not used as official language or as language in schools, or alternatively the use of a language or dialect is accompanied by reprisals. In many regions in the world, the extinction of a language is directly connected to colonialisation and the building of nation-states that aim for a unification of language and culture (Dittwald et al., 2007). We have to be aware that linguicide is cultural genocide (Hall & Tandon, 2017). The English language has been particularly forced on many people. We have to ask ourselves whether we as arts managers are complicit, then, in using a language that is so deeply rooted in privilege and linguistic oppression.

There are even more 'subtle' ways regarding how, in the name of integration for instance, the abandonment of a language is pursued. There is little doubt that acquiring the language of the country in which you live is essential for educational as well as economic success and well-being, and is therefore pursued with much effort by many migrants and refugees. However, the still widespread idea of assimilation as forcing people to give up their native languages is as irresponsible as it is dangerous and proves that the concept of diversity is not yet fully understood.

There is a substantial amount of literature on intercultural and transcultural arts projects, particularly on those projects that involve participants from diverse ethnic backgrounds (Borwick, 2012; Bishop, 2012; Pilic & Wiederhold, 2015; Ziese & Gritschke, 2016). However, the important aspect of multilingualism in this context needs further research (Jacobsen, 2015, 2018; Jullien, 2018).

Sensitivity

The issue concerning languages is not only one about which language or even how many languages should be used. It is also about how we use the language selected in a sensitive or reflexive manner. For several years, gender-neutral language has been debated at length. The generic masculine is still widespread in German but there is an increasing awareness to use gender-balanced forms in official documents and publications. We have also seen some progress in our terminology concerning issues of migration or development always striving to be as 'politically correct' as possible. One of the more prominent examples is the shift from the 'developing or third world country' to a county of the 'Global South'. The term 'developing country' has a rather problematic political history as well as being part of a thinking pattern, which, nowadays, raises critical questions (Korf & Rothfuß, 2015, p. 165). This questioning is related to the long-standing and widespread idea that there can only be one form of development, which means that some countries are more advanced than others (Shome, 2012). Closely related is a discussion that interrogates the use of the 'developed world' as a role model against the background of the ecology and climate debate, which argues that, in terms of, for example, a sustainable economic system, countries like the USA are 'developing countries' (Henze, 2017a). Critics argue that this linguistic finesse does nothing to challenge the situation of these countries, which are now admittedly awkwardly called the 'Global South'. One still finds the term 'developing country' in official documents of UNESCO for instance. Several of the authors in this book have also decided in favour of using this term, which shows that many of us in the profession have—for various reasons that will be further explored—different sensitivities when it comes to issues of terminology.

We surely also have particular blind spots and fault lines in our rhetoric on 'participation'. However, it would be incorrect to argue that radicalism with words serves only as a mask for our incapacity, or even worse, our unwillingness to break out of existing power structures, since operating within them has been quite comfortable for many years in our still too homogenous sector. Without being paralysed by 'political correctness', striving for more sensitivity and reflexivity concerning our expressions is about building awareness of privileges as well as prejudices. I have challenged the terminology used by students and colleagues numerous times. These debates have always been fruitful. What starts as a discussion about a term is necessarily followed by a discussion about underlying concepts, assumptions, and belief systems—and these discourses, that unveil different understandings, standpoints, and philosophies, which have been disguised or blurred by language, are perhaps even more important than finding the 'correct' term.

Terminology in Arts Management

Particularly in the contexts of globalisation, internationalisation, migration, and digitalisation, we have seen particular 'hot topics' to emerge during the last years. As a result, several new terms have been introduced into our discourses. The terms 'empowerment', 'inclusion', 'migration' or 'artivism' are, for instance, missing in Bennet, Grossberg, and Morris's (2005) book *New Keywords: A Revised Vocabulary of Culture and Society*, which was published less than 14 years ago. The rapidness with which new terms emerge causes confusion, particularly because these terms are mostly coined in English and it takes time for non-native speakers to catch up—not only with the term as such but with the concept that needs critical reflection in the respective context. But even more difficult and as such, more interesting, is that arts managers and researchers all around the world might use the same terms but intend something different because of certain different narratives, ideas, and methodologies that form part of their professional canon, and that might inter alia be shaped by the country in which they work or have been trained. It is this local, regional, and national background within the global context of which we urgently need to be aware (Latour, 2011; Hall, 2000). The aim of this research is therefore not to come up with another glossary that tries to find a common denominator. On the contrary, it strongly argues in favour of examining the differences and the reasons for our different takes on particular terms in order to be able to learn from one another.

Methodology

In order to explore how arts management researchers define certain terms, 21 arts management researchers from Argentina, Australia, Austria, Bulgaria, Cameroon, Columbia, Denmark, Finland, Ghana, Germany, Hong Kong, Malta, the Netherlands, Puerto Rico, Singapore, Slovenia, Spain, Taiwan, Turkey, the UK, and the USA, as well as four practitioners from Brazil, France, India, and Lebanon, have been asked to provide spontaneous ideas, feelings and/or definitions for terms assigned to them.

The interviews were conducted via email in order to allow the participants space to consider and phrase their responses, which the majority of participants formulated in a language that was not their first (James, 2016; Meho, 2006). It was not the primary intention of this research to compare differences between practising arts managers and academics, although there are interesting differences to be found.

The respondents were asked to share insights regarding the following terms: arts management, transcultural arts management, equality, inclusive society, empowerment, post-colonialism, and social impact. These terms were selected because they have appeared frequently in discussions of the Arts and Humanities Research Council (UK)-funded network, *Brokering Intercultural Exchange* during the last two years (Durrer & Henze, 2018). Respondents were explicitly asked not to refer to any literature or do any research, but rather to give spontaneous answers, ideas, and impressions of these terms. In asking for responses in this manner, the focus of the study has been on their perception of the term, as they understand it in their everyday work.

There are some limitations to the data presented here. Arts management researchers, particularly from Europe, are well represented in this research, whereas the number of participants from countries in the Middle East and Africa is unfortunately small. Extending the reach to as yet unheard voices in the field of arts management still proves to be particularly difficult, as has been described by Durrer and Henze (2018, p. 3). Furthermore, there might again be a language barrier that hinders participation. This underlines the importance of the above-mentioned (financial) support for translation in arts management research.

Arts Management

The first term to be explored is arts management. Although this term defines the discipline, there is ample proof that we might have very different understandings of what exactly should be part of an arts management education and what constitutes the role of arts managers (Durrer, this volume).

Participants from Germany, Malta, the UK, the USA, and Lebanon refer to the difficulty of combining technical management with liberal arts, as well as to the ambiguous relationship that both still have.

A colleague from Lebanon states that it is:

...[a] hard position because it juggles two extremes. The role suits those who have a structured mind but also a high appreciation for the art and the artists as well as an admiration for beautiful chaos.

A colleague from the UK explains:

Arts management as a term is certainly present in the UK, and there has been a proliferation of post graduate programmes using the title. The US appears to have stuck with arts administration. I find it interesting that a number of the Arts management programmes in the UK are far more Arts and Cultural Policy as far as I am concerned (in terms of their content). I also find this at cultural policy conferences where questions often appear to be ones of management but are presented as ones of policy. But then I think that a lot of people working in this area do not want to acknowledge that they are management scholars (because of the acrimonious relationship that the 'arts sector' appears to have with managers/management/administrators).

Whether the observation that arts administration is still the title of choice in the USA is correct is doubtful. Obviously, the Association of Arts Administration Educators (AAAE) in the USA still uses this term. This might be due to the fact that the network was already established in 1975—and as such at a time when most European programmes were either not yet on the market or at the very beginning. According to Tonks (2016, p. XVI), the shift from 'administrator' to 'manager' had to do with the professionalisation of the discipline. It seems as if even the term 'management' is already outdated and has been replaced by leadership in many programmes—not particularly in Canada and Australia but also in the USA. Even AAAE's slogan is "Training cultural leaders is at the heart of all we do."

Management as such seems to have negative connotations for many in this research, as has been explored by the colleague from the UK. This does not really come as a surprise, when one takes into account the fact that arts management programmes, particularly in Europe, were established in order to make arts organisations more efficient, effective, and fit for competition with the growing leisure sector during the prime time of New Public Management (Durrer, this volume).

Respondents from Spain, Turkey, Slovenia, Germany, Puerto Rico, and Argentina underline that they prefer the term 'cultural management' to 'arts management'.

For example, the colleague from Turkey states:

> Arts management is a US term. We use 'cultural management'. Whenever I hear arts management, I think of US programmes and Americans for the Arts ... I feel restricted and prefer not to use it if not in the above-mentioned US context.

The respondent from Argentina makes a remarkable point about how the entire field in his country seems to have been influenced by programmes run by the University of Barcelona:

> Arts management is by large not a term used on a daily basis. The category that emerged through the last thirty years—and the influence of the University of Barcelona is clear in this process—is cultural management...

Programmes by Spanish universities—among them also the Universitat Oberta de Catalunya—seem to have a huge influence in the Spanish-speaking countries in South America. The Universitat Oberta de Catalunya in cooperation with the Universitat de Girona runs an online master for arts managers in Spanish/Catalan and has an enormous outreach in the entire Spanish-speaking world (Universitat Oberta de Catalunya, 2019). The fact that arts/cultural managers from South and Central America tend to be more inclined to participate in Spanish programmes most likely has to do with the common language. Particularly for Argentina, the reasons for this influence of Spanish universities on the arts sector might even be more complex and geopolitical. In the 1990s, several Spanish companies started to reach out to the South American market. A large portion of Argentinian public services, among them services in telecommunications or water supply, are run by Spanish companies. At the same time, in Spain, these companies—with the help of foundations they established (one of the best-known ones being Fundación Telefónica)—began to influence the cultural and artistic sector that the Spanish state had largely abandoned. In this context, cultural management was born as a professional field and exported to Argentina. That European approaches do not necessarily fit in this context is something that the Argentinean arts sector discusses fiercely (Castineira de Dios, 2009). That we have to be cautious when exporting narratives, methodologies, and models around the world has recently been stressed by an increasing number of authors (de Sousa Santos, 2014; Hampel, 2014, 2016; Henze, 2017b; Dragićević-Šešić & Mihaljinac, this volume; Durrer, this volume).

The respondent from Puerto Rico clarifies that a different framework of work in the cultural sector has been developed in that region, which comprises not only of the arts manager but also of the cultural agent and the cultural entrepreneur:

> *I always associate arts management with very traditional (functional) management. Because of this, I always think in museums, orchestras and big arts institutions. Arts management to me is when you have to deal with operations, human resources, marketing and operations in a very traditional way... In Puerto Rico we differentiate the concept from cultural agency and cultural entrepreneurship (for more self-managed operations).*

It is exactly these concepts that need further exploration (Hernández-Acosta, this volume), since they provide opportunities to challenge the role of arts managers. DeVereaux (2009) has, for example, claimed that arts management has for too long been a discipline that constantly reacts to, rather than sets, agendas and often even fails in envisioning new forms of collaboration. New impulses concerning role models for instance are therefore urgently needed.

Apart from a commonly acknowledged need to differentiate from US-based arts management concepts by broadening out to other forms of cultural expressions, all respondents agree that an integral part of arts management is "… ensuring everything runs smoothly, catering in a balanced way for the expectations of all stakeholders involved", as a UK colleague put it.

Most respondents agree that arts management has—at least to a certain extent—used tools borrowed and redefined from management (Chong, 2010; Henze, 2014). The respondent from Columbia called arts management a "dual concept", again referring to the two parts of the discipline today, arts and management.

Transcultural Arts Management

In the German context, we have seen a shift from intercultural to transcultural arts management in recent years. The term 'transcultural' refers to its coinage by Welsch (1994) some twenty-five years ago. Transcultural seems better suited to define collaborations that aim at creating something new with an inhomogeneous group of participants. Whereas 'intercultural' has more of a project character with a somehow pre-defined idea and end, 'transcultural' refers to an open process where the multiple competencies that the artists, participants, and organisations bring are considered as assets for co-creation. Whereas the term is common in German-speaking countries, it seems not to have made ground in other parts of the world for different reasons.

A colleague from the UK explains that 'transcultural' is:

… [n]ot something that really features very strongly in my own lexicon of teaching. Also, not something that I find a lot of students are specifically thinking about. While many are motivated by managing organisations and events that facilitate intercultural dialogue/exchange or even transcultural projects, the idea of transcultural arts management does not really hold much meaning for me.

In regards transnational arts management as a term/concept I would basically be making up an understanding of it on the basis of what transnational means—I would suppose that it referred to the management of arts organisations/projects that involved representatives from more than one culture or was taking place in/located in more than one culture. But as I say, I have never used the term myself!

In contrast, a practitioner from France with work experience in several European countries knows the concept well. She articulated strong dependence on raising funds from funding bodies that seem to use the term frequently:

Transcultural is one of these trendy terms that just appear [sic] one day, one of those that you absolutely have to use to characterise your work when applying to EU funds. I remember when everyone working in cultural cooperation started to use this term. I was living and working in Poland at the time, and suddenly all cross border projects became transborder cultural cooperation, our festival was not pluri- or multi-disciplinary anymore, but trans-disciplinary. There are countries where the translation just does not work, and I believe "transcultural" is not really accepted in conservative societies, people often associating the term with transgender. Additionally, as for the arts management part, in the French context, this is not really a term we use, as our way of working with arts and culture is still very sectored, and therefore not very "trans".

Apart from learning that arts management in France is siloed without much exchange between the different cultural sectors, this respondent makes us aware that sometimes terms are used as labels because they are considered "trendy". This is something often referred to as "ticking boxes" in application processes. Challenging the terminology as well as the underlying concepts of funders can be a delicate but necessary thing to do (Henze, 2018a).

An inspiring definition comes from a colleague in Singapore,

Like water temple networks that manage the ecology of rice terraces in some parts of Southeast Asia, where small groups of farmers focus on their own irriga- tion problems for their communities, and yet somehow work together to opti- mise rice harvests in dozens of villages. A transitory pattern of order that offers everyone involved a new way of thinking or rethinking about how people inter- act with the environment or ecosystem.

It is the practice of arts management with a focus on the regional and/or international scope, not merely on a national level, and yet is community-specific.

An intercultural working using adaptable communications that then becomes transcendent as communities are integrated.

It becomes apparent, therefore, that the idea of community engagement, which is closely linked to the idea of transcultural arts management, has a long-standing tradition in Asian arts management (Liu, 2014). Unfortunately, there is not enough literature on this available to 'Western' scholars. Where Zheng (2019) has undertaken an effort to introduce Chinese scholars to 'Western' arts management concepts, and while we find several arts management programmes in China, Hong Kong, Taiwan, and Singapore inviting 'Western' experts (mainly from the USA and UK) to lecture, there is still a lack of mutual exchange and a lot to learn from Asian narratives and methodologies (Liu, 2014).

Equality

The important difference between equality and equity does not exist in the German language. This absence results in German scholars using equality when speaking or writing in English, although they might actually be referring to equity. Where equity describes an approach that focuses on fair outcomes for all by applying measures that differ according to the respective needs, equality is about equal measures for all regardless of their individual needs.

A colleague from the USA refers to this issue in the following way:

This word immediately makes me think of separate but equal pre-civil rights in the U. S. Essentially, it's ensuring that everyone has the same thing. For example, access to education. But, I wonder if equality is ever really equal?

The practitioner from France, like many other participants, also doubts whether equality can ever be achieved:

First thing that comes to my mind is the French motto "Liberty, Equality, Fraternity", and I would define it as considering and giving opportunities to every human being regardless of their gender, belief, nationality, age, place of living, etc. This is one of the biggest issues of our modern societies, and when I look at what is happening today, I have no idea how we can reach equality. Education is definitely a way.

The colleague from Taiwan also underlines that we are not there yet:

Equal access to opportunities, disregarding gender, race, age, social status. To me, this has never happened. It is more like a process of people looking for ways to exclude factors such as power, social-economic-cultural capital differences in the field, in order to find a balance (or acceptable relations and solutions) among stakeholders of different positions.

That our definitions are also shaped by race, gender, and religious belief is equally important to recognise in our debates about specific concepts and terms, as was underlined by the Canadian colleague:

Equality—this term means that people should be treated equally despite their differences in gender, race, ability and any other situations that might put them at a disadvantage compared to the mainstream. Equality for me, as a woman of colour means that despite my gender and race it should not be seen negatively and that people like me should have the same fairness in all situations including personal and professional.

Overall, it becomes obvious that the definitions of equality in this study are relatively similar. What stands out is that all respondents consider achieving it to be a huge challenge.

An Indian practitioner explains:

Equality for me is lived through representation—something we struggle to ensure in the art world. Let us not just highlight diverse stories but create opportunities and spaces for practitioners from diverse backgrounds, and take art to diverse communities so more people can be involved in the practice of making and sharing art.

A colleague from Finland considers the Declaration of Human Rights as giving the sector the mandate to pursue its work:

> *The Universal Declaration of Human Rights from 1948, Article 27, says that everyone has the right to participate freely in the cultural life of the community, to enjoy and to share in scientific advancement and its benefits. It also includes a statement on the protection of artistic production. In times of financial cuts, cultural political decision-making, strong marketing orientation, etc., this gives us the reason and argumentation, we may need, as well as it requires from us a whole bunch of actions and activities.*

Social Impact

Few terms have caused as much activism, as well as many mixed feelings, as the term 'social impact'. Although the topic is by far a new one (Landry, Bianchini, & Maguire, 1993; Matarasso, 1997), a lot of research—particularly on how to measure social impact—has been conducted in Europe and the USA during recent years (Walmsley, 2013; O'Brien & Oakley, 2015; Newsinger & Green, 2016; Svensson, 2018; Belfiore & Bennett, 2007). One of the most recent and prominent works is the Arts and Humanities Research Council-funded Cultural Value Project in the UK (Crossick & Kaszynska, 2016). However, in South East Asia, arts organisations are faced with having to measure their impact as well. For example, in Singapore, several government agencies such as the Singapore Tourism Board and the National Art Council look into the outcome or results of arts projects supported by public arts funding. Many of these measurements look into economic gains, and levels of accessibility and participation of audiences in Singapore. In the Philippines, the National Commission for Culture and the Arts is tasked with evaluating and measuring the outcomes of publicly funded projects or agency initiatives. Interestingly, the topic seems to feature less prominently in China. If you search for evaluation of arts projects on CNKI—the Chinese journal article network—you get only six hits. Two of those reports are about evaluation of arts projects in the 'West'. This does not mean that evaluation as such is not a topic, but perhaps evaluation may be mainly aimed at measuring the market value of art works and it may otherwise be responsive to the particular context in that country.

In practice, it often seems as if the social value of the arts is taken for granted, and it is just a question of how to deal with the nuisance of funding bodies that ask for evaluations in order to justify their and the tax payers' contributions. That this approach might be too superficial is proved by several of the respondents' answers.

The majority of the participants, particularly the practitioners, react positively towards the term that is for many of them closely linked with community building and participation.

A Ghanaian researcher answers:

Social impact is about how do we monitor or evaluate the influence of the arts on the social well-being of people/how does it improve their lives?

An arts manager from Canada states:

Social impact—is making a community a better place through building a type of organization, group or collective of individuals. Social impact is such a solid way to connect with individuals and working towards a common goal that benefits a larger segment of a society. For me, social impact is conducted all the time and we might not even know it. It could be working for a non-profit organization and building homes or be a collective of women working with their ethnic community and engaging ideas, stories and promoting their culture to a younger generation.

Equally positive is the practitioner from Lebanon:

… it makes me think of a positive change in society as well as of active participation of individuals in a given society…

An Australian participant explains:

Social impact, while perhaps for some a broad and amorphous term, for me is easy to see—and actually not that hard to achieve if the community has agency and some power and the creative resources are focussed to that end rather than simply making art in a community.

A Columbian colleague associates social impact with:

> ... [w]ellbeing, nontraditional value creation, positive externalities.

Only two participants refer to negative effects. For example, a colleague from the UK remarks:

> A problematic term that is used liberally (and without enough specificity) and one which arts management students need to become critical users of. It is connected to discussions around instrumentalism, evaluation methods, and the mission/vision of arts organisations. I find that students often come to the programme with a 'belief' in the social impact of something called 'art' but that upon further investigation they have given little significant thought to it. Impact is also always assumed to be positive, and too little/no consideration is given to potentially negative impacts/ethical issues around the relationship between arts organisations/projects and the social spheres with which they interact.

A practitioner from France explains:

> This is a very strong aspect of my everyday work, something that I have always taken into consideration all along my professional career. Being aware that we, as arts managers, can have both negative and positive social impacts through our actions, like disturbing the local community while organising a music festival, or on the contrary working with the local community from the very beginning while putting an event together.

These last two comments are of particular interest. While there has been a lot of enthusiasm concerning community or participatory arts projects, particularly among practitioners (Henze, 2017a), and while most of those in the sector are fierce believers in what is sometimes somewhat nebulously called "the power of the arts", it is important to raise awareness of the fact that not all participatory or community arts projects are sustainable and that they might even perpetuate imbalances and create rejection (Canas, 2015, 2017; Henze, 2018b; Rush, this volume; Durrer, this volume). The dilemma is it is exactly this increasing scepticism concerning long-term effects that results in the idea of evaluating in order to be sure that the desired impact—desired by those that provide the funds—is achieved. Moreover, this leads to the difficulties of how to measure, for example, emotions and feelings that art works might arouse in individuals. How should one measure long-term impacts that even the respective individual might have difficulties to name, as a direct result of an artistic experience? (Walmsley, 2013)

A term closely related to 'social impact' is 'inclusive society'. It appears as a kind of vision for all those that believe in the social impact of arts projects for the well-being of individuals and societies.

Inclusive Society

Several respondents refer to the topic of migration and nationality when defining inclusive society.

A Brazilian practitioner hints at something that is widely discussed in the literature (Canas, 2015, 2017; Terkessidis, 2015; Mörsch, 2016; Henze, 2017a; Rush, this volume), by critiquing inclusion as being just about including those often presumed as 'others' into the mainstream, rather than addressing broader issues of social justice. According to her,

Rather than providing conditions for citizenship deprived minorities to be incorporated or absorbed into the dominant social fabric, an ideally inclusive society would be one in which the idea of majority and minority is discontinued in favour of another model of collective existence based on the multitude—as an open sum of interconnected singularities. Full citizenship should be a common right to all singularities, regardless of identity, belief, gender, education, social grouping or territory. A truly inclusive society would abolish concepts of border and nationality to favour a more universalist approach to unite mankind across its cultural differences.

Similarly, an Argentinian respondent explains:

An inclusive society (a concept that I am particularly interested in) is supposedly one that guarantees citizens to participate equally in various areas: education, culture ...

To achieve a (more) inclusive society, it is necessary to focus on issues such as access to education and employment, something difficult to offer when governments face the global migration crisis as a security problem or risk to national sovereignty.

Where many respondents referred to the responsibility of the state, only one colleague from the Netherlands mentioned the role that the arts sector plays in achieving what many have called a utopian idea.

For me this term relates to a society in which cultural work relating to the expression of identity constructively contributes to a national or transnational societal fabric.

Empowerment

Most participants underline the positive aspects of empowerment and the role it plays in community projects, as was stated by the colleague from Canada:

Empowerment—this term means to give power to those who might not feel that they have it and encouraging those people to take the power. Empowerment is one of the most useful tools to build a community, it could mean empowering the working class to have a voice in their place of employment and empower them to make a change towards their employer. It could also mean for me, as a young person to empower others to create a change and make a positive impact.

Some make more direct references to their respective countries or the region they come from, such as a colleague from Argentina:

For me, it is a process in which different tools are provided to an individual, a community or a social group to give them voice, strength, to improve their capabilities, etc. Always aiming to improve their social, political or economic situation. One case is the female empowerment at a global level and how this process affected the debates on state policies that are taking place in a large part of Latin America.

Three participants from Denmark, Germany, and Brazil remark on the one-sidedness of empowerment and refer to participatory arts projects critically.

The colleague from Denmark states:

What interests me is the fact that empowerment is always for someone else. No one says, "I want to be empowered". And is it at all possible to empower other people? I have just written an article about this—in relation to participatory art practices. If empowerment is about strengthening agency and the ability to achieve self-defined goals, how can we transfer that to other people? I think it's very important to move away from the deficit model and recognize the (various) skills and powers that all people have.

The German participant draws attention to a paternalism she sees as inherent in this concept:

I assume that empowerment is supposed to be a good thing. It is about giving a voice to those that have not yet had one in the discourse. However, being empowered does not mean that you have power. When having a closer look at some participatory arts projects or even worse at cultural policy to me it seems to be a huge fad. Give them a good feeling but do not change anything. I furthermore think it has something paternalistic. It is again those within the sector that decide that they have to empower others.

The Brazilian practitioner summarises the concerns raised by her two European counterparts:

Is empowerment: to concede power? to claim power? to conquest power? to redistribute power? to re-signify power? Is empowerment a matter of who versus who based on a sort of "inequality is the rule" paradigm?

If we admit "inequality is the rule", therefore inequality will be always present somehow. Would there be an alternative paradigm (that would drive to unexpected results) instead of the "inequality as rule" minorities empowering approach?

Instead of playing the "one side empowering"/"other side weakening" game—based on "inequality is the rule" paradigm—what if we could imagine a sort of redistribution of the sensible based on the premise that equality is the original landscape / inequality is the exception (a huge exception indeed) / and work—somehow—towards a return to an original "equality as rule" multitude landscape?

The final term 'post-colonialism' has been prominent for decades, particularly due to the outstanding works by Stuart Hall, that have appeared on many literature lists in arts management curricula.

Post-colonialism

That the geographic background plays a significant role became most nuanced with the term post-colonialism. For example, the American colleague refers to race and to how to deal with the devastating effects that colonialism has created:

In reflecting on this word, the question, "is there any place on the planet that people of colour can go where they do not have to engage with Whiteness or the implications of it," came to mind. To me, it is how victims of colonialism make sense of their experience.

The colleague from Puerto Rico refers to the work of institutions like the World Bank or the International Monetary Fund:

I always believe in post-colonialism as [a] mental state, where knowledge [is] still subject to that influence and not necessarily based on local needs or knowledge development. For example, we always talk about post-colonialism in economic development strategies in Latin America when it comes to IMF or World Bank initiatives (mostly because of a Eurocentric view, very different from regional development reality).

The respondent from Australia refers to his countries' historical connection and still existent ties to the British Empire, which has a particular long history in colonialisation:

Perhaps ironically in the Australian context, the term/topic/idea is not as prevalent in arts and cultural discourse as it once was. I could be wrong but my sense of it is that Australia is no longer preoccupied by its rear view mirror as it moves forward. While still part of the British Commonwealth and previously oriented to it, Australia now looks more like the USA, more recently its orientation has shifted towards Asia (its own region).

Where some may see the relevance of the topic in decline, others—particularly those living in former colonies—underline the relevance of it up to the present day. A practitioner from India explains:

Post colonialism is still relevant particularly when it comes to the idea of hybrid identities- and as artists we can find spaces of liminality and hybridity to challenge set notions of identity, community, personal and collective.

A participant from Ghana defines it as such:

It is about how the aftermath of colonialization/the colonial legacy affects the African understanding of the arts.

A participant from Cameroon, a county with a century long history of colonialisation, defines the term without any reference to his country of origin:

Post colonialism is a theory or field of study that looks at how formerly colonised societies are faring in today's world, perhaps with focus on the cultural influence on these societies and how it helps (or not) in the integration of these societies in today's global world.

A colleague from Columbia, a country that owes its name to Christoph Columbus, interestingly does not refer to Columbia's long history as a Spanish colony, but to Africa and Europe when he is asked to spontaneously give his thoughts on the term post-colonialism:

Africa, Europe migration, conflict and wars

The colleagues from Northern countries, by contrast, do not relate much to the term. The colleague from Denmark states, by way of example:

It is not a word that I use very often. What pops up is an artwork by Jeanette Ehlers 'Whip It Good', a Caribbean diaspora artist born and based in Denmark. It is a live performance where she re-enacts the whipping of enslaved people by whipping a white canvas with a whip rubbed in charcoal. After having done that several times (very strongly!), she invites the audience to take the whip and do the same. I couldn't!

A German arts management researcher explains:

For years the concept did not feature in my courses. Only when I started to become more involved in international arts management it became of interest to me. I would make a difference between post-colonialism which is in my eyes how to deal with the devastating effects that colonialism has caused particularly by destroying cultural identities and neo-colonialism which I personally think is a concept still too often (involuntarily) applied by e.g. the Goethe Institut.

Conclusion

Language as such and multilingualism in particular both need greater reflection in our discourses. Languages are transmitters of cultures as well as integral part of (cultural) identities (Hall, 2000; Zou, 2012). More research on multilingualism can therefore benefit (participatory) arts projects that strive to involve more people from diverse ethnic backgrounds. In arts management research, greater and deeper reflection on the language and terminology, as well as on the frames of reference we use, will help us to experience new narratives and approaches that we have been indifferent to for too long. In the study presented, it became apparent that the understanding of certain terms, that stand for specific concepts in arts management, does not differ as much as was presumed with regard to where we are actually based. This might in part be explained by the fact that most of the respondents have been engaging with other cultures and languages for years in their profession. Several of them have been trained or worked outside of their country of origin. Almost all of the researchers involved participate in international arts management conferences. However, there are obviously references to the particular country the person comes from. This is not surprising since our environment shapes our understanding. Without being aware of this and working out these differences, we would most likely agree on a common denominator that can never reflect the variety inherent in our understandings. Instead, we should accept that definitions and concept are never valid and applicable for everyone.

The fact that arts management concepts from Europe have been exported to, for example, Argentina where they do not fit and cause resistance in the sector is as revealing as is the different professional roles that have emerged, in, for example, Puerto Rico. That post-colonialism and all it implies seems more relevant to those that have somehow experienced it is of huge interest for the work in the international field. It is once again about sensitivities. Nevertheless, it is obviously not only geography that shapes our ideas, views, and philosophies. As has been shown in this research as well, a great deal of discussion has been based on race, age, and gender, for instance. Hall (2000, p. 21) has stressed this already years ago by saying: "We all write and speak from a particular place and time, from a history and a culture which is specific. What we say is always 'in context,' positioned".

What follows from this? Will we always be lost in 'translation' and never really be able to understand what someone of, for example, a different origin, gender, religious belief, or ethnicity wants to express? The answer might be—unsurprisingly—yes. However, this is an amazing chance if we are willing to learn as much as we can by working out these differences. Being sensitive to these differences and learning from them is surely a valuable quality to foster relationships, shared beliefs, and common goals in the entire discipline.

A Taiwanese respondent explained transcultural arts management in this research as such:

> the recognition and acceptance of different ways of arts management in different cultures, i.e. collaboration and coordination without harmonisation.

This is exactly what we should all be striving for.

References

Abbas, A., & Erni, J. (2005). Introduction: Internationalising cultural studies. In A. Abbas & J. Erni (Eds.), *Internationalising cultural studies* (pp. 1–12). Malden, MA: Blackwell Publishing.

Belfiore, E., & Bennett, O. (2007). Rethinking the social impacts of the arts. *International Journal of Cultural Policy, 13*(2), 135–151.

Bennet, T., Grossberg, L., & Morris, M. (2005). *New keywords. A revised vocabulary of culture and society.* Malden, MA: Blackwell Publishing.

Bishop, C. (2012). *Artificial hells: Participatory art and the politics of spectatorship.* London and New York: J.P. Tarcher/Putnam.

Borwick, D. (2012). *Building communities, not audiences: The future of the arts in the United States.* Winston-Salem: ArtsEngaged.

Canas, T. (2015). 10 things you need to consider if you are an artist—Not of the refugee and asylum seeker community—Looking to work with our community. Retrieved June 23, 2016, from http://riserefugee.org/10-things-you-need-to-consider-if-you-are-an-artist-not-of-the-refugee-and-asylum-seeker-community-looking-to-work-with-our-community/#

Canas, T. (2017). Diversity is a white word. Retrieved February 19, 2017, from http://www.artshub.com.au/education/news-article/opinions-and-analysis/professional-development/tania-canas/diversity-is-a-white-word-252910

Castineira de Dios, J. L. (2009). *Crítica* de la *Gestión Cultural pura.* Revista Aportes, No. 23. Venezuela, Argentina, 79–92. Retrieved February 20, 2019, from https://www.asociaciong.org.ar/pdfaportes/23/07.pdf

Chong, D. (2010). *Arts management.* London: Routledge.

Crossick, G., & Kaszynska, P. (2016). AHRC Cultural Value Project. Final report. Retrieved January 26, 2019, from http://www.ahrc.ac.uk/documents/publications/cultural-value-project-final-report/

De Sousa Santos, B. (2014). *Epistemologies of the South: Justice against epistemicide.* London: Routledge.

DeVereaux, C. (2009). Cultural management and the discourse of practice. In *Jahrbuch für Kulturmanagement 2009* (pp. 155–167). Bielefeld: Transcript Verlag.

Dittwald, R., Genc, S., Haude, K., Kutscher, S., Lehmann, K., Schultze-Bernd, E., et al. (2007). *Sprachen Verschwinden. Gesellschaft für bedrohte Sprachen.* Köln: Institut für Lingusitik. Retrieved February 21, 2019, from http://gbs.uni-koeln.de/wordpress/wp-content/uploads/2017/06/Broschure.pdf.

Dragićević-Šešić, M., & Mihaljinac, N. (this volume). Cultural management training within cultural diplomacy agendas in the MENA region. In V. Durrer & R. Henze (Eds.), *Managing culture: Reflecting on exchange in our global times* (pp. 205–231). Basingstoke: Palgrave Macmillan.

Durrer, V. (this volume). A call for reflexivity: Implications of the internationalization agenda for arts management programmes within higher education. In V. Durrer, & R. Henze (Eds.), *Managing culture: Reflecting on exchange in our global times* (pp. 173–203). Basingstoke: Palgrave Macmillan.

Durrer, V., & Henze, R. (2018). Leaving comfort zones. In *Arts Management Quarterly*, Leaving comfort zones. Cultural inequalities, no. 129, June 2018, 3.

Gutiérrez, J., Grant, P.S., & Colbert, F. (2016). Arts management in developing countries: A Latin American perspective. *International Journal of Arts Management*. Special Edition Latin America. HEC Montreal, *18*, 6–17.

Hall, B. L., & Tandon, R. (2017). Decolonization of knowledge, epistemicide, participatory research and higher education. *Research for All, 1*(1), 6–19.

Hall, S. (2000). Cultural identity and diaspora. In N. Mirzoeff (Ed.), *Diaspora and visual culture: Representing Africans and Jews* (pp. 21–34). London and New York: Routledge.

Hampel, A. (2014). *Fair Cooperation—Partnerschaftliche Zusammenarbeit in der Auswärtigen Kulturpolitik*. Wiesbaden: Springer VS Verlag.

Hampel, A. (2016). Kooperationskultur in den Künsten: Perspektiven am Beispiel deutsch-indischer Partnerschaften. In W. Schneider and A. Kaitinnis (Eds.), *Kulturarbeit in Transformationsprozessen. Innenansichten zur ›Außenpolitik‹ des Goethe-Instituts* (pp. 155–160). Wiesbaden: Springer VS Verlag.

Henze, R. (2014). *Kultur und Management: Eine Annäherung*. Wiesbaden: Springer VS Verlag.

Henze, R. (2017a). *Introduction to international arts management*. Wiesbaden: Springer VS Verlag.

Henze, R. (2017b). Why we have to overcome paternalism in times of populism. In M. Dragićević-Šešić (Ed.), *Cultural diplomacy: Arts, festivals and geopolitics* (pp. 73–87). Belgrade: Ministry of Culture Republic of Serbia & University of Arts.

Henze, R. (2018a). The master's tool will never dismantle the master's house. *Arts Management Quarterly*, Leaving comfort zones. Cultural inequalities, no. 129, June 2018, 29–35.

Henze, R. (2018b). Kultur mit allen statt Kultur für alle. Demokratisierung von Kunst und Kultur im 21. Jahrhundert. In Jahrbuch für Kulturpolitik

2017/2018. *Thema Welt.Kultur.Politik. Kulturpolitik in Zeiten der Globalisierung* (pp. 329–341). Bielefeld: Transcript Verlag.

Henze, R. (2018c). Eurocentrism in European arts management. In M. Dragićević-Šešić & J. Vickery (Eds.), *Cultural policy and populism* (Cultural Policy Yearbook 2017/2018, pp. 31–43). Istanbul Bilgi University. Istanbul: Iletisim.

Hernández-Acosta, J. (2013). Differences in cultural policy and its implications for arts management: Case of Puerto Rico. *The Journal of Arts Management, Law, and Society, 43*(3), 125–138.

Hernández-Acosta, J. (this volume). Navigating between arts management and cultural agency: Latin America's contribution to a new approach for the field. In V. Durrer & R. Henze (Eds.), *Managing culture: Reflecting on exchange in our global times* (pp. 271–291). Basingstoke: Palgrave Macmillan.

Jacobsen, U. C. (2015). Cosmopolitan sensitivities, vulnerability, and Global Englishes. *Language and Intercultural Communication, 15*(4), 459–474.

Jacobsen, U. C. (2018). Language in art and cultural management. In *Arts Management Quarterly*, Leaving comfort zones. Cultural Inequalities, No. 129, June 2018, pp. 17–23.

James, N. (2016). Using email interviews in qualitative educational research: Creating space to think and time to talk. *International Journal of Qualitative Studies in Education, 29*(2), 150–163.

Jullien, F. (2018). *Es gibt keine kulturelle Identität*. Berlin: Edition suhrkamp.

Korf, B., & Rothfuß, E. (2015). Nach der Entwicklungsgeographie. In T. Freytag, H. Gebhard, U. Gebhard, & D. Wastl-Walter (Eds.), *Humangeographie kompakt* (pp. 164–182). Wiesbaden: Springer Spektrum.

Landry, C., Bianchini, F., & Maguire, M. (1993). *The social impact of the arts: A discussion document*. Stroud: Comedia.

Latour, B. (2011). Waiting for Gaia. Composing the common world through arts and politics. A lecture at the French Institute, London, November 2011. Retrieved February 20, 2019, from http://bruno-latour.fr/sites/default/files/124-GAIA-LONON-SPEAP_0.pdf

Liu, J. (2014). ReOrienting cultural policy. Cultural statecraft and cultural governance in Taiwan and China. In L. Kim & H. K. Lee (Eds.), *Cultural policy in East Asia. Dynamics between the states, arts and creative industries* (pp. 120–138). London: Palgrave Macmillan.

Mandel, B. (2016). *Arts/cultural management in international contexts*. Hildesheim: Georg Olms Verlag.

Matarasso, F. (1997). *Use or ornament: The social impact of participation in the arts.* London: Comedia Publishing Group.

Meho, L. I. (2006). E-mail interviewing in qualitative research: A methodological discussion. *Journal of the American Society for Information Science and Technology, 57*(10), 1284–1295.

Mörsch, C. (2016). Refugees sind keine Zielgruppe. In M. Ziese & C. Gritschke (Eds.), *Geflüchtete und Kulturelle Bildung. Formate und Konzepte für ein neues Praxisfeld* (pp. 67–74). Bielefeld: Transcript.

Newsinger, J., & Green, W. (2016). The infrapolitics of cultural value: Cultural policy, evaluation and the marginalisation of practitioner perspectives. *Journal of Cultural Economy, 9*(4), 382–395.

O'Brien, D., & Oakley, K. (2015). Cultural value and inequality: A critical literature review. A report commissioned by the Arts and Humanities Research Council's Cultural Value Project. Retrieved February 12, 2019, from https://ahrc.ukri.org/documents/project-reports-and-reviews/cultural-value-and-inequality-a-critical-literature-review/

Pilic, I., & Wiederhold, A. (2015). *Kunstpraxis in der Migrationsgesellschaft. Transkulturelle Handlungsstrategien am Beispiel der Brunnenpassage Wien.* Vienna: KunstSozialRaum Brunnenpassage.

Rösler, B. (2015). The case of the Asialink's arts residency program: Towards a critical cosmopolitan approach to cultural diplomacy. *International Journal of Cultural Policy, 21*(4), 20–30.

Rowntree, J., Neal, L., & Fenton, R. (2011). *International cultural leadership: Reflections, competencies and interviews. British Council.* https://creativeconomy.britishcouncil.org/media/uploads/files/International_Cultural_Leadership_report.pdf

Rush, K. (this volume). Value as fiction: An anthropological perspective. In V. Durrer & R. Henze (Eds.), *Managing culture: Reflecting on exchange in our global times* (pp. 81–96). Basingstoke: Palgrave Macmillan.

Shohat, E., & Stam, R. (2005). De-eurocentricizing cultural studies: Some proposals. In A. Abbas & J. Erni (Eds.), *Internationalising cultural studies* (pp. 481–498). Malden, MA: Blackwell Publishing.

Shome, R. (2012). Asian modernities: Culture, politics and media. *Global Media and Communication, 8*(3), 199–214.

Svensson, J. (2018). *Die Kunst, Kultur (nicht nur) zu messen. Evaluation im Theater- und Kulturbetrieb.* Münster: Lit Verlag.

Terkessidis, M. (2015). *Kollaboration.* Berlin: Suhrkamp Verlag.

Tonks, A. (2016). *The A to Z of arts management. Reflections on theory and reality.* Prahran: Tilde Publishing and Distribution.

Universitat Oberta de Catalunya. (2019). Retrieved February 21, 2019, from https://estudios.uoc.edu/es/masters-universitarios/gestion-cultura/itinerario

Walmsley, B. (2013). Whose value is it anyway? A neo-institutional approach to articulating and evaluating artistic value. *Journal of Arts & Communities, 4*(3), 199–215.

Welsch, W. (1994). Transkulturalität—die veränderte Verfassung heutiger Kulturen. In *Sichtweisen, Die Vielfalt der Einheit.* Weimar: Weimarer Klassik.

Zheng, J. (2019). *Cultural management: Evolution and education in the world.* Hong Kong: Chung Hwa Book Co. (H.K.) Ltd.

Ziese, M., & Gritschke, C. (2016). *Geflüchtete und Kulturelle Bildung. Formate und Konzepte für ein neues Praxisfeld.* Bielefeld: Transcript.

Zou, H. (2012). Language identity and cultural difference. *International Journal of Social Science and Humanity, 2*(6). Retrieved February 21, 2019, from https://www.researchgate.net/publication/286258662_Language_Identity_and_Cultural_Difference

4

Value as Fiction: An Anthropological Perspective

Kayla Rush

Introduction

In this chapter, I take as my object of study a rather slippery concept: that of 'value'. Anthropologists tell us that value is a notoriously difficult term, encompassing as it does so many aspects that give shape to human life and society: ideas about morality, aesthetics, economic or monetary worth, priorities shared among the members of a particular social or cultural group and so on (Graeber, 2001; Herzfeld, 2004; Miller, 2008; O'Brien, 2014). Value is, moreover, ubiquitous. We make value judgments every day. We evaluate the world around us, both knowingly and unconsciously. We use our evaluations and ideas about value to make decisions large and small. This ubiquity extends to contemporary arts and cultural management practice. It seems that arts and cultural managers are constantly making, or are expected to constantly make, value arguments regarding their own work—to colleagues, to peers, to government institutions, to funders, to board members, to potential or current

K. Rush (✉)
Clark State Community College, Springfield, OH, USA
e-mail: Krush03@qub.ac.uk

© The Author(s) 2020
V. Durrer, R. Henze (eds.), *Managing Culture*, Sociology of the Arts,
https://doi.org/10.1007/978-3-030-24646-4_4

transnational partners, to artists, to audiences and to the public—that is, to all key stakeholders in their work.

Preponderance of discussion, however, does not guarantee clarity, for within these constant valuings and evaluations remains the difficulty of determining precisely what we mean. When an arts manager speaks of the value of her work, is she referring to its economic worth? And how might that be determined? By economic activity generated in a certain area, by the resale value of the finished artistic product, by the financial stability with which her pay will hopefully provide her? Or is she referring to the aesthetic value of a work, programme or project, a vague measure at the best of times, and one which has been notoriously contested throughout history? All of this means that, in practice, when discussing value it becomes easy for stakeholders of arts and culture to speak past each other: using the same language and rhetoric, but not always in the same way, or with the same understanding.

The language of value in arts and cultural management has come to the fore in recent decades, particularly in the United Kingdom (UK) context, where my own research has been based. A few brief notes on the particular UK policy context are required here to situate the discussion that follows. It will also demonstrate some of the ways in which arts and culture stakeholders end up embroiled in discursive contestation and talking past each other. While my own reasoning has been indelibly shaped by its particular context, it is my intent that the discussion in this chapter be of interest and relevance to artists and arts managers who hail from and work within a wide diversity of cultural and intercultural contexts.

In recent years, value in arts and culture has often been glossed as 'cultural value'. Cultural value is viewed as distinct from, though still entangled with, economic or monetary value (Throsby, 2001; Hutter & Frey, 2010). At its core, this notion asserts that the value of arts and culture cannot be measured merely in currency, but rather that they tap into some sort of intangible, unquantifiable value, one that makes human life more meaningful. The cultural value discourse is best exemplified by a series of well-funded and -publicised research projects in the UK such as the *Warwick Commission on the Future of Cultural Value* (Neelands et al.,

2015) and the Arts and Humanities Research Council *Cultural Value Project* (Crossick & Kaszynska, 2016; see also Crossick & Kaszynska, 2014).

Cultural value is a culturally and politically specific notion, emerging out of the UK cultural policy context in response to other, previously dominant (and still highly influential) types of valuing and evaluation, particularly those which arose in the latter half of the twentieth century. The history of this development has been discussed at length in a number of scholarly publications (see below) and is beyond the scope of this chapter. Most important to note here, however, is that in the UK a public policy and managerial emphasis on the social value of arts and culture emerged roughly in the 1980s, focusing on the ability to effect 'impact' by contributing to broader policy aims such as welfare, economic development and healthcare. This was closely tied to, and thus further propagated by, the aims of the New Labour government from 1997 to 2010 (Hesmondhalgh, Oakley, Lee, & Nisbett, 2015). Cultural value incorporates these ideas about social value, but attempts to broaden them, to take a much wider view of what 'value' might mean, one grounded more in individual experiences without losing sight of wider-spread 'impact' (Crossick & Kaszynska, 2016).

While readers' own policy contexts may differ, debates of this sort on the nature of value in arts and culture are found throughout the world (Bianchini & Parkinson, 1993; Matarasso, 1997; Gray, 2007; UNESCO, 2013, 2014; Hesmondhalgh et al., 2015). This is especially, though not exclusively, true in places where arts and culture receive some form of public subsidy (see e.g. Hillman Chartrand & McCaughey, 1989; Lim, 2014; Durrer, Miller, & O'Brien, 2018). More specifically, Şuteu (2006), Nisbett (2013), Dragićević-Šešić (2015) and Durrer (2018) have discussed the ways in which the work of arts and cultural managers in different national contexts has become connected to—and thus valued according to—such diverse areas of government concern as economic development, community and social cohesion, reconciliation and cultural diplomacy. Difficulties in pinning down the meaning of 'value', in other words, are global in occurrence, and even localised debates may have far-reaching international resonances or effects.

My goal in this chapter is not to unify the language of value, which would at any rate be an impossible task. My aim is rather to pull on these threads, using the specific lens provided by anthropological investigation, which is my own discipline. To speak as a disciplinary outsider is, perhaps, an unusual approach to the themes of this volume; however, anthropology has long traded on the idea that the cultural outsider, in observing the everyday lives and experiences of those other than herself, has the potential to see with fresh eyes that which those others might take for granted—to bring to the discussion another perspective.

In this chapter, I will first argue that 'value' is a fundamentally fictitious concept, rooted in the subjective experiences of individuals of different perspectives and cultural backgrounds. Following that, I will introduce a new concept for discussing, analysing and making sense of the multiple value fictions we encounter, a concept that I have termed the 'cracked art world'. I will argue that value conflict is inherent to art worlds and thus colours all aspects of arts management practice. In this discussion, I attempt to bring together anthropological theory with the everyday lived experiences of arts and cultural management, suggesting that the former might provide linguistic and analytical tools for better explaining the often-frustrating realities of the latter. I will conclude the chapter by making suggestions for some ways in which these ideas and their application might foster new debates about the nature and practice of intercultural arts management—that is, arts management practices which traverses national and cultural boundaries.

Value as Ethnographic Fiction

We anthropologists have long claimed 'culture' as our purview—culture conceptualised quite broadly, including not just the arts and cultural industries, though those are of course part of it; but rather the whole of human sociocultural experience: ways of life, social relationships, language, patterns of thought, "body, evolution, origins, tools, art" and so on, "as parts or aspects of a general pattern, or whole"—that is, as partial aspects of the whole of human experience (Wagner, 1981, p. 1).

In the pursuit of knowledge about these varied aspects of culture, many anthropologists pursue a particular type of methodology called 'ethnography'—a sort of intensive 'being there', of experiencing everyday life, both exciting and mundane, alongside our cultural others. Ethnographic research methods, long the province of anthropologists but increasingly employed by those in other disciplines as well, are rooted in the idea that long-term engagement with a group or groups of people will provide the researcher with insights that she could not otherwise gain (Willis & Trondman, 2000). Readers with backgrounds in artistic practice may recognise these ideas, as ethnographic methods have grown increasingly prominent within contemporary art practice since the late twentieth century (sometimes called the 'ethnographic turn'; see Foster, 1996, pp. 171–203; Coles, 2000; Desai, 2002; Schneider, 2008). With regards to arts management specifically, ethnography has been variously deployed to inform understandings of organisational work culture (Stadler, Reid, & Fullagar, 2013; Schlesinger, Selfe, & Munro, 2015), public safety (Mackellar, 2013) and audience experience (Walmsley, 2011). Crossick and Kaszynska (2016) have also indicated its usefulness in understanding cultural value.

Viewed through the lens of anthropological and ethnographic research, 'value'—particularly as it relates to culture—is ultimately a fiction. I use 'fiction' here not in the sense of falsehood, per se, but rather in the sense of a thing crafted to serve a purpose. Ethnographers have long recognised the constructed, and thus inherently 'fictitious', nature of their work. Given that the medium of research is the ethnographer's own mind and body, her own personal experience while doing life with and alongside her interlocutors, the knowledge produced will always be subjective, 'inherently partial—committed and incomplete' (Clifford, 1986, pp. 6–7). In describing this phenomenon, anthropologists have repeatedly referred to ethnographic knowledge as fictitious (Geertz, 1973, p. 15; Conquergood, 1989, p. 83) and invented (Wagner, 1981).

In the same way that ethnography is invented or fictitious, so too is value. Like ethnographic knowledge, value is not a fixed, objective measure, but is rather made up, constructed according to evaluators' ideas about what is important and worthwhile. Like ethnographic knowledge, understandings of value—and relatedly, of what is valuable, or of how evaluation ought to be conducted—do not exist separately from individual human perspectives; rather, they are mediated through the evaluators' own bodies, experiences and cultural understandings. Like ethnographic research in anthropology, value in arts and cultural management is partial, grounded in particular, subjective points of view. Value is, thus, an ethnographic fiction: each idea or argument about value in arts and culture

> has been crafted based on the skills and dispositions of its author, while recognising that [s]he believed it to be, for the most part, the truth as [s]he understood it. (Hansen, 2009, p. 35)

With these ideas in mind, we might take the argument one step further still, arguing that value is, moreover, a science fiction, in that it is often portrayed as something 'scientific'—something to be measured and quantified; something objective, inherent or unchanging. The subjective nature of value frequently finds itself at odds with such calls for objective measures of value—that is, for 'facts'. Such 'facts' are often gathered and evaluated in order to ensure a financial return on investment for public funding (Belfiore, 2004), so that arts and cultural managers are engaged in constant processes of data-gathering and -sharing as a way of legitimising their labour and practice. And yet these facts are constructed, based on the evaluators' particular ethnographic notions of what is valuable. The nature of these facts is culturally relative, and they shift according to prevailing political and social ideas. Thus, artists and arts and cultural managers must frequently adjust to new value regimes, to new science fictions that dictate their ability to carry out their work.

The science fiction of value is particularly evident in arguments based in economics or measures of instrumentality. It has risen to considerable prominence, especially within the UK, but also in relation to European cultural funds, through the increasing prevalence of 'audit culture'—a phenomenon which anthropologists Shore and Wright (2015) describe as

> the process by which the principles and techniques of accountancy and financial management are applied to the governance of people and organisations. (p. 24)

Put more cynically, audit culture is the result of an

increasing fetishisation of statistical measurement and competitive ranking as robust and reliable instruments for calculating (and enhancing) what are largely qualitative features such as 'excellence', 'quality', 'value' and 'effectiveness'. (Shore & Wright, 2015, p. 22)

What these authors, and others, argue is that a certain type of evaluation, one presumed to be based in objective 'fact' and usually tied to quantitative measurements, has become a central part of the ways in which both the public and private sectors conduct themselves and present themselves to the world as ordered, efficient and, ultimately, valuable (see also Strathern, 2000, 2016; Selwood, 2002; Belfiore, 2004; Karttunen, 2012; Ladkin, McKay, & Bojesen, 2016). While the *Cultural Value Project* in the UK (Crossick & Kaszynska, 2016) sets an important precedent in calling for qualitative and especially ethnographic research into the value of arts and cultural activity, and thus in recognising that value is not always quantifiable, qualitative research alone does not signal a departure from audit culture.

Audit culture is not inherently a bad thing, although many of the academics writing on it do tend to view it in a negative light, often due to their own experiences in their workplaces (e.g. Spooner, 2018). What it *is*, however, is a fiction—one grounded in particular, largely Eurocentric cultural ideals about how businesses, governments and sectors should be run, what they should produce and what they should expect in return. It is one among many available ethnographic fictions that speak to the topics of value and evaluation.

The Cracked Art World

These fictions of and about value exist within what I call 'cracked art worlds'. 'Art worlds' is drawn from Becker (1982), who characterises an art world as the sum total of the individuals and institutions whose ideas and labours are necessary for a work of art to be conceived, created, circulated and critiqued. The *cracked* art world is precisely that, but splintered, misaligned: an art world in which the many players do not always see eye to eye. The cracked art world is much like a cracked mirror. When a mirror is cracked, the images on either side of the crack will never quite align. While the mirror remains functional, still fulfilling its role of reflecting an image back to the viewer, the two sides will never be perfectly joined. The image is misaligned; while it is whole, it has an uncanny quality—it feels not-quite-right.

The metaphor can easily be applied to art worlds and the different stakeholders therein. Arts managers engaged in intercultural partnerships know from experience that different individuals or groups of people experience arts and culture in different ways. I can never experience life as anyone other than myself, and so I must employ imagination and empathy to feel something of the experiences of others. While my imagination can be quite successful in doing this, my experience is never precisely the same as that of another. And this is true of value as well: my own values as regards arts and culture, and my evaluations thereof, will likely share similarities with those of others, but they will never be precisely the same, as each of our perspectives will be shaped by life experiences, cultural norms, social conditioning and a host of other factors. As with the cracked mirror, art worlds still function despite these differences, which can range from the barely perceptible hairline fracture to more jagged breaks. (And it is worth noting that only in very rare cases does an art world shatter completely and cease to exist.) Art worlds carry on and continue to make art in spite of—and even, perhaps, because of—these differences. And yet the cracks cannot be ignored, for they are endemic to art worlds, and they give it its shape.

Values and evaluation are culturally learned and conditioned phenomena, and our cultures' values influence our individual decision- and value-making. They also influence policy-making and other collaborative or societal acts of ascribing and measuring value. We can see this in the case of UK audit culture described above; the move towards audit culture and its particular values has been informed by cultural values such as efficiency, financial expediency and specific ideas about the role of government. As each individual person, group, organisation or institution approaches questions of and discourses about value from different, ethnographically situated perspectives, so too will their ideas about value all be unique. And while there may be widespread agreement about certain things—an overall picture that will more or less come into focus—these ideas will never quite fully align, as the images on either side of a crack in a mirror will never fully align. The cultural value discourse in the UK is one example of this phenomenon: since its emergence in the early 2000s, ideas about cultural value have been contested, shaped by the divergent views of different arts and culture stakeholders (O'Brien, 2014, pp. 122–125).

The cracked nature of art worlds, and thus of various stakeholders' approaches to and understandings of value and evaluation, is precisely what makes value discourse so difficult. As Proctor (2015) tells us, discourses that are nominally about the same thing diverge and twist around each other fractally—similar and yet 'not self-identical' (p. 295). Value discourses simultaneously intersect and splinter along the fault lines of the cracked art world; this is how differently positioned speakers or evaluators, while ostensibly addressing the same subject, can easily end up talking past one another. Much of the language with which we discuss value is similar, but it also diverges; it repeats itself, but it also changes according to the position of the speaker; and it replicates itself across time and space, raising the same core questions in new iterations.

Funding Applications as Tournaments of Value

This fragmentation, this splintering and misalignment, is always present in art worlds; it is inevitable. It also has real-world implications. Ideas about value within cracked art worlds meet and compete in what Appadurai (1986) calls 'tournaments of value': "complex periodic events that are removed in some culturally well-defined way from the routines of economic life" (p. 21). According to Appadurai, what is principally at stake in tournaments of value is "the disposition of the central tokens of value in the society in question" (p. 21). Though tournaments of value are set apart from the quotidian norm,

> their forms and outcomes are always consequential for the more mundane realities of power and value in ordinary life. (p. 21)

Funding applications at local, national and international levels comprise perhaps the best-known tournaments of value within art worlds. These are high-stake games, in which the success or failure of value arguments is often tied to increased or decreased funding for arts and cultural organisations and transnational partnerships. Funding applications are set-apart spaces in which one organisation or institution manifests its particular set of values, and in which those manifest values meet those of another institution or organisation—the funder, as well as the other institutions against whom the applicant is competing for the funder's limited support. As argued by Jhunjhunwala and Walker (this volume) and Hampel (2017), not all participants in a tournament of value are equal. In any meeting of values, there are dominant and marginal discourses that underpin not only funding practices and distribution but also conceptual frames for project objectives, as well as routinised arts and cultural management practices. This becomes even more apparent, and more complicated, when the tournament of value occurs within transnational contexts, where the tournament's players must also navigate complex differences in cultural values (see e.g. Aragon & Leach, 2008).

Imbalances of power are inherent in the artistic encounter. The artist, and/or the arts manager, depending on the structure and hierarchy of a given project, is always a figure of authority, even where that authority might be "decentered" (Desai, 2002, p. 310). Power flows unevenly towards those conceptualising, framing and leading a project, and away from those who engage with it, whether as participants, co-creators or audience members. These positions of power include the ability to decide what is and is not valuable, and what constitutes a valuable project. Those in positions of power are also, typically, more involved in the evaluation process than their less powerful collaborators or interlocutors, a reality that can further exacerbate issues of power.

In speaking of intercultural work, it is also worth bearing in mind that the arts management sector is far less diverse than the general population, and its diversity has "contracted" in recent years (Neelands et al., 2015, p. 35). This is further exacerbated by the overwhelming dominance of the English language in scholarship, and in cultural exchange more generally (Proctor, 2015; Henze, 2018), as well as in the increasingly dominant role played by European and North American third-level institutions in educating arts and cultural managers (Durrer, Chap. 8). Where English is valued above other languages—even when only valued as a *lingua franca*, and not necessarily because of cultural imperialism—it stands to reason that the values associated with English-speaking might rise to the fore and thus potentially eclipse others (Henze, Chap. 3). Where education at an Anglophone university represents a highly prized commodity, and even in some cases a necessary requirement for accessing full-time work in the arts and culture sector, such institutions will play a disproportionate role in determining the values that shape intercultural exchanges and the methods by which these works are evaluated.

Thus, as power flows (as it is naturally inclined to do) towards arts managers and cultural producers, as well as scholars of arts management and cultural policy, it also flows towards an increasingly homogenised creative workforce, whose values may not match up entirely with those of their cultural interlocutors. This is, to my mind, the most important caution raised by a cracked art world analysis, for without recognising the differences of value, valuing and evaluation that exist within art worlds, we run the risk of repeating the value regimes of the dominant majority, and in so doing perhaps obscuring those of the less powerful, of the cultural 'other'.

This is where recognising the shape of the cracked art world becomes vitally important, especially for artists and arts managers who work interculturally or are interested in doing so. A tournament of value occurs upon an inherently unequal playing field. When taken uncritically, a tournament of value has the potential to drown out more marginal voices and values, to declare victory to those who conform to dominant norms and values in intercultural exchanges (see Vidmar-Horvat, 2012; Henze, 2017, 2018). Recognising where values diverge along sociocultural lines presents a vital challenge for arts management.

Conclusion: Some Implications for Arts and Cultural Management

The discussion in this chapter proffers a new set of linguistic and discursive tools with which to describe the value conflicts that we all experience within art worlds in our daily lives. While we cannot escape the cracked nature of value, nor the disproportionate power that certain stakeholders wield within art worlds, I suggest that having language with which to analyse these disconnects is itself useful. It allows us to more clearly describe the ways in which our own notions of value do not always align with those of other stakeholders with whom we collaborate and engage in dialogue, or from whom we receive support. This new language can also provide insight into how value conflicts reify or are inscribed onto other social divides and inequalities.

Moreover, reorienting our understanding of value, by coming to view it as fundamentally fictitious, opens up new possibilities for creativity in our practice—discursive, aesthetic, pedagogical and even political. Whereas 'fact' is often conceptualised as something to be taken very seriously, 'fiction' connotes a certain playfulness that can be beneficial to artists and arts managers who feel constrained by particular regimes of value. Art world stakeholders are creative people, and a more creative linguistic approach can potentially open up new avenues of enquiry and thought. While a new language for discussing and understanding value cannot itself change these structures to which we are subjected and within which we are mired, it just might provide a way forward towards new ways of thinking about value and evaluation in intercultural arts management practice.

References

Appadurai, A. (1986). Introduction: Commodities and the politics of value. In A. Appadurai (Ed.), *The social life of things: Commodities in cultural perspective* (pp. 3–63). Cambridge: Cambridge University Press.

Aragon, L. V., & Leach, J. (2008). Arts and owners: Intellectual property law and the politics of scale in Indonesian arts. *American Ethnologist, 35*(4), 607–631.

Becker, H. S. (1982). *Art worlds*. Berkeley: University of California Press.

Belfiore, E. (2004). Auditing culture: The subsidised cultural sector in the new public management. *International Journal of Cultural Policy, 10*(2), 183–202.

Bianchini, F., & Parkinson, M. (1993). *Cultural policy and urban regeneration: The West European experience*. Manchester: Manchester University Press.

Clifford, J. (1986). Introduction: Partial truths. In J. Clifford & G. E. Marcus (Eds.), *Writing culture: The poetics and politics of ethnography* (pp. 1–26). Berkeley: University of California Press.

Coles, A. (2000). *Site-specificity: The ethnographic turn.* London: Black Dog.

Conquergood, D. (1989). Poetics, play, process, and power: The performative turn in anthropology. *Text and Performance Quarterly, 1*(1), 82–95.

Crossick, G., & Kaszynska, P. (2014). Under construction: Towards a framework for cultural value. *Cultural Trends, 23*(2), 120–131.

Crossick, G., & Kaszynska, P. (2016). *Understanding the value of arts and culture: The AHRC Cultural Value Project.* Swindon: Arts and Humanities Research Council.

Desai, D. (2002). The ethnographic move in contemporary art: What does it mean for art education? *Studies in Art Education, 43*(4), 307–323.

Dragićević-Šešić, M. (2015). Capacity-building programmes: Keeping institutional memory and regional collective consciousness alive. In P. Dietachmair & M. Ilić (Eds.), *Another Europe: 15 years of capacity building with cultural initiatives in the EU neighbourhood* (pp. 101–117). Amsterdam: EU Cultural Foundation. Retrieved May 18, 2016, from www.culturalfoundation.eu/library/another_europe

Durrer, V. (2018). The relationship between cultural policy and arts management. In V. Durrer, T. Miller, & D. O'Brien (Eds.), *The Routledge handbook of global cultural policy* (pp. 64–85). London: Routledge.

Durrer, V., Miller, T., & O'Brien, D. (Eds.). (2018). *The Routledge handbook of global cultural policy.* London: Routledge.

Foster, H. (1996). *The return of the real.* Cambridge, MA: MIT Press.

Geertz, C. (1973). *The interpretation of cultures.* New York: Basic.

Graeber, D. (2001). *Toward an anthropological theory of value: The false coin of our own dreams.* New York: Palgrave.

Gray, C. (2007). Commodification and instrumentality in cultural policy. *International Journal of Cultural Policy, 13*(2), 203–215.

Hampel, A. (2017). *Fair cooperation: A new paradigm for cultural diplomacy and arts management.* Brussels: Peter Lang.

Hansen, W. (2009). *When Tengu talk: Hirata Atsutane's ethnography of the other world.* Honolulu: University of Hawai'i Press.

Henze, R. (2017). Why we have to overcome paternalism in times of populism. In M. Dragićević-Šešić (Ed.), *Global culture: Arts festivals and geopolitics* (pp. 73–88). Belgrade: Ministry of Culture Republic of Serbia/University of Arts in Belgrade.

Henze, R. (2018). The master's tool will never dismantle the master's house: How language and terminology in international arts management perpetuate inequalities. *Arts Management Quarterly, 129*, 29–34.

Herzfeld, M. (2004). *The body impolitic: Artisans and artifice in the global hierarchy of value*. Chicago: University of Chicago Press.

Hesmondhalgh, D., Oakley, K., Lee, D., & Nisbett, M. (2015). *Cultural policy under new labour*. Basingstoke: Palgrave Macmillan.

Hillman Chartrand, H., & McCaughey, C. (1989). The arm's length principle and the arts: An international perspective—Past, present and future. In M.C. Cummings, Jr., & J.M.D. Schuster (Eds.), *Who's to pay for the arts: The international search for models of support*. New York: American Council for the Arts. Retrieved February 23, 2019, from https://www.americansforthearts.org/sites/default/files/ArmsLengthArts_paper.pdf.

Hutter, M., & Frey, B. S. (2010). On the influence of cultural value on economic value. *Revue d'économie politique, 120*(1), 35–46.

Karttunen, S. (2012). Cultural policy indicators: Reflections on the role of official statisticians in the politics of data collection. *Cultural Trends, 21*(2), 133–147.

Ladkin, S., McKay, R., & Bojesen, E. (Eds.). (2016). *Against value in the arts and education*. London: Rowman & Littlefield.

Lim, L. (Ed.). (2014). *Cultural policy in East Asia: Contemporary issues and trends*. London: Routledge.

Mackellar, J. (2013). Participant observation at events: Theory, practice and potential. *International Journal of Event and Festival Management, 4*(1), 56–65.

Matarasso, F. (1997). *Use or ornament: The social impact of participation in the arts*. Stroud: Comedia.

Miller, D. (2008). The uses of value. *Geoforum, 39*(3), 1122–1132.

Neelands, J., Belfiore, E., Firth, C., Hart, N., Perrin, L., Brock, S., et al. (2015). *Enriching Britain: Culture, creativity and growth*. Warwick: University of Warwick.

Nisbett, M. (2013). New perspectives on instrumentalism: An empirical study of cultural diplomacy. *International Journal of Cultural Policy, 19*(5), 555–575.

O'Brien, D. (2014). *Cultural policy: Management, value and modernity in the creative industries*. London: Routledge.

Proctor, L. M. (2015). English and globalization in India: The fractal nature of discourse. *Journal of Linguistic Anthropology, 24*(3), 294–314.

Schlesinger, P., Selfe, M., & Munro, E. (2015). Inside a cultural agency: Team ethnography and knowledge exchange. *The Journal of Arts Management, Law, and Society, 45*(2), 66–83.

Schneider, A. (2008). Three modes of experimentation with art and ethnography. *Journal of the Royal Anthropological Institute, 14*(1), 171–194.

Selwood, S. (2002). The politics of data collection: Gathering, analysing and using data about the subsidised cultural sector in England. *Cultural Trends, 12*(47), 13–84.

Shore, C., & Wright, S. (2015). Governing by numbers: Audit culture, rankings and the new world order. *Social Anthropology/Anthropologie Sociale, 23*(1), 22–28.

Spooner, M. (2018). Pushing boundaries: Academic de-institutionalization and our radical imagination vs. ourselves and audit culture. In N. K. Denzin & M. D. Giardina (Eds.), *Qualitative inquiry in the public sphere* (pp. 25–37). New York: Routledge.

Stadler, R., Reid, S., & Fullagar, S. (2013). An ethnographic exploration of knowledge practices within the Queensland Music Festival. *International Journal of Event and Festival Management, 4*(2), 90–106.

Strathern, M. (Ed.). (2000). *Audit cultures: Anthropological studies in accountability, ethics and the academy.* London: Routledge.

Strathern, M. (2016). The authority of value and abjection from value. In S. Ladkin, R. McKay, & E. Bojesen (Eds.), *Against value in the arts and education* (pp. 37–44). London: Rowman & Littlefield.

Şuteu, C. (2006). *Another brick in the wall: A critical review of cultural management education in Europe.* Amsterdam: Boekmanstudies.

Throsby, D. (2001). *Economics and culture.* Cambridge: Cambridge University Press.

UNESCO. (2013). *Culture: A key to sustainable development.* Hangzhou: UNESCO. Retrieved May 2, 2015, from www.unesco.org/new/fileadmin/MULTIMEDIA/HQ/CLT/pdf/final_hangzhou_declaration_english.pdf

UNESCO. (2014). *Action plan for the international decade for the rapprochement of cultures (2013–2022).* Paris: UNESCO. Retrieved April 13, 2015, from http://unesdoc.unesco.org/images/0022/002266/226664e.pdf

Vidmar-Horvat, K. (2012). The predicament of intercultural dialogue: Reconsidering the politics of culture and identity in the EU. *Cultural Sociology, 6*(1), 27–44.

Wagner, R. (1981). *The invention of culture* (Revised and Expanded ed.). Chicago: University of Chicago Press.

Walmsley, B. (2011). Why people go to the theatre: A qualitative study of audience motivation. *Journal of Customer Behaviour, 10*(4), 335–351.

Willis, P., & Trondman, M. (2000). Manifesto for *ethnography*. *Ethnography, 1*(1), 5–16.

Part II

Practice

5

Affective Arrangements: Managing Czech Art, Marginality and Cultural Difference

Maruška Svašek

Entering the building, I show my invitation to a man behind the desk, and am given access through a turning gate to the space where the opening ceremony will take place. It is 12 April 2017 and I have arrived at the Egon Schiele Art Centrum in Český Krumlov, a town in southern Bohemia that is situated about 40 kilometres from the Austrian border. Despite the fact that I have conducted research into Czech arts for many years, it is my first visit. The day after the opening, director Hana Jirmusová will tell me enthusiastically that she regards the Centre as "a child of the Velvet Revolution", as its establishment was directly related to the political shifts of the late 1980s: the ending of the Cold War and the collapse of state-socialism in Czechoslovakia. The Centre's website explains that,

M. Svašek (✉)
School of History, Anthropology, Philosophy and Politics, Queen's University Belfast, Belfast, UK

The Senator George J Mitchell Institute for Global Peace, Security and Justice, Queen's University Belfast, Belfast, UK
e-mail: m.svasek@qub.ac.uk

V. Durrer, R. Henze (eds.), *Managing Culture*, Sociology of the Arts,
https://doi.org/10.1007/978-3-030-24646-4_5

99

[t]he Egon Schiele Art Centrum owes its foundation in 1992/93 to the private initiative of several individuals who recognized the uniqueness of the situation after the fall of the Iron Curtain. They dedicated themselves to the idea of an international culture centre in one of the most beautiful Renaissance towns in Europe.

The statement reminds us that initiatives in the sphere of the arts are always taken by people whose personal and professional lives unfold against the background of wider societal and political developments. As emphasised in this chapter, so does the status of artists and works of art. In the context of the overall theme of this edited collection, what needs to be investigated is the ways in which art managers operate within dynamic historical settings as they shape artistic processes and develop their own careers. To what extent are they able to influence the reputations of the art producers and artworks they work with, and how does this process evolve in changing political circumstances? How do existing and emerging hierarchies in art worlds intersect with hierarchies and power distribution in (interconnected) realms of local, national and international politics? To find answers to these questions, the analysis draws on a mixed-method, ethnographic approach, including participant observation, recorded interviews, informal chats, visual analysis, textual analysis and archival study. The account forms part of a research project that explores interconnections between Czech art production and political dynamics from 1918 (the year when Czechoslovakia was established) to 2018 (Svašek, 1996a, b, 1997a, b, c, 2000, 2001, 2002, 2019 forthcoming).

The first section of the chapter will present the theoretical approach. After that, an insight will be provided into the tumultuous historical setting in which Jirmusová was able to establish the Egon Schiele Art Centrum with two other art managers from abroad. What follows is an investigation of the significance of Český Krumlov's geographical location and its heritage status to the success of the centre. The remainder of the chapter will offer a detailed analysis of the opening ceremony of the exhibition on 12 April 2017. Connecting the perspectives of 'art world' and 'affective arrangement', it will show that the opening provided a dynamic social and material setting in which discourses of freedom and democracy were propagated and reinforced.

Theoretical Approach

The analysis draws on arguments made by numerous scholars. In the 1980s, sociologist Howard Becker rightly criticised the dominant tendency by art historians to solely focus on artists and their works, as this approach uncritically reflects Romanticised notions of artistic genius. Becker (1982, p. 18) argued that the career trajectories of artists unfold in 'art worlds' that comprise of many different actors who "routinely participate in the making of art works". In addition to artists, these worlds include art educators, dealers, curators, critics, audiences, buyers, collectors, museum directors, art policymakers and other actors. Becker contended that, to find out who constitutes an art world at any moment in time, we need to investigate "who actually does what with whom" (Becker, 1982, p. 18). From this perspective, arts managers, policymakers and intellectuals engaged in artistic research all need to pay critical attention to their own role in art world dynamics. Furthermore, they must reflect on the ways in which their own activities contribute to the production and reinforcement of (politically relevant) artistic hierarchies.

Besides investigating social entanglements and actions of human actors, it is crucial to also explore the 'social lives' of works of art (Appadurai, 1988). As potentially powerful actants in 'transit' and 'transition', art works actively co-constitute affective encounters with members of the public. Transit, in this context, refers to artefacts' temporal and spatial movements, and transition alludes to transit-related changes in meaning, value and efficacy (Svašek, 2012, 2016). Evidently, art works do not have inherent affective power. As material presences in social environments, they have the potential to impress audiences, but their impact is situational and partially dependent on the onlookers' dispositions and understandings of art. In addition, curatorial acts of selection and discursive framing influence the ways in which beholders evaluate exhibits, although individual viewers may, of course, disagree with the curatorial interpretations. Nevertheless, art managers' choices often help shape longer term artistic reputations, a process that may be part and parcel of a wider politics of in/visibility. As we will see, the curatorial framing of works by the two Czech artists central to this chapter, Pavel Brázda and

Věra Nováková, reinforced their post-1989 transformation into artistic creators of almost iconic significance.

Referring to Bourdieu's influential work on social and symbolic capital in fields of cultural production, art sociologist Vera Zolberg (1990, p. 24) has argued that art works are active players in artistic fields. She employed the term 'careers' to refer to the process whereby works of art gain or lose art historical status and investment value. The career trajectories of artists *and* their products are often interlinked, for example when an artist and her works are deemed more important after a solo exhibition in a major gallery, leading to an increase in their status and commodity value.[1] Anthropologist Arjun Appadurai (1988) has examined the value potential of different kinds of artefacts, arguing that objects gain or lose value as they are appropriated by, and circulated in, specific cultural economies. In his theoretical framework, the perspective of 'value' does not necessarily refer to fluctuating prices but explores a broader dynamics of exchangeability and demand.

In this chapter, I am specifically interested in the ways in which the exhibition in the Egon Schiele Art Centrum presented and validated the works of the two artists. The analysis will specifically focus on the opening ceremony, regarding the event as a dynamic social environment that produced a diversity of affective processes. The analysis will draw on Jan Slaby and Birgitt Röttger-Rössler's (2018, p. 9) definition of 'affective arrangement' as a

> dynamic formation comprising persons, things, artifacts, spaces, discourses, behaviours and expressions in a characteristic 'intensive' mode of composition, demarcated from its surroundings by shifting thresholds of intensity.[2]

As will become clear, intensity was generated through the unique co-presence of artists, speakers, works of art, and audience members and was intensified through performative acts of curatorial framing.

Expertise, Enthusiasm and Shared Aims

To understand the affective dynamics of the opening that I was about to attend, it is necessary to provide some background information about the establishment of the art centre in 1992, and the life trajectories of those involved: the Czech Hana Jirmusová, the Austrian Gerwald Sonnberger, and the Austrian-American Serge Sabarsky. Although only Jirmusová was present during the opening in 2017, it was through their combined efforts that the centre had materialised.

By the late 1980s, the three had lived most of their adult lives in the geopolitical context of the Cold War (1947–1991).[3] The oldest, Sabarsky, was born in 1912 in Vienna, at the time the political and cultural centre of the Habsburg Empire. When the empire collapsed in 1918, three new nation states were established: Czechoslovakia, Austria and Hungary. Vienna remained an important centre of high and popular culture and the Jewish Sabarsky found employment as a clown and set designer with cabaret Simplicissimus.[4] When Hitler rose to power in neighbouring Germany, he escaped the horror of the expanding Third Reich and ended up in New York, where he became a successful contractor who began collecting Austrian and German Expressionist art. In 1988, he established Neue Galerie, a gallery that specialised in this genre, proudly displaying the kind of art that had been banned under the Nazis (Haider & Stoll, 2002).[5] The surviving works, in other words, resonated with the story of Sabarsky's own survival.

The 38 years younger Austrian Sonnberger was born in 1950. A curator of Austrian art, he got to know Sabarsky in 1988 and was well positioned to serve as one of the key contacts for Neue Galerie in Austria. In 1990, he became director of the newly established Museum of Modern Art in the German town of Passau. The distance between the museum and the Czechoslovak border was only 70 km. Reacting to possibilities offered by the dismantling of the Iron Curtain, the heavily secured border between the Communist bloc and the capitalist West, Sonnberger promoted the museum as a 'forum of modern and contemporary art on the doorstep of Eastern Europe', one of its aims being to facilitate exchanges between 'East and West'.[6] His intention to reach out to people on the other side of the Czech-German and Czech-Austrian borders must be placed in the wider context of cross-border movements, especially those by people of Sudeten German background.

After the ending of the Second World War, over three million ethnic Germans were expelled en masse from Czechoslovakia (Svašek, 2005, p. 197). Hoping they would soon regain ownership over their lost properties in the Sudetenland, many expellees had settled in Bavaria, close to the Czechoslovak border. In 1990, after visa restrictions were lifted, many decided to make return trips to their old homeland (*Heimat*). While most were driven by nostalgia (visiting their family homes, the graves of their ancestors, and in numerous cases getting involved in reconciliatory events with Czech who now occupied their houses), some were engaged in the politics of *Heimatrecht*, trying to get compensation for what they saw as illegal theft. The majority, however, were supportive of Czech attempts to breathe new life into a region that, as a marginal space marking the outer border of the Eastern bloc, had been neglected under Communism (Svašek, 1999, 2005, p. 204, 2014).[7] This supportive attitude was also reflected, for example, in an article in the official *Sudetenpost*, published by the Austrian Sudetenlandsmannschaft, that reported positively about Sonnberger's efforts to cooperate with Czechs (unauthored 1993).

Jirmusová, the youngest of the three, was born in 1963 in the small Czech town of Boskovice and studied History and Czech at the South Bohemian University in Český Budějovice at the time when Serge and Gerwald got acquainted in 1988. She completed her studies not long before the 1989 Velvet Revolution which made an end to the Communist system. The three met by chance in 1990 in a park in Český Krumlov, when the two men visited the city to admire views they knew so well from paintings by the well-regarded Austrian Expressionist artist Egon Schiele (1890–1918). Sharing enthusiasm for the artist's work, and spotting an opportunity for East-West cooperation, the three decided to plan an exhibition of Schiele's works in Český Krumlov (Wischin, 2010). The location was ideal, Jirmusová told me, not only because it was the artist's mother's place of birth and Schiele had depicted the town, but also because most Czechs did not know the artist as a result of forty years of censorship. Especially during the grim Stalinist 1950s, she explained, Expressionism had been deemed 'bourgeois', and the artist had been ignored in official art history. The chance to travel to the West and see his work had been limited. To Jirmusová, presenting Schiele to Czech audiences was clearly linked to her enthusiasm about the end of Communism. In her own words, it was "high time to make things right".

While Sabarsky, Sonnenberger and Jirmusová had different life experiences, the chemistry of their combined hopes, skills and energy drove them to work together to take the idea to exhibit Schiele in Český Krumlov further. Their synergy, or 'immanent causality' (Mühlhoff & Slaby, 2018, p. 157), came about as they shared time and bounced off one another's ideas. In the process, they did not only identify with each other's goals but also reacted to each other's suggestions. Enabled by the changed political environment, the initial idea to organise an exhibition of Schiele's work in Český Krumlov grew into a determinate plan. Looking for an exhibition space, they soon realised that there was no acceptable existing site in town, which is how the idea to establish their own gallery was born.

Finding Political and Financial Support and Dealing with Unexpected Challenges

To establish an art centre in Český Krumlov they needed financial and organisational support. Luckily, so soon after the Velvet Revolution, many politicians and civil servants in Czechoslovakia were keen to support initiatives that echoed the new slogans of freedom and democracy. As Jirmusová remembered,

> The city was in the middle of post-revolutionary euphoria, and the city council offered us a choice of various buildings (...) It was a time when anything was possible. I know that it is hard to explain today, but I partly still live off it, even today, because I still have the enthusiasm.

The three looked at numerous buildings "but it soon became clear that we did not want those that were occupied, we did not want to force people to move. So we were left with the huge sixteenth century brewery". When Sabarsky objected, saying "Hana, please, it is gigantic. What are we going to do with it?", Sonnberger, who had been trained as an architect, pointed out that the roof was in good condition, so they agreed to "give it a go".

To cut a long story short, the Egon Schiele Centrum[8] was established in 1992. Jirmusová told me proudly:

We slowly did it up and already opened three halls in 1993, three spaces with a huge Schiele exhibition. About 100 works on paper, drawings and watercolours. And gradually, each year we repaired another part of the building.

To encourage international exchange, part of the museum complex was converted into studios for study and working visits by artists from Eastern and Western Europe. The Centrum became a hub of activity.

The expression on Jirmusová's face changed when she explained that, as the gallery was beginning to build a name for itself, disaster struck. Within five years, she lost both co-founders. In 1996, the 84-year-old Serge Sabarsky died unexpectedly, and in 2000, Gerwald Sonnberger got seriously ill.

He had a brain tumor and they gave him a few weeks to live. He survived a year and a half, it was a very difficult time. When he died, I wasn't sure whether or not to continue.

She decided to carry on with the help of the Austrian Ingeborg Habereder, one of Sonnberger's acquaintances from Austria, who had experience in the organisation of a number of art festivals focused on women's art. As Jirmusová remembered, "he kept believing that he would live, but he said, 'if anything happens to me, she can help you, she is a good girl'". The cooperation turned out to be successful. Jirmusová told me that they were not only colleagues who co-designed the exhibition programme but that they had also become good friends.

Yet another major disaster struck when the building was affected by the floods in 2002. The water reached two metres high, completely flooding the ground floor, resulting in damage of 20 million crowns. In unusual circumstances, endangered art worlds can, however, trigger overwhelming responses across national borders and geographic territories. Jirmusová fondly recalled that,

[a]fter the floods I got help from all over the world, from Canada, from the whole of Europe up to Estonia. Estonia gifted us, our building, one million crowns. And artists who had worked in our studios collected money for us.

To save the building, they organised auctions to support us financially. It is hard to close down if the whole world is helping you!

The disaster also generated 'a specific energy' at local and national level, she added.

Everybody got together and helped each other. People who I didn't know at all came to help, and didn't want anything in return, they helped cleaning up and so on. The government gave us also ten soldiers who helped cleaning up the mud, and to remove the wooden floors that were all twisted and dirty. So suddenly the enthusiasm returned, we helped each other, and we got going again.

The above illustrates how human and non-human environments are entangled in dynamic affective relations. Having invested so much time and emotional energy into the art centre, which in itself indexed her attachment to her deceased colleagues, Jirmusová regarded the building as an extension of her own being. Faced with the damage of a building that they perceived as 'their' cultural centre, locals felt the urge to help putting it back into order. In the process, they developed a strong personal link to the place and the people connected to it. Their situationally specific 'affective capacity' (Mühlhoff & Slaby, 2018, p. 157) at the time of the floods, in other words, turned them into active players in its continuing social and artistic relevance.

Non-local Audiences and the Attraction of Český Krumlov

Situated so close to the Austrian and German border, the aim to attract international audiences had been realistic. In a feature produced for Radio Prague in 2017, Jan Velinger pointed out that during the first years after the Velvet Revolution, most visitors to Český Krumlov were Sudeten Germans whose families had been expelled from Czechoslovakia after the Second World War, many of them having lived in 'Krumau' and the surrounding 'Böhmerwald' (the German names for Český Krumlov and the

Šumava).[9] A second wave of mostly Americans followed, with many working or volunteering in Prague. Some settled permanently in the town, attracted by the romance of faded glory. At the time, several buildings were still in a state of dereliction after years of negligence by the former communist regime. Having spent three weeks in Český Krumlov for holidays in 1974 with my mother, sister and Czech grandmother, I personally remember the charm of the run-down, dilapidated historic buildings. The impression that this was a marginal, forgotten part of the world was strengthened by the dominant presence of soldiers who were based in military barracks, situated close to the Iron Curtain.

When I arrived at the train station on the evening of the opening, I vividly remembered how the town had looked in the 1970s. Walking down the hill, I could not believe my eyes. Instead of soldiers, I saw tour buses and large groups of mostly Asian tourists, strolling around and taking pictures. The buildings had all been done up, and the town gave the impression of an outdoor museum. Apart from those aimed at tourists, there were hardly any shops, and it took me quite a while to find a Czech-speaking local who could direct me to my hotel. In the interview with Radio Prague, Český Krumlov's Mayor Dalibor Carda referred to the large tourist crowds.

> When it comes to tourism, the biggest changes are in the last three years, when there was a big increase in the number of visitors from Southeast Asia, due to a deal of Czech Airlines with Korean Air. So we have a lot of tourists from South Korea and Japan. We have also attracted many more tourists coming from China. That is the newest wave from the last few years.[10]

The town had also gained increased exposure to wider global audiences after gaining UNESCO status in 1992. One of the attractions is the truly stunning thirteenth-century castle.[11] The medieval town has also attracted countless politicians, ambassadors and royalties, including Prince Charles (1992), Princess Margaret (1992), the Queen of Denmark (1994), the King and Queen of Sweden (1995) and US Secretary of State Madeleine Korbel Albright (1997).[12] Celebrities also paid visits to the Egon Schiele Centrum. Jirmusová remembered officials from many different countries, but noted that to her personally, one of the most memorable visits was that of President Václav Havel in 1993. Her experience was of course strongly influenced by her euphoria about the recent political change. The transformation of the former dissident writer into the leader of a democratic country, and his presence in gallery space, powerfully symbolised the end of Communism. The event also made a long-lasting impression on Serge, she recalled, who up to the day of his death, always carried a photograph of the encounter with him.[13]

The willingness of high-status personalities to visit the Egon Schiele Centrum increased the prominence of the museum. So did the many exhibitions curated by Jirmusová and her colleagues, displays that mostly focused on artists who had worked in the parallel sphere of 'unofficial culture' before 1989.[14] Arts management at the Centre thus actively contributed to the re-evaluation of their works, and the rewriting of Czech art history.

The Launch: Art World Rituals as Affective Arrangements

The large display, spread out over the three floors of the museum, shows works by two Czech and two Swiss artists. I am early, and the room on the ground floor where the opening will take place is still only half-full. On the walls, I see large paintings by the Swiss art duo M.S. Bastian and Isabelle L. A towering assemblage of different smaller paintings stands in the middle. Executed in a comic strip style, the works confront viewers with nightmarish scenes of bulgy eyed monsters, grinning skeletons and sharp-teethed beasts that remind me of Breughel's hellish scenes. The creatures, some straight from the Mexican Day of the Dead, stare and growl at the audience, fighting for attention.[15] The apocalyptic scenes strongly contrast with the structured ongoings in the room. Familiar with the ritual of exhibition openings, all those present know what to expect. A steady stream of invitees sit down on neat rows of chairs, leaving reserved seats for the curators, artists and local dignitaries. Some audience members walk up the stairs that lead to an open walkway and find a place on the first floor. All those present patiently wait for the launch to start, quietly talking with their neighbours. The press and a television crew are ready, taking a few shots of the ambiance.

Then suddenly, the cameras, my own included, begin to click frantically when the artists and invited speakers appear and take their seats on the front row (Fig. 5.1). I smile at Pavel Brázda and Věra Nováková, whom I got to know a few months earlier. It is for them that I have made the three-hour train journey to Český Krumlov. When I last spoke with them in their Prague home, Věra told me about the upcoming exhibition and gave me an invitation for the opening.

The first speaker is the mayor of the city, Dalibor Carda. Dressed in a formal suit, he enthusiastically welcomes the public to the city, to "one of its most beautiful buildings, filled with art". He emphasises the importance of the Egon Schiele Centrum, not only to the city but also to him personally, and praises director Hana Jirmusová and her colleagues for the organisation of "yet another attractive display". His public expression of support

Fig. 5.1 Dalibor Carda, Věra Nováková, Pavel Brázda, Marcel Sollberger (M.S. Bastian) and Isabelle Laubscher (Isabelle L.). (Photograph by the author)

is important, as it reinforces the significance of the art centre, which by now has gained museum status, as a major cultural hub in the region.

Jirmusová begins her speech thanking the Mayor and handing him a small gift, the booklet *A Walk with Egon* (*Procházka s Egonem*) by Toybox that contains illustrations referring to Egon Schiele's sojourns in Český Krumlov. The act does not only demonstrate the importance of gift-giving to the maintenance of networks in art worlds but also shows how the supposed link between past and present is used to naturalise particular images of its dynamics. The focus on the past movements of the famous Austrian artist through Český Krumlov, and the suggestion that we can get closer to the artist's perception if we follow 'Egon's' footsteps, creates a bridge between then and now. When Jirmusová speaks about Schiele's frequent travels between Vienna and Český Krumlov, she reinforces the image of the Czech town as a dynamic cultural environment, connected to art worlds outside the region:

> "You know very well", she says, "that every year, we try to offer you artists from abroad and artists from the Czech Republic. This year, we have brought you art works by the Czech couple Pavel Brázda and Věra Nováková, and by the Swiss authors Bastian and Isabelle".

The capacity to do so is of course tightly interwoven with the end of Communism, and Jirmusová sketches an optimistic picture of democracy when she introduces the Swiss couple. Asking her assistant to hand them a bunch of purple and yellow irises, she says:

> When we hear the word 'Switzerland', most of us will imagine a free, successful, rich country. And the life of these two artists resonates with this image. They have studied what they wanted and were able to visit Paris and New York. They have traveled around the world.

The image of a happy, free life intensifies when she contrasts the successful career history of the Swiss duo with the tough life that Brázda and Nováková had during 40 years of state-socialism. With a sense of drama, she recounts how, soon after meeting each other at the Academy of Fine Art in Prague, the couple was told to leave.

The Communist coup came in 1948, and shortly afterwards, the so-called purges began. In fact, both artists were kicked out of the academy for political reasons from the academy for their views. They were forbidden to study at any college. (see also Fiedor & Brázda, 2013, p. 14)

Speaking about "the terrifying 1950s", she also mentions people's fears for a third world war. These circumstances impacted on the two artists' creative imagination. "Věra Nováková", Jirmusová says,

> created a large drawing entitled, "Thus Passes the Glory of the World (Sic Transit Gloria Mundi)" (*Tak končí sláva světa*). In the middle she depicted an explosion and around it are people whose faces show expressions of terror.

Hearing these words, I cannot help but look at the apocalyptic scenes behind her that resonate with her description of Nováková's painting (Fig. 5.2). I begin to understand why the exhibition has brought works by the Swiss duo in conversation with those by Nováková and Brázda, as some of their shared subject matter has strong apocalyptic dimensions.

I later spot *Thus Passes the Glory of the World* in the exhibition, and I am able to study it in detail. On the right, a stern-looking cyborg rests a claw-like hand on a globe. Mounted on the globe, a flag sporting the image of a skull flutters in the wind. The words "Sic Transit Gloria Mundi" are printed over clouds of smoke, caused by a large explosion. Bodies and stones fall into all directions and a terrified mass of people run away in despair. Jirmusová's introduction, mentioning fear for another world war, has sensitised me to the wider political context of the Cold War. The curator also mentioned in her introduction that Nováková, driven by her despair about the impact of Stalinism on Czechoslovak society, converted to Christianity. I see that this is also reflected in the painting. On the left, people huddle around a crucified Jesus. Rays of light radiate from his body (Fig. 5.3).

During her opening speech, Jirmusová also draws attention to another one of Nováková's works, the 1952 painting, 'After the End (Hic Iacet Omnipotens Sapiens) (Po konci)'. "You see a bleak dark blue landscape", she says, "and two very slender people, practically still children, walk

Fig. 5.2   Jirmusová at the opening. (Photograph by the author)

hand in hand, with a guardian angel floating above them". The painting provides a powerful biblical image of hope, indirectly referring to God's expulsion of Adam and Eve (Fig. 5.4). In fact, the striking image is deeply engraved in my memory, making a strong impression when I first saw it on the cover of her 2010 catalogue (Nováková, 2010). Its 'internalised presence' (Svašek, 2010) clearly illustrates the affective potential of artistic imagery. I am not surprised that this painting has been chosen to be reproduced as poster, for sale in the Egon Schiele Art Centrum's shop.

Jirmusová then speaks about Nováková's husband, Pavel Brázda, drawing attention to what she calls "one of his iconic works", *Five Minutes Before the End of the World* (1953–1966) and *The Monster Waits, the Monster Has Time, Self Portrait of P.B.* (1949).[16] Seeing the first painting in the exhibition, I notice that it is as Breughelesque as the works by the Swiss duo. The head of one of the figures is made up of a large nose and a thick-lipped mouth, and its armless torso shows seven breasts. Several humanoids can be seen, including aggressive flying machines with large teeth and tongues. Behind two round windows, constructed in a hollow

Fig. 5.3 Thus Passes the Glory of the World (Sic Transit Gloria Mundi) by Věra Nováková. (Photograph © Libor Sváček, archive Egon Schiele Art Centrum)

Fig. 5.4 After the End (Hic Iacet Omnipotens Sapiens) by Věra Nováková. (Photograph © Libor Sváček, archive Egon Schiele Art Centrum)

winged earth that is placed on a Roman pillar, Hitler and Stalin stare at the scene. A naked man on a ladder looks down at the spectacle with an expression of despondency. When I see the second painting (Fig. 5.5), my eyes are captured by the grim-looking eyes of the artist. His face, a reflection, is bordered by the round rusty metal frame of a mirror. One of the eyes is wide open, in shock. The other is squeezed, critically observing—looking at himself and the viewing public. The mirror blocks the head of a female figure, who carefully holds a bird's nest with two turtle dove headed lovers, lying in a tender embrace. "The body is Věra's",

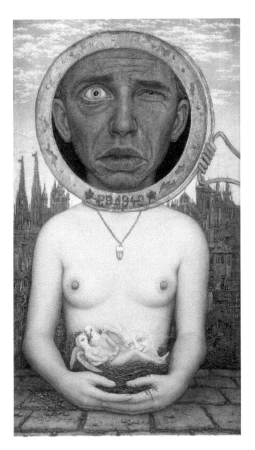

Fig. 5.5 'The Monster Waits, the Monster Has Time, Self Portrait of P.B.' (1949). (Photograph © Libor Sváček, archive Egon Schiele Art Centrum)

Jirmusová says when she introduces the work, "and the painting expresses the contrast between the couple's love and the horror of the Communist regime". A reproduction of *The Monster Waits, the Monster Has Time, Self Portrait of P.B.* is also available as poster in the museum shop. As with Nováková's *After the End*, the choice demonstrates the potential of visual images to captivate viewers. Unsurprisingly, the painting has also been used as cover image on several of Brázda's catalogues.

When Jirmusová continues her introduction, she provides more details about the struggle of the two artists under Communism. With a more upbeat tone, she speaks about the liberal 1960s and their first trip "beyond the Iron Curtain" in 1967. Her voice gets a darker tone when she refers to Czechoslovakia's invasion by the Warshaw Pact army in 1968 that made an end to the Prague Spring:

> Family Brázda seriously considered emigration but they had a five-year old daughter and in the end decided to stay. A period of censorship followed and because they could not exhibit, they started organising exhibitions on the landing in their house. They exhibited regularly, and a kind of philosophical circle was formed, they met up with some former students and later with important personalities. Occasionally professor Patočka gave lectures in their house.

For those who know Czech history, the reference to Patočka (1907–1977) is highly evocative, as he was one of the initiators of Charter 77, a document that called for human rights and criticised the persecution of Czechoslovak citizens (Brikcius, 2017). Soon after meeting the Dutch Minister of Foreign Affairs Max van der Stoel (1924–2011), an event through which the signatories of Charter 77 gained international support for their cause, the philosopher was arrested. After "an exhausting interrogation by members of the State Security", he had to be admitted to the hospital and died a few days later (Tuckerová, 2017, p. 70). The philosopher had urged citizens to live "in truth", take responsibility for their actions and become aware of the widespread passive acceptance of oppressive politics (Tuckerová, 2017, p. 47).

Jirmusová continues her introduction, mentioning a trip to relatives in the United States in 1987 after the two artists had retired, "when the regime allowed them to travel". She also speaks about their hope that the regime would collapse. When that happened in 17 November 1989, "especially Mr. Brázda was very engaged" in the transformation of the political system. As pointed out in earlier research (Svašek, 1996a, b), the end of state-socialism created many opportunities for artists who had been marginalised under Communism. The political change also radically impacted on the careers of Brázda and Nováková. The couple "got their first studio space in the 1990s", says Jirmusová, and their first exhibition in Prague had 'cultic' proportions. "I heard from witnesses that there were long queues", she says, "and the exhibition then toured to a number of other cities". Through her narrative, the curator strongly endorses the artists' growing reputation, enthusiastically explaining that Brázda was offered a large retrospective exhibition in the Trade Fair Palace in Prague, and that artists produced major catalogues. Referring to their ongoing activities, she emphasises that both are still working, and indeed, producing innovative works. Brázda, for example, has recently experimented with digital graphics (see also Drury, 2013, p. 6).[17]

The Czech curator ends saying that the story she just told about the life of the two artists is "very important because it will help you to understand and interpret the hundreds of works you will see upstairs". Her Austrian co-curator, "Mrs Habereder", takes over and emphasises the connection between the works of the two Czech and two Swiss artists, explaining that the artists themselves have recognised a similar approach in each other's work. Her words increase the affective resonance and interplay of the apocalyptic paintings in the exhibition.

Jirmusová then introduces "the most important, best-known speaker", former art academy and museum director Milan Knížák. At the start of my own research on Czech art and politics, I first met Knížák in 1992, two years after he had been elected director of the prestigious Academy of Fine Art in Prague. In fact, he was the first director appointed after 1989, and his sudden appearance from the margins of the official Czech art world illustrates how radically the Czech art world changed as a result of democratisation. Most 'conformist' artists who had been Communist party members lost their positions in the art educational system, and artists like Knížák, who at the time of the Normalisation (1969–1989) could only create and show works outside the official Communist art world, replaced them.[18] Knižák headed the Academy of Fine Art from 1990 to 1997, and became the director of the Trade Fair Palace (*Veletržní palác*) in 1999, an important museum of contemporary art in Prague.[19] In 2006–2007, he organised a large retrospective exhibition of Brázda's work, which is why he had been invited to give a speech at the opening. Jirmusová already knew him well, as she had curated a solo exhibition of Knižák's work in the Egon Schiele Centrum in 2004/2005.[20]

At the start of his talk Knižák apologises to Nováková, saying that he will most of all talk about her husband as he does not know her work very well. His confession reflects the fact that, so far, Brázda's work has received far more attention than his wife's. When I interviewed Haberer the next day about the exhibition, she criticised the gender bias in art worlds and pointed out that one of the reasons why they had included both artists in the show was to address this problem. Nováková, she said, produced high-quality work and deserved a place in art history. In her view, the joint exhibition clearly showed the mutual influences between her work and that of Brázda and showcased her individual talent. The curatorial approach indeed increased Nováková's artistic reputation, as, in reaction to the exhibition, both artists were given much attention by the media.[21] Even though more space was given to Brázda's work in the gallery, the show provided a good overview of Nováková's artistic developments. At the start of his speech, Knižák gives her a compliment, saying that some of the works made a strong impression on him when he saw them earlier. He then concentrates on Brázda, emphasising his significance to global art history. "Brázda", he says, "is the first artist who created pop art, his work *Great Astronaut* (1954) being an early example" (see also Vlček, 2014, p. 37). "This needs to be acknowledged by Western art historians as they generally assume that all creative innovations are rooted in Western Europe or the United States". Importantly, Knižák's remarks destabilise dominant Western-oriented art historiography, thus influencing the way in which those present at the opening ceremony perceived the artist, placing him not only in the history of Czech art, but also framing him as an artist of international quality.

When Knižák ends his speech, the audience applauds and the exhibition is declared 'open'. Over the next two hours, people young and old stroll through the different exhibition spaces, admiring the works on display. No doubt, the words of the four speakers still echo in their heads, as they do in mine. No doubt, their curatorial framing and public endorsement have reinforced, and indeed increased, the artists' significance in the Czech art world and beyond, as evidenced by the exhibition *Brázda is here!* in Birmingham a few months later.[22]

Conclusion

This chapter has investigated art managerial practices as evolving affective relations between people, objects and places. The analysis has demonstrated the potential of this perspective to disentangle interactions between human and non-human actants, in this case curators, artists, visitors, a building and the exhibits. As such, the approach can be employed in other research settings to explore the ways in which the people and things that comprise specific art worlds influence, and are influenced by, each other's activities and presences.

This particular analysis showed that the end of the Cold War and the disappearance of the Iron Curtain created an opportunity for new art managerial initiatives. The three art managers central to the chapter first found each other in their shared admiration for Egon Schiele, and influenced by each other's professional disposition, expertise and enthusiasm, decided to work together. The chemistry between them generated enormous energy. Their shared ambition to link up 'East European' and 'Western' art worlds grew over time, reflecting a strong belief in democracy and artistic exchange. Their determination was partially fuelled by their personal histories, including embodied memories of totalitarianism and regional marginality. These experiences added a political dimension to their aims.

Gaining support from local and national authorities, the Centrum was officially established and transformed into an active museum. Soon, the chosen building provided a spatial, material and discursive focus for artistic reputation building. On the one hand, the curators broadened audiences for already world-famous artists such as Schiele. On the other, they increased the exposure of the public to Czech artists who had not been able to exhibit officially in Czechoslovakia before 1989. In addition, artists from different national backgrounds were invited to work and exhibit.

The case presented was particularly striking as Brázda and Nováková had been virtually unknown before 1989. While Jirmusová and Habereder were not the first curators to pay attention to their work, their decision to invite them for an exhibition reinforced the artists' growing reputation as highly significant artists of international standing. The process of rewriting communist art history had started in the early 1990s, when their art made a remarkable transition from hardly known, marginal works, to becoming celebrated icons of nonconformist creativity. Shown in combination with the works by the Swiss art duo, the curators emphasised dystopian dimensions in their art. Curatorial framing did not, of course, fully determine people's understanding of the works. The exhibition and the opening ceremony did, however, create a moment of concentrated focus on specific artistic and political values, promoting a belief in the power of artistic freedom and creativity. It produced an affective environment in which those present were reminded of the widespread euphoria and optimism of the first post-Cold War years.

Notes

1. The careers are also affected by comments by influential critics and can be shaped by change of ownership and museum acquisition. Career developments are not, of course, necessarily uniliniary. Even when art works are included in the 'permanent' displays of prestigious art institutions, changing artistic policies or the introduction of political censorship may result into a fall from grace, leading at best to disappearance into storage space.
2. To analyse how people affect things, and vice versa, a distinction has to be made, of course, between the distinct ontological status of humans and non-humans. While humans are intentional, breathing, ageing, mortal beings, artefacts are physically dead, even if they have biographies and social lives, and may be perceived in some settings to have human or supernatural agency. Artefacts do, however, have a power that humans lack, namely the potential to outlive their makers.
3. The Cold War was the geopolitical, ideological and economic struggle between two world superpowers, the United States and the USSR, that involved many countries in their sphere of influence. It started in 1947

at the end of the Second World War and lasted until the dissolution of the Soviet Union in 1991.

4. For an interview with Serge Sabarsky, conducted by Rose Carol Washington-Long for the Archives of American Art, Smithsonian Institution on April 22, 1993, see https://www.aaa.si.edu/collections/interviews/oral-history-interview-serge-sabarsky-13032#transcript. See also: http://www.kabarettarchiv.at/Ordner/history.htm, last accessed 01/10/2018.

5. "Neue Galerie New York was conceived by two men who enjoyed a close friendship over a period of nearly thirty years: art dealer and museum exhibition organizer Serge Sabarsky and businessman, philanthropist and art collector Ronald S. Lauder. Sabarsky and Lauder shared a passionate commitment to Modern German and Austrian art, and dreamed of opening a museum to showcase the finest examples of this work. After Sabarsky died in 1996, Lauder carried on the vision of creating Neue Galerie New York as a tribute to his friend". https://www.neuegalerie.org/news, last accessed 06/10/2018. See also https://www.nytimes.com/1999/11/12/arts/inside-art.html, last accessed 09/11/2018.

6. "Es versteht sich selbst als Forum moderner und zeitgenössischer Kunst am Tor zu Osteuropa und hat sich die Annäherung von Ost und West zum Ziel gesetzt". https://regiowiki.pnp.de/wiki/Museum_Moderner_Kunst_W%C3%B6rlen_Passau, last accessed 06/10/2018.

7. See also https://gfx.sueddeutsche.de/politik/sudetendeutsche/, last accessed 29/01/2019, for an example of personal stories about the expulsion.

8. It was first called The Egon Schiele Foundation and International Cultural Centrum (Nadaci Egona Schieleho a mezinárodní kulturní centrum v Českém Krumlově) but was renamed in 1998.

9. https://www.radio.cz/en/section/travel-tip/cesky-krumlov-an-historic-but-heavily-visited-jewel, last accessed 09/11/2018.

10. https://www.radio.cz/en/section/travel-tip/cesky-krumlov-an-historic-but-heavily-visited-jewel, last accessed 09/11/2018.

11. As posted on the UNESCO website, "[t]he Historic Centre of Český Krumlov is an outstanding example of a small Central European medieval town whose architectural heritage has remained intact thanks to its peaceful evolution over more than several centuries. This feudal town, a former centre of a large estate owned by powerful noble families who played an important role in the political, economic and cultural history

of Central Europe, was founded in the Middle Ages and underwent Renaissance and Baroque transformations. As it remained almost intact, it has retained its street layout, which is typical of planned medieval towns, as well as many historic buildings including their details such as the roof shapes, the decoration of Renaissance and Baroque facades, vaulted spaces, as well as original layouts and interiors" (https://whc. unesco.org/en/list/617, last accessed 07/10/2018).

12. http://www.ckrumlov.cz/uk/mesto/soucas/i_vynami.htm, last accessed 07/10/2018.

13. http://www.jihocesi2012.cz/osoby/255/hana-jirmusova-lazarowitz, last accessed 07/10/2018.

14. The exhibitions focused, for example, on Jiří Kolář, Aleš Veselý, Karel Nepraš, Milan Knižák and František Skála.

15. Their work was described as follows by Widewalls, a digital network for artists and galleries: "The mutual passion for advertising and the world of comics allowed them to overcome limits of the classic narratives, and create special visual art, full of freshness and details. This commitment can be seen in a project called *Bastokalypse*, which is actually a series of canvases made over several years. This collage can be considered as an encyclopaedia of diverse images that reflect aspects of the modern world, media and culture, in which idealism and utopia collide with human destruction and terror. It erases the line between the high and low, by combining Ronald McDonald, Pablo Picasso, Mark Beyer, Ghost face and Jack altogether. The final outcome is a 52-metre monumental avant-garde work that recreates chaos and apocalypse of today" (http://www.widewalls.ch/artist/m-s-bastian-and-isabelle-l/, last accessed 15/04/2017).

16. See also https://vimeo.com/166475502, to hear the artist comment in Czech on his work in a video produced in 2016 by the Gallery of the Central Bohemian Region.

17. Pavel Brázda sadly passed away in December 2017.

18. In the 1960s, Knížák had been a founding member of the Czech art group Actual that organised happenings and other events, and also became involved in Fluxus, an international (anti-)artistic community of music, actions and poetry. Fluxus included artists from the United States, Western Europe and the Eastbloc, and in 1965, director George Maciunas appointed him Director of Fluxus East.

19. He held this position till 2011.

20. To access photographs of the opening of this exhibition, see https://www.bing.com/images/search?view=detailV2&id=79993E7CD9D6C70D6CAABF37D159D6470B4052ED&thid=OIP.y6hiu9ey7nl3jcY1eWRh6wHaE8&mediaurl=http%3A%2F%2Fwww.schieleartcentrum.cz%2Fimg%2F2004091345b.jpg&exph=500&expw=750&q=Kni%c5%be%c3%a1k+egon+schiele&selectedindex=24&qpvt=Kni%c5%be%c3%a1k+egon+schiele&ajaxhist=0&vt=0&ccid=y6hiu9ey&simid=608048100786111749, last accessed 08/09/2019.
21. See, for example, https://www.idnes.cz/ceske-budejovice/zpravy/brazda-schiele-centrum-krumlov.A170418_2319630_budejovice-zpravy_epkub
22. To know how the exhibition was advertised, see, for example, https://www.youtube.com/watch?v=Gb0Xly0oGJI

References

Appadurai, A. (1988). *The social life of things*. Cambridge: Cambridge University Press.
Author unknown. (1993). Schiele's Rückkehr nach Krumlau. *Sudetenpost, 7*(39), 6.
Author unknown. (undated). Heimat im Kopf. *Süddeutsche Zeitung*. Retrieved January 29, 2019, from https://gfx.sueddeutsche.de/politik/sudetendeutsche/last
Becker, H. S. (1982). *Art worlds*. Berkeley: University of California Press.
Brikcius, Z. (Ed.). (2017). *Charta story. The story of Charter 77*. Prague: National Gallery.
Drury, R. (2013). Introduction. In R. Rozbroj & A. Wincencjusz-Patyna (Eds.), *Pavel Brázda: Malarstwo i grafika* (pp. 4–7). Wrocław: Galerie Miejska we Wrocławiu.
Fiedor, J., & Brázda, P. (2013). Jiří Fiedor talks with Pavel Brázda. In R. Rozbroj & A. Wincencjusz-Patyna (Eds.), *Pavel Brázda: Malarstwo i grafika* (pp. 10–28). Wrocław: Galerie Miejska we Wrocławiu.
Haider, H., & Stoll, D. (2002). *Serge Sabarsky: A full life*. New York: Neue Galerie.
Mühlhoff, R., & Slaby, J. (2018). Immersion at work: Affect and power in post-Fordist work culture. In B. Röttger-Rössler & J. Slaby (Eds.), *Affect in relation: Families, places, technologies: Essays on affectivity and subject formation in the 21st century* (pp. 155–174). New York: Routledge.
Nováková, V. (2010). *Věra Nováková*. Prague: Argo.

Slaby, J., & Röttger-Rössler, B. (2018). Introduction: Affect in relation. In B. Röttger-Rössler & J. Slaby (Eds.), *Affect in relation: Families, places, technologies: Essays on affectivity and subject formation in the 21st century* (pp. x–x). New York: Routledge.

Svašek, M. (1996a). *Styles, struggles and careers. An ethnography of the Czech art world, 1948–1992*. Unpublished PhD thesis, University of Amsterdam.

Svašek, M. (1996b). What's (the) matter? Objects, materiality and interpretability. *Etnofoor, 9*(1). Theme issue on 'Words and Things', pp. 49–70.

Svašek, M. (1997a). The politics of artistic identity. The Czech art world in the 1950s and 1960s. *Contemporary European History, 6*(3) (November 1997). Theme issue on 'Intellectual Life and the First Crisis of State Socialism in East Central Europe, 1953–1956' (G. Péteri, ed.), pp. 383–403.

Svašek, M. (1997b). Visual art, myth and power. Introduction. *Focaal. Journal of Anthropology, 29* (May 1997). Theme issue on 'Visual Art, Myth and Power' (M. Svašek & G. van Beek, eds.), pp. 7–24.

Svašek, M. (1997c). Gossip and power struggle in the post-Communist art world. *Focaal. Journal of Anthropology 29* (May 1997). Theme issue on 'Visual Art, Myth and Power' (M. Svašek & G. van Beek, eds.), pp. 101–122.

Svašek, M. (1999). History, identity and territoriality: Redefining Czech-German relations in the post-Cold War era. *Focaal. Journal of Anthrolopology, 32*, 37–58.

Svašek, M. (2000). Les monuments à la glorie de l'Armee Rouge en Tschéquie. *Les Annales de la Recherche Urbaine, 85*, 111–118.

Svašek, M. (2001). The politics of artistic identity. The Czech art world in the 1950s and 1960s. In G. Péteri (Ed.), *Intellectual life and the first crisis of state socialism in East Central Europe, 1953–1956* (pp. 133–153). Trondheim: Norwegian University of Science and Technology.

Svašek, M. (2002). Contacts. Social dynamics in the Czech state-socialist art world. *Contemporary European History*. Theme issue on 'Artistic and Academic Patronage in State Socialist Societies' (G. Péteri, ed.).

Svašek, M. (2005). The politics of chosen trauma: Expellee memories, emotions and identities. In K. Milton & M. Svašek (Eds.), *Mixed emotions: Anthropological studies of feeling* (pp. x–x). Oxford: Berg.

Svašek, M. (2010). In the field: Intersubjectivity, empathy and the workings of internalised presence. In D. Spencer & J. Davies (Eds.), *Anthropological fieldwork: A relational process* (pp. 75–99). Cambridge: Cambridge Scholars Press.

Svašek, M. (Ed.). (2012). *Emotions and human mobility. Ethnographies of movement*. London: Routledge.

Svašek, M. (2014, Summer). Forced displacement, suffering and the aesthetics of loss. *Open Arts Journal, 3*, 137–156.

Svašek, M. (2016). Introduction. Creativity and innovation in a world of movement. In M. Svašek & B. Meyer (Eds.), *Creativity in transition. Politics and aesthetics of cultural production across the globe* (pp. 1–32). Oxford: Berghahn.

Svašek, M. (2019, forthcoming). (Memories of) monuments in the Czech landscape: Creation, destruction and the affective stirrings of people and things. In Ø. Fuglerud, K. Larsen, & M. Prusac-Lindhagen (Eds.), *Negotiating memory from the Romans to the twenty-first century: Damnatio memoriae*. New York: Routledge.

Tuckerová, V. (2017). Charter 77 and art. In Z. Brikcius (Ed.), *Charta story. The story of Charter 77* (pp. 23–118). National Gallery: Prague.

Vlček, T. (Ed.). (2014). *Modern and contemporary Czech art 1890–2010: Part two*. Prague: National Gallery.

Wischin, F. E. (2010). *Schiele and Krumlov*. Český Krumlov: Egon Schiele Art Centrum.

Zolberg, V. (1990). *Constructing a sociology of the arts*. Cambridge: Cambridge University Press.

6

The 'West' versus 'the Rest'? Festival Curators as Gatekeepers for Sociocultural Diversity

Lisa Gaupp

Introduction

This chapter analyses how sociocultural diversity is standardized through conventions in the performing arts. It examines how sociocultural diversity is curated at renowned international performing arts festivals. As used here, sociocultural diversity refers chiefly to artists and audiences with different sociocultural backgrounds and to different art forms and aesthetic expressions. These festivals present a variety of performances, with art forms ranging from contemporary theatre, dance, music, to visual arts and many others. Generally, such festivals take place annually or bi-annually and are funded mainly by public or other third-party funding bodies. These are international festivals featuring artists from all over the world. In this contribution, the focus is on the so-called non-European or non-Western performances and on the figure of the festival curator, understood as cultural broker, cultural intermediary as well as cultural gatekeeper. This chapter considers whether or not curators of

L. Gaupp (✉)
Leuphana University of Lüneburg, Lüneburg, Germany
e-mail: gaupp@leuphana.de

© The Author(s) 2020
V. Durrer, R. Henze (eds.), *Managing Culture*, Sociology of the Arts,
https://doi.org/10.1007/978-3-030-24646-4_6

festivals taking place in Europe or the 'West' define and normalize what is considered to be diversity and how it is programmed in the arts. In the tradition of Eurocentric and postcolonial critique, the issues of who, and on which grounds, holds the power to define conventions in the art world of the performing arts are discussed. The case studies presented serve as a basis to ask how, in general, international performing arts festivals are curated or managed and which sociocultural conventions are applied, and through that application, which conventions are reinforced.

In international art worlds, "diversity is almost considered to be a value in itself" (Peres da Silva & Hondros, 2019, p. 19). At the international performing arts festivals analysed in this case study, attempts to achieve diversity are based on diversifying the audience as well as achieving a "greater visibility of work by artists with a 'non-Western' background" (Westen, 2012, p. 78). Different worldviews and challenging perspectives are welcomed or even the explicit goal of festival organizers. Diversity is most often understood as diversity in the national or ethnic origins of the performing artists. Diversity can also be about addressing and involving audiences with, from an intersectional perspective, different social identity markers such as gender, ethnicity, race or sexual orientation. Some festivals also strive for greater linguistic diversity by translating performances and marketing material. Still others want to diversify by introducing art forms into their programmes that are new to the region (Gaupp, 2020). However, it will be shown that the conventions defining the boundaries of sociocultural diversity at these festivals are mostly oriented towards the norm that art should be different, but not too different.

Most festivals communicate that the national origin of their artists is unimportant, that their mission is to present the 'best' artists, and art, regardless of national origin or any other affinity to a geographical location. But this image, essentially a marketing device, will be questioned by discussing how specific social processes and organizational structures seem to nevertheless lead to a 'Western-centric' canon at these performing arts festivals. In its analysis of the organizational structures and processes of these festivals, this chapter queries two issues. First, whether the public presentation of these festivals is aligned with the practices acted out at these festivals, or secondly, whether there are segregational tendencies dividing European or 'Western'-based festivals, curators, artists and art forms from 'the rest' (Hall, 1994), understood as an epistemological object constructed in opposition to an imaginary 'West' (Said, 1991). Through analysing the institutionalizing practices of the sociocultural conventions that influence how diversity is displayed, the chapter explores what role festival curators play when it comes to normalizing diversity and how other gatekeeping processes determine which groups will be produced at the festivals.

It seems that, on the one hand, there is a strongly Eurocentric or 'Western'-centric canon with regard to what kind of aesthetic forms are being curated. On the other, and on the level of formal organization, there seems to exist both normative ideological definitions of diversity as well as conventions of diversity based on the global circulation of financial capital. It will be shown whether these assumptions of how diversity is curated prove to be true and which organizational processes form the basis of these developments.

The gatekeeping and other power relations involved in the setting up of festival programmes will be analysed. How diversity is defined in the curatorial practice at performing arts festivals is deeply dependent upon the cultural and social capital, tastes, dispositions, beliefs and perceptions of individual curators, who are understood as cultural intermediaries (Bourdieu, 1984). But it is not the curators alone who define diversity but rather the complex processes and structures surrounding curatorial practices. As such, in this chapter, both the curator and the curatorial strategies of the festivals are analysed.

It is not possible to determine whether a festival is curated in an Eurocentric perspective or is situated in imaginary spaces seemingly outside Europe. What can be determined is that art worlds construct diverse spaces of globalization, transcultural spaces in-between, and that they are themselves in a constantly changing mode. The perspective of 'Europe or the West versus the rest' falls short. Speaking with Derrida, "every seemingly strong and irreducible opposition is declared a 'theoretical fiction'" (2004, p. 135).

For example, reflecting on the work of curation, the founding director of the *International Festival Performing Tangier*, and former director of *Tangier's Professional Theatre Festival*, Khālid Amīn, turns to the postcolonial concept of *double critique*, advanced by the Moroccan sociologist

Abdelkebir Khatibi, to develop a view that could be called transcultural diversity:

> Double critique calls for the rethinking of the supremacy of the West and the subordination of the East, the Orient, the Third World, the South, or any of the other names used by the West to designate areas that lie outside of it. It also calls for rethinking the Maghreb, the home country, and for considering it as it currently is, with all of its elements of diversity, difference, and plurality. (Amīn, 2014, p. 36f)

So, it is not enough to criticize neo-colonial power hierarchies in the art world of performing arts festivals. We must also look at how sociocultural norms, or conventions, come into being and especially how they can be changed. The 'West' and the 'rest' should not be put into a static dichotomy. Neither should diversity be understood as a mere plurality of differences, as if there were no conflict involved in the cross-cultural contacts taking place at these festivals. Moreover, Amīn questions:

> Do we have to consider hybridity as the ultimate and inexorable condition of all postcolonial subjectivities? Or shall we think of it as a road map leading to alternative exchanges? (Amīn & Laamiri, 2010, p. 7)

In this sense it will be argued that while it is still necessary to lay open and question the continuing biases underlying curating processes at international performing arts festivals, it is also important to demonstrate that diversity is not something that is definable. It can lead to processes of transcultural diversity that allow for the development of dynamic spaces-in-between in which critique and conflicts are major driving forces. The conclusion is that arts management in general and curatorial practices in particular must respond to the realities of today's post-migrant social processes. Likewise, it will be important to examine how a transcultural perspective provides an alternative view of curatorial practices and arts management. This view entails the rejection of Eurocentric or 'Western'-centric assumptions and a focus on decentred postcolonial analysis, instead of the conventional model of core, semi-periphery and periphery countries (Wallerstein, 1990).

Curatorial Practice at International Performing Arts Festivals

Curators embody a special role in arts management. And the same is true for the curators' organizational field of performing arts festivals in the context of international art production. Curators are important gatekeepers for upcoming artists if they are to be produced on an international level. The festivals they curate form an art world in Howard Becker's sense (2008 [1982]). Drawing on the philosopher Arthur C. Danto, who understands an art world as something institutionalized by conventions constructed in arts organizations (1964), Becker extends this conventionalist and institutionalist view by introducing the network relations of art worlds. For Becker, art is not the product of a single artist but rather a collective action of a cooperative network (2008 [1982]).

Festivals, as one of the most common organizational structures in the art world of performing arts, can thus be seen as a social practice, as 'a temporally unfolding and spatially dispersed nexus of doings and sayings' (Schatzki, 1996, p. 89). Through the analysis of the social practices at festivals, one can find out a lot about how people interact, communicate, socialize etc. when participating in performances. As such, festivals provide a space for identity construction:

> The contemporary festival … becomes a potential site for representing, encountering, incorporating and researching aspects of cultural difference. (Bennett, Taylor, & Woodward, 2014, p. 1)

Festivals offer a valuable insight into questions such as whether "the festivals express our zeitgeist" (Willnauer, 2007, p. 11). Thus, festivals have become a key influence on artistic cultural life. Like other art forms, performing arts have been increasingly staged in economic contexts, leading to a discussion of the 'festivalization of culture' (Bennett et al., 2014). Many of today's arts festivals have been founded in the last 30 years, a trend reinforced by funding bodies, public authorities and cultural institutions, which show a tendency to focus on annual or bi-annual festival series or the like, mainly due to funding structures that depend on annual

budgets for a single festival edition. With a festival, a cultural organization can often attract more visitors in a short period than with single
events throughout the year and can therefore raise more interest in their
programme and mission.

This chapter focuses on performing arts festivals with cultural, national
and artistic diversity as part of their mission statement. This means that
these festivals present themselves as featuring artists from around the
world with diverse cultural backgrounds and programmes devoted to
multiple art forms and the crossing of art genre boundaries. Performing
arts at these festivals do not only encompass productions in music, drama
and dance but also include contemporary performances such as site-specific shows, installations with performances and discursive programmes
such as panel discussions on the topics of the respective festival. Similar
to approaches in contemporary music, performing arts question what
theatre, dance or music should be and tend to develop new approaches to
art production.

> Historically, performance art has been a medium that challenges and trans-
> gresses boundaries between disciplines and genders, between private and
> public, between everyday life and art, and that follows no rules. In the
> process, it has energized and affected other disciplines—architecture as
> event, theater as image, photography as performance. (Fischer-Lichte &
> Roselt, 2001, p. 241)

With this approach to questioning enduring concepts of more 'traditional' art forms, performing arts are very much a suitable research field
for analysing how different approaches to diversity in the arts are enacted.

The curator's role is clearly one of the most urgent ones to be discussed
when analysing the field of arts management. The professional field of the
curator has become one of the most desired jobs in these globalized times
as, since about the 1970s, the boundaries between curator and artist have
become blurred. "The bearer of an artistic 'skills set' replaces the exclusive
figure of the original artist" (Reckwitz, 2012, p. 115). With their responsibility for selecting and setting new trends, curators act, and sometimes
live, like internationally successful DJs, flexibilized global nomads and

social networkers (Timm, 2011). Curators therefore carry symbolic capital in the art field as embodying the 'entrepreneurial self'.

> The potential of curating on the one hand is based in its strong interconnections with artistic practice both historically as well as regarding status, and on the other hand because it connects—as an organisation, social networking, contextual association, motivation, facilitating and interpreting practice—social and self-technologies that meet the current demands of economical management. (von Bismarck, 2003, p. 83)

Curators no longer focus solely on visual arts but mix genres and work outside the art field or rather aestheticize every part of social life in the paradigm of the 'creativity dispositif' (Reckwitz, 2012), where it "seems closer to a basic requirement that everyone develop curatorial skills, or at least curate their own profile" (Beyes, 2018, p. 112f). This diversity in the approach to curating is reflected in a diversity of labels within the art field comparable to the artistic directors, programmers or bookers found in the field of popular music. Since 2009, the founding of new curatorial study programmes at universities in Berlin, Frankfurt, Leipzig, Zurich, London, New York or Hamburg testifies to the 'curatorial turn' (O'Neill, 2012) in a globalized art field.

Rather than examining the curating of a festival, "the technical modality of making art go public" (Lind, 2012, p. 11), 'the curatorial' is studied as a complex

> field of overlapping and intertwining activities, tasks, and roles that formerly were divided and more clearly attributed to different professions, institutions, and disciplines. (von Bismarck et al., 2012, p. 8)

Curatorial strategies are seen as a social practice that construct and deconstruct identities, symbols and relations in the performing arts. In other words, the curatorial is understood as a complex field in arts management of different intermingling practices, multiplex network relations, persons and institutions where dominant ideologies, terminologies, habits etc. are produced and reproduced, but where the curator also embodies a special role when it comes to defining (social) conventions in the respective field. Related to Pierre Bourdieu's understanding of a field, the curatorial has "social and political implications" (Rogoff & von Bismarck, 2012, p. 37) where curators and other field participants define and redefine the rules and by doing so "create differences, deviances, and frictions with the existing conditions" (Rogoff & von Bismarck, 2012, p. 37). Bourdieu's cultural intermediaries are also embedded in a complex field of organizations that influence ideas of taste channelled by the cultural intermediary.

Another interpretation of the curatorial is found in Michel Foucault's concept of the 'dispositif' (1978). The curatorial, so to speak, not only includes specific artistic programming decisions taken by an artistic director or curator, but it also takes into account all the different and complex, intertangled sets of institutional, political, economic, architectural and social conditions influencing these processes.

At the same time, the organizational structures of the festivals enable and limit curatorial strategies. By studying the curatorial strategies employed in these festivals, one is able to detect certain meanings of diversity construction and analyse the gatekeeping processes and power relations that form the base of every curatorial decision. What is revealed is how the conventions of fostering diversity at performing arts festivals are influenced by the complex field of the curatorial. In the following, the figure of the curator and the concept of the curatorial are both understood as meaning that every curator is influenced by the complex conditions surrounding their work and the curatorial is intermeshed with power relations.

Curators as Gatekeepers

We will now explore the power of conventions in order to demonstrate the complexity of relations in the curatorial and the art world of international performing art festivals. The curatorial practice employed within such festivals is analysed both with regard to their formal organizational structures (Reed, 1992) as well as the organizational processes underlying every curatorial strategy (Beyes, 2007, 2016; Langley & Tsukas, 2017; Helin, Hernes, Hjorth, & Holt, 2014). The first perspective looks at festivals as formal organizations with their (financial) infrastructure, policies etc., whereas the latter perspective allows a 'deeper' look at 'circulating scripts' (Latour, 2013, p. 50), such as the conventions involved in the curatorial.

The more important festivals are for the cultural landscape, and so for the field of arts and cultural management, the more significant the figure of the curator is. Even though there are about "a few thousand curators worldwide" who belong to the art world of international performing arts festivals, there are only "about 20 persons in Germany" (curator interview 10-6-2017). These few curators, seen internationally, act as both gatekeepers and brokers. These are key terms in the analysis of power relations in networks (Burt, 2004). Gatekeepers are seen as having a crucial position in granting or denying access to a network. For instance, a curator can decide which upcoming artist is going to be produced at their festival, and so gain admittance to the international festival network, and which artist will not.

Becker (2008 [1982], p. 93ff) also sees a gatekeeper's role in the distribution of art as someone who enacts power while controlling access to valuable resources. In social network analysis, by contrast, a gatekeeper is a type of broker. So, a curator acts as a broker by arranging contact between an artist and another gatekeeper or someone similar. Brokers plan and act on the basis of power decisions (Burt, 1992). Power is established and de-established by assigning differences, by controlling and sanctioning deviance. This can lead to standardization and thereby to the institutionalization of diversity. For instance, "in music practice, the position of the broker is called, amongst others, the multiplier" (Dollereder, 2018, p. 60), information is multiplied by the broker in communicating to other network members. Further, information from outside the network or from other networks is communicated by the broker. The broker can thereby fill so-called structural holes (Burt, 1992), gaps in social relations between network members. Curators, for example, rely on their colleagues' advice to find 'new' artists. But the broker only bridges structural holes in their own interest, thus acting as a gatekeeper in Becker's (2008 [1982]) sense for weaker network members dependent on the broker's decisions if they are to be admitted to the network.

Power is key to social network theory, in that it encompasses the ability of the brokerage to concurrently understand different levels of networks and to think in the context of multiplex network structures. (Dollereder, 2018, p. 167)

'Multiplex' is used here to describe 'layered relations'. In the curatorial brokerage takes place on different levels, for example, by providing access to artist networks, connections to funding organizations, entry to political networks etc. This means that in the international network of performing arts festivals, some curators have stronger positions than others; depending on their ability to use network structures on multiplex levels, they can enact more power than others. One can either zoom in to a microlevel on the relations of the broker and their relations to other curators or artists or zoom out to a macrolevel and focus on the position of the broker in the art world or the network of performing arts festivals.

Curators are also described as cultural intermediaries (Bourdieu, 1984), as taste makers who define what is legitimate and illegitimate art. Cultural intermediaries

construct value by mediating how goods (or services, practices, people) are perceived and engaged with by others. … Cultural intermediaries are defined by their professional expertise in taste and value within specific cultural fields. (Smith Maguire & Matthews, 2014, p. 2)

Accordingly, cultural intermediaries, drawing from their personal habitus, which includes cultural capital and subjective dispositions, can assign cultural legitimacy to an art form or an artist but they can equally exclude art forms or artists by constructing them as illegitimate (Bourdieu, 1984). Cultural intermediaries also work as 'power brokers' between, or rather bridging, the spheres of production and consumption, thus filtering information and products from the area of artists to the area of their audiences (Featherstone, 2007).

Brokerage involves how the relations between the single actors are constructed on a qualitative level and can take place on many different levels. "A social network is a network of meanings" (White, 1992, p. 65f), and these meanings are stabilized by conventions. As Becker puts it:

> Every art world uses, to organise some of the cooperation between some of its participants, conventions known to all or almost all well-socialized members of the society in which it exists. (Becker, 2008 [1982], p. 42)

Becker describes how the entire art organization is influenced by the development and impact of these conventions. At first, processes of construction take place in the interactions of the stakeholders who define the social, political, aesthetic and evaluating criteria of art. These criteria are often unquestioned and have normative effects through their institutionalization. In a second step, the gatekeepers of an art world take up these criteria and together with the producers and mediators of the arts negotiate, in another complex interactive process, their symbolic meanings as conventions. These conventions are not static though; they can be changed or discarded with the agreement of a majority of participants in the art world. Depending on what promises a better outcome for the stakeholder, social status, and with it power, can be achieved or increased both by adjusting and by flexing the established conventions. But most often in an art world conventions only change very slowly (Gaupp & Kirchberg, 2017).

Following a French strand of sociology, conventions are not understood as fixed standards or traditions but rather serve as a socioculturally based logic of action that

> enables the participants to coordinate themselves actively in situations characterised by conditions of uncertainty in order to realize a common intention. Conventions serve participants in situations as a collective interpretative frame for the evaluation of appropriateness and the value of actions, persons, objects and conditions. (Diaz-Bone, 2011, p. 23)

How does innovation happen in the art world? In other words, how can conventions be changed? Becker (2008 [1982]) calls innovators in the art world 'mavericks', people who are able to bend the conventions but who still have to be part of the art world by following the organizational rules. They "violate the conventions of art world practice, but ... do so selectively ....abid[ing] by most of them" (Becker, 2008 [1982], p. 242f.). Only if the change introduced by a maverick also "develops an adequate organisational support system" (Becker, 2008 [1982], p. 242f.) will the change last and survive and thereby succeed in establishing new conventions.

Deviance, which itself is dynamic and flexible, occurs when someone does not follow the normative conventions, rules or values followed by the majority of an art world, or some part thereof. If we are interested in nonconformity to conventions, we must also pay attention to the processes that first led to establishing the conformity rule. Bending or breaking rules also implies that someone has had the social power to define and impose these rules in the first place. The curators and others involved in gatekeeping and brokering information in the art world of performing arts have set the conventions of how to act in this art world, penalizing at the same time nonconforming, deviant artists. Deviance here is generally sanctioned by not being granted entrance into the network.

In the classic sociological theory of deviance, Durkheim (1973) defines it as nonconformity to generally accepted norms. However, he also examines how deviance brings about innovation. Apart from this functionalist theory, other sociological explanations can be taken into account to understand deviant behaviour and to draw a thin line between deviance and innovation. For example, subculture theories see deviant behaviour as something that, while it does not conform to the majority's values, can be perfectly accepted in a subcultural frame with different norms and values (Raithel, 2002). As the term 'subculture' implies a normative understanding of 'one culture dominating another', again drawing from Becker's symbolic interactionist approach in *Outsiders* (1963), labelling theory can offer a valuable understanding of deviance in art worlds. It is the people with more power who are able to label another person (or art form) as too different, not fitting in, or deviant. So, it is not the artist or the art form itself that is deviant but instead the interactionist process of labelling an art form or the reactions of the more powerful gatekeeper towards the art form or the artist. The question is who defines the conventions and what are their interests and intentions.

As such, politics and domination are at the centre of these practices. The establishment of standards and norms of deviancy can lead to an intrinsic artistic censorship. In order to be able to participate in the art worlds of performing arts, artists must adapt to established conventions. This is not to say that different productions are explicitly forbidden, only that their artists would be less likely to succeed in having their work produced. Following Pierre Bourdieu, acquiring a certain habitus is essential to joining the respective field (1984). This means that to gain acceptance or higher status in the field, artists unconsciously conform to a certain behaviour—including lifestyle, clothing, speech and taste—to display the social status of the artist.

Methodology

This chapter deals with how conventions in the curation of performing arts festivals develop, and it examines the interdependencies among diversity, the performing arts and the curatorial. This is done by combining performance, cultural, organizational and postcolonial studies with sociological theories and methodological approaches. The arguments are based on an empirical qualitative study in the field of international performing arts festivals conducted from 2014 until 2018. On the whole, 26 qualitative expert interviews were conducted with 22 curators and dramaturges of 13 festivals based mainly in Europe, West Asia and North Africa. In addition, four artists and representatives of five more cultural organizations active in the field of music and performing arts were interviewed. These data are backed by the analysis of seven public discussions, lectures and published interviews of curators from these festivals as well as press publications of the festivals. The notions of diversity discussed earlier are then used as a grid for analysis of this data corpus. Most of these festivals and events were attended for one or several days of participant observation. In one festival, the author participated in a production as a singer in the choir. In this chapter, two of these festivals are used as exemplary cases to highlight the findings discussed below.

Network Relations

While it may seem that festivals taking place in Europe are dominated by artists from European countries and that this representation of how diversity should be staged has become the norm, it cannot be stated that it is always and only 'European or Western festivals versus the rest'. There are far more complex network processes at work, which are again influenced by multiple power structures and broker positions as well as funding structures, language and cultural policies, and festivals mission statements. But these processes also generate synergetic effects and opportunities for upcoming artists and smaller festivals, as will be shown in this section.

One of the main structural influences on these organizations is the number of in-house productions and co-productions in comparison to presentations of guest performances. In essence these approaches differ. While in-house productions and co-productions typically involve a specific show being developed in cooperation with a specific curator, guest performances generally consist of existing works with no intended link to the specific festival. Most curators who took part in this study indicated a preference for co-producing over presenting guest performances, as "in-house productions in particular incorporate the nimbus of commitment and aesthetic vision, as only they are the 'product' of a single festival" (Elfert, 2009, p. 127). Curators normally work with 'their' artists over the course of several years to develop a new production. If in the talks with the artists an idea seems to be very interesting, it may be postponed to a later date, due to budgeting or scheduling constraints or if the idea does not fit into the upcoming festival programme.

Very often such in-house productions are too expensive to be produced by a single festival organization. This is one of the most important reasons for the development of festival networks, which co-produce one or several works in order to share production costs by showing the same production at the cooperating festivals. One result of this strategy is that there are fewer performing arts groups and fewer productions in the festival calendar. On the one hand, co-productions are … promotionally effective as they unite renowned partners … saving costs compared to many in-house productions and [through the collaboration with partners from different countries] attract funds from companies and private foundations more easily. (Elfert, 2009, p. 127)

On the other hand, this can lead to festivals losing their individuality and their unique selling position. A canonized performance landscape takes shape, with the same groups being produced at a majority of these festivals and a corresponding loss in diversity of cultural expression.

But the majority of this study's interview partners acknowledge the positive aspects of such cooperation. From 2007 until 2017, eight European festivals of performing arts united in the network *Nxt.Stp* and received funding from the European Commission totalling of 2.5 million euros. This development gives upcoming artists the opportunity to be produced on a European level without having to conduct lengthy production negotiations. This network encompasses many of the major festivals in Europe: *kunstenfestivaldesarts* (Brussels, Belgium), *Alkantara Festival* (Lisbon, Portugal), *Baltoscandal festival* (Rakvere, Estonia), *Göteborgs Dans & Teater Festival* (Goteborg, Denmark), *De Internationale Keuze van de Rotterdamse Schouwburg* (Rotterdam, Netherlands), *steirischer herbst* (Graz, Austria), *Théâtre national de Bordeaux en Aquitaine* (Bordeaux, France) and, in the second funding period, *Noorderzon Performing Arts Festival* (Groningen, Netherlands). Associated festivals that did not receive EU funding but participated in the network meetings were *Dense Bamako Danse* (Bamako, Mali), *On Marche* (Marrakesh, Morocco), *Kyoto Experiment* (Kyoto, Japan) and the *Panorama Festival* (Rio de Janeiro, Brasil) (https://www.nxtstp.eu/). The substantial funding from the EU, in addition to their existing festival budgets, means that a large part of the performing arts world in Europe is joined in an institutionalized network.

The funding scheme reveals a deeply Eurocentric bias. Not only had the non-European festival representatives to pay for their own travels to network meetings, they also had no influence in deciding which artists were produced. Such a network seems to be a closed circle, inevitably facilitating a European canon of performing arts. But this is relativized because *Nxt.stp* is not the only the network in which these festivals participate. It is more accurate to say that curators come together in a number of non-institutionalized networking groups, joining one for a period time because a specific theme is attractive and then in the following season finding other partners. As former co-director of the *Berliner Festspiele* and former head of general project funding at the *German Federal Cultural Foundation* Torsten Maß (cited in Elfert, 2009) explains,

> There are always new alliances emerging. The curator discovers new, fresh, and unknown groups, and not by chance. Constellations form, ideas arise, which are meaningful for some time, and then the group splits up again and reunites in a different form. (p. 336)

So, new network contexts are continually established, which in turn strengthen the position of the respective curator as a broker. Artistic director of the international centre for the finer arts in Hamburg *Kampnagel* Amelie Deuflhard (cited in Elfert, 2009) explains,

> in the past [the 1990s] it was like this: five partners united and showed a production one after the other. Nowadays, networks are not closed circles any more but instead are open for no matter how many partners. … I build up a new network for every new project. (p. 340)

Social network analysis indicates that with each new project the network is expanded, especially as the former network partners still have strong ties to the curator due to the trust they built up in the former project (Kadushin, 2012). This approach was widely recognized by other curators in this study. As such, there are several strategies in the curatorial that not only depend on funding schemes and financing issues but also on several other influences, such as following a specific theme.

For instance, the *kunstenfestivaldesarts* in Brussels is seen as the trendsetter in the art world of international performing arts festivals. Curators from festivals around the world, given sufficient travel funds (curator interview, 28 May 2015), attend to see what is being staged. The curator of the *kunstenfestivaldesarts* has a very strong and central position as a broker in the festival network and his ideas as to which artists are recognized as 'new' and 'emerging' are highly valued by the other and weaker network members. One aspect of the *kunstenfestivaldesarts*'s strong broker position is its relationship to networks of artists. This status allows the festival team to more easily confirm bookings or the production of new work from those artists in whom they are interested. Other curators with equally strong broker positions are not influenced by the *kunstenfestivaldesarts*'s choices; on the contrary, they go there to find out which groups they should not curate themselves so that they can differentiate their own festivals from the '*kunsten*'.

In addition, the ambition or mission of a curatorial also contributes to how much and what notions of diversity are being practised at these festivals. For instance, the goal of the festival *theaterformen* in Hanover/Brunswick, Germany is to show new, often emerging, productions and as the curator disposes over sufficient travel funds she is able to personally learn about new productions all over the world. The goal of the curator of the *D-CAF festival* in Cairo, Egypt, is to stage mostly established artists 'from the West' for Egyptian audiences, as the majority of his festival audience does not have the possibility to travel and see those productions otherwise. In order to make contact with these groups, the curator travels only to the big European festivals staging these artists. The festival *Performing Tangier* in Morocco in turn is not free to develop its own programme with artists from outside Morocco as it is dependent on institutional and financial relationships, for example with the *Institut Français*. These European funding organizations influence the choice of which non-Moroccan artists are programmed. Apart from these 'international' acts, the festival's programme is dominated by Moroccan acts due to fierce internal budget constraints. Then again, the artistic curator of the *KunstFestSpiele Herrenhausen* in Hanover, Germany, is first interested in the artistic idea and only then addresses how to finance its production. Similarly, the approach of the *kunstenfestivaldesarts* in Brussels focuses on the artists and understands the festival as an experimental field for both established and emerging artists. Although this involves the possibility failure, artists are allowed to experiment with the new and unusual, leading in turn to more artistic diversity and the bending or even breaking of art world conventions.

Even though these institutionalized networks are open to new members and sometimes provide valuable opportunities for unknown artists to be produced on a wider international scale, there is nevertheless a national focus in this process. Former director of the festival *Steirischer Herbst* and Viennese city councillor for culture Veronika Kaup-Hasler expresses this aptly:

> The biggest challenge for the arts is an increasing nationalism in all matters. Due to the financial crisis, the national funding bodies insist more and more on national production—foreign participation is of course welcome in financial terms, but there is less interest in co-financing new works by non-resident artists. (Kaup-Hasler, 2012, p. 5)

As can be seen in some of the examples, brokerage and gatekeeping depend heavily on who is funding the festival. One might assume that the bigger the budget of a festival, the greater the diversity of the artists in its programme. However, this view falls short as the funders' mission, and funding schemes also have to be taken into account.

Sociocultural Conventions

A review of the programmes of what the majority of the interviewed curators consider as most important performing arts festivals over the last ten years indicates that a western canon of artists is emerging. Despite a growing focus on artists from Latin America, especially Argentina, such as *Mariano Pensotti*, programmed artists and art groups featured are mainly from 'Western' countries or at least based in the 'West'. These include *Forced Entertainment* (UK), *SheShePop* (Germany), *Rimini Protokoll* (Germany), *Jan Lauwers & the Needcompany* (Belgium), *Anne Teresa De Keersmaeker* (Belgium), *the Wooster Group* (USA), *Nature Theater of Oklahoma* (USA), *Boris Charmatz* (France) and *Milo Rau* (Switzerland). In addition to the structural reasons outlined above, 'aesthetic barriers' are a cause behind this development. 'Aesthetic barriers' hinder non-European works from being presented at major festivals. In fact, there is "strong Eurocentrism in the field" (Husemann, 2012, p. 276f) and this takes place even amongst curators of Europe-based festivals who are from non-European countries. Husemann (2012) explains,

> Works from other continents get easily labelled as either 'outdated' in comparison to work based in Europe or as 'too specific' to be presented next to European works without also creating access to their 'original' local context. ... Even European curators who decide to focus on works from non-European regions often have to defend their programme from accusations of being 'an easy way out' or pure 'exoticism'. (p. 276f)

Such generalizations have to be critically examined. First of all, a statement that equates the country of origin of an artist or curator with their artistic practice equally exoticizes ethnicity and race. It is equally arguable as to whether or not there is such a thing as 'non-European art'. An artist could practice an art form, wherever its traditions might be rooted in the world, once this artist has acquired a certain level of capital in the respective field of art. In addition, art itself is not static but instead it is constantly changing not least traveling; every art form is a dynamic transcultural practice with no pure topographic origin (Gaupp, 2016). Nevertheless, the processes of assigning a certain meaning in the production, distribution and consumption are subject to the established sociocultural conventions. This is why equating an art form with a country of origin is wide spread. Johannes Ismaiel-Wendt calls these othering processes in music practices 'topophilia' (Ismaiel-Wendt, 2011). Still, even when a curator does not engage in such practices, aesthetic barriers may still come into play when the art form does not comply with the established standards and norms of the (European) art world.

Sociocultural conventions serve as an interpretative framework that ultimately decides what is appropriate to programme and what is not. The actions of a curator, understood as a cultural intermediary in Bourdieu's sense, reveal how conventions are not simply routinized procedures but rather formed and legitimized by taste. After all, a cultural intermediary is often striving to legitimate the 'not-yet-legitimate' (Bourdieu, 1984, p. 326). The curator's work as a taste maker reconfirms his own cultural capital and thus his position as cultural intermediary. He reproduces and legitimizes social stratification through notions of taste

(Bourdieu, 1984). The conventions that define how diversity is staged and perceived within the field of international performing arts festivals are strongly oriented towards a norm that attempts to stress that national origin is irrelevant, and a festival should be a space of inclusion with the greatest possible diversity of art forms and artists. Yet, when it comes to valuing differences, curators tend to only include productions that are different enough to fulfil the demand for the unfamiliar while not too different from the known. Art must still fit into the circulating organizational scripts.

For instance, a curator participating in this research indicated he would not programme an 'African' artist whose aesthetics might be too 'boring' for the audience, as a long explanation contextualizing the work would be required (curator interview, 13 March 2017). The curator argued that the audience of this festival would be too unfamiliar with the requisite 'African' aesthetic language to be able to understand the conventions in that field. The curator went on to say that other cultural organizations, such as *Mousonturm* in Frankfurt, could show such artists, as they have— for at least 20 to 30 years—a tradition of educating their audiences to appreciate an art form with which they may be unfamiliar.

At the same time, bending of moral conventions may be seen as acceptable when those conventions are understood within a particular sociocultural context. For the same festival, a European artist who displayed scenes on stage, involving her vagina and her own blood, was chosen as a featured artist. The artist's work was both critically celebrated (Schlagenwerth, 2015) and condemned (Luzina, 2015). In fact, while many people in her audience left her shows, audiences and critics are still familiar with the sociocultural conventions surrounding such a piece, programmed as it was by way of an organizational network of established 'Western'-centric conventions, where critique of, for example, religious norms through theatrical means has a longer tradition (see the development of the so-called in-yer-face theatre in the 1990s in the United Kingdom: Sierz, 2001; Case, 1990). So, in this case a feminist critique of religion can be programmed, even if it employs theatrical means that may be shocking or offensive to some, but the production of an art form thought to be unfamiliar to an audience is declared too deviant from this norm and excluded.

Another issue that needs to be addressed in this context is the diktat in contemporary art worlds to produce something innovative or creative (Reckwitz, 2012). In the art world of contemporary performing arts, innovations can be introduced if they are supported by the organizational system of the curatorial and if they still work with the known conventions, even while bending or breaking them, "as long as the change in perception does not lead to radical practice" (Büscher-Ulbrich, Kadenbach, & Kindermann, 2013, p. 11). If an innovation does not refer to any standards within this art world—no matter if this reference involves conforming to or breaking the rules—it is highly unlikely to be included into a festival programme. Perhaps even more urgent is the question of what happens to critical or subversive art forms when they become an 'innovation' in the art world they were once opposed to (Boltanski & Chiapello, 2007).

Only a person with a strong broker position is able to introduce something more or less unknown or critical into this art world. This means that it takes the social relations of a gatekeeper to introduce a cultural innovation, in the sense of an unknown aesthetic convention, into an art world. But if there is no social relationship, then it is nearly impossible to bridge such a structural hole and the cultural innovation is unlikely to be established. So if an 'African' artist practices an art form outside of the art world of international performing arts festivals in Europe, this practice will not change the conventions and aesthetic expectations in this art world. Only if this art form is being brokered by a cultural intermediary is it possible for it to be accepted for programming. Again, as intermediaries curators are able to change the conventions and norms of the art world. So if there is to be innovation in 'Western'-centric art worlds, it is exactly these curators who need to be even more self-reflective about the underlying biases that inform every process in the curatorial in order to reverse "the relation between norm and deviance" (von Osten, 2003, p. 7).

One might think that the opportunity to promote one's own work through online channels would make it easier for artists from outside an art world to enter, but the position of curators as cultural intermediaries remains largely unaffected by digitalization for three reasons. Firstly, curators simply do not look for new artists online nor do they necessarily have time to watch all the videos sent to them by unknown artists.

Instead, they depend on their own experiences or personal relationships with other curators or trusted experts in the field. Normally, a curator only becomes aware of an artist if they have already been recommended by a trusted broker (curator interview, 26 May 2015). Secondly, even in the face of the decentralizing potential of digitalization, topographic space remains important, as cultural intermediaries and other helping hands are still regionally clustered (Hracs, 2013). Thirdly, an artist's symbolic capital depends on their personal relationships to cultural intermediaries in the field, providing them access to festival networks and programmes (Lizé, 2016). Following in the conclusion, the possibilities of a transcultural curatorial practice in the field of arts management will be considered.

Conclusion

This chapter discussed how different concepts of diversity are played out in the curatorial practice of performing arts festivals. As postcolonial critique or *double critique*, it was argued that this practice is deeply influenced by power relations, conventions, network structures and network processes as well as other organizational issues. These power hierarchies are unlikely to change in the near future as the majority of performing arts festivals are financed by 'Western'-centric funding bodies and organized by established curators able to strongly influence the conventions governing this art world. This makes it all the more imperative for research into how cross-cultural cooperation can be made fruitful for all parties involved, whether artist, festival organizer, audience and curator. In a transcultural perspective, it will be crucial to lay open, critique and question the structures, conventions and processes in the curatorial of the art world of performing arts festivals in particular and in arts management in general in order to decolonize international arts management a bit more and achieve something resembling a true diversity.

The research presented here indicates that arts management needs to adapt to the realities of today's post-migrant social processes (Gaupp, 2016). Diversity understood from a transcultural perspective means that differences are not reduced to national or ethnic differences but are seen for what they are, a manifold and multilayered intersectionality in each individual. These differences are not categorically ascribed to artists or art forms. The curator anticipating that the 'African' artist would be too 'boring' for their audiences should rather focus on the commonalities between the 'African' artist and the audience and build a bridge to the more established conventions in this art world.

It is indeed possible to change or at least expand the prevailing convention of 'different enough-but not too different' in the curatorial of performing arts festivals through conflict and critique, questioning the established concepts of diversity and imagining alternative point of views and alternative exchanges. The curatorial is not a fixed dichotomy of Eurocentric or 'Western'-centric curators working 'against' non-European or non-'Western' artists and art forms, it is not Europe or the 'West' versus 'the rest' but rather a transcultural way of inclusion that involves critique as a major driving force. Such a transcultural curatorial practice would legitimize conflict as part of engaging with 'new' art forms. So the feared unfamiliarity of an 'African' art form or even the unconscious biased conventions within curatorial practice could themselves become topics of exploration in festival programmes, creating new meeting places for the performing arts. Transcultural diversity in this sense does not mean that social inequalities or discrimination processes are ignored, but rather that they are at the core of a transcultural diversity-sensitive approach. In this context, diversity is not a given entity but rather a condition for life in today's societies, "a matter of cultural overlaps, border spaces and spaces-in-between, of crossings and simultaneous affiliations" (Yıldız, 2013, p. 144).

References

Amīn, K. (2014). Postcolonial modernity. Theatre in Morocco and the interweaving loop. In E. Fischer-Lichte, T. Jost, & S. I. Jain (Eds.), *The politics of interweaving performance cultures: Beyond postcolonialism* (Routledge Advances in Theatre and Performance Studies, Vol. 33) (pp. 25–41). New York: Routledge.

Amīn, K., & Laamiri, M. (2010). *Performing cultural diversity: Critiquing post-colonialism* (Series: Conderences and Colloquia) (1st ed.). Tetouan: Université Abdelmalek Essaâdi, Faculty of Letters and Humanities, Research Group of Performance Studies.

Becker, H. S. (1963). *Outsiders: Studies in the sociology of deviance* (Social Theory). London: Free Press of Glencoe.

Becker, H. S. (2008). *Art worlds.* Berkeley, CA; London; Los Angeles, CA: University of California Press.

Bennett, A., Taylor, J., & Woodward, I. (Eds.). (2014). *The festivalization of culture.* Surrey and Burlington, VT: Ashgate.

Beyes, T. (2007). Organisationstheorien von Agamben bis Žižek. Auf dem Basar der Organization Studies. In T. Eberle, E. Walter-Busch, & A. Sousa-Poza (Eds.), *Fokus Organisation. Sozialwissenschaftliche Perspektiven und Analysen* (pp. 65–86). Konstanz: UVK.

Beyes, T. (2016). Art, aesthetics and organization. In B. Czarniawska (Ed.), *A research agenda for management and organization studies* (Elgar Research Agendas) (pp. 115–125). Cheltenham: Edward Elgar Publishing Ltd.

Beyes, T. (2018). Curating. In T. Beyes & J. Metelmann (Eds.), *The creativity complex. A companion to contemporary culture* (Kulturen der Gesellschaft) (1st ed., pp. 109–113). Bielefeld: Transcript.

Boltanski, L. & Chiapello, È. (2007). *The new spirit of capitalism* (1st Publ.). London: Verso.

Bourdieu, P. (1984). *Distinction. A social critique of the judgement of taste.* Cambridge, MA: Harvard University Press.

Burt, R. S. (1992). *Structural holes. The social structure of competition.* Cambridge, MA: Harvard University Press.

Burt, R. S. (2004). Strucural holes and good ideas. *American Journal of Sociology, 110*(2), 349–399.

Büscher-Ulbrich, D., Kadenbach, S., & Kindermann, M. (2013). Einleitung: "The more things change". In D. Büscher-Ulbrich, S. Kadenbach, & M. Kindermann (Eds.), *Innovation—Konvention. Transdisziplinäre Beiträge zu einem kulturellen Spannungsfeld* (Kultur- und Medientheorie) (1st ed., pp. 7–20). Bielefeld: Transcript.

Case, S.-E. (1990). *Performing feminisms. Feminist critical theory and theatre.* Baltimore, MD: Johns Hopkins University Press.

Danto, A. C. (1964). The artworld. *The Journal of Philosophy, 61*(19), 571–584.

Derrida, J. (2004). *Die différance. Ausgewählte Texte.* Stuttgart: Reclam.

Diaz-Bone, R. (2011). Einführung in die Soziologie der Konventionen. In R. Diaz-Bone (Ed.), *Soziologie der Konventionen: Grundlagen einer pragmatischen Anthropologie* (Theorie und Gesellschaft, Vol. 73) (pp. 9–41). Frankfurt am Main: Campus.

Dollereder, L. (2018). *Netzwerkbildung im Musiksektor von Niedersachsen. Funktionsweisen und Mechanismen Sozialer Formationen.* Lüneburg: Leuphana University of Lüneburg.

Durkheim, É. (1973). *Moral education. A study in the theory and application of the sociology of education* (1, Free Press paperback ed.). New York: Free Press.

Elfert, J. (2009). *Theaterfestivals. Geschichte und Kritik eines kulturellen Organisationsmodells* (Vol. 16). Bielefeld: Transcript.

Featherstone, M. (2007). *Consumer culture and postmodernism* (Theory, Culture & Society). London: Sage Publications.

Fischer-Lichte, E., & Roselt, J. (2001). Attraktion des Augenblicks—Aufführung, Performance, performativ und Performativität als theaterwissenschaftliche Begriffe. In *Theorien des Performativen* (pp. 237–253). Berlin: Akad.-Verl.

Foucault, M. (1978). *Dispositive der Macht. Über Sexualität, Wissen und Wahrheit* (Merve titel, Vol. 77). Berlin: Merve.

Gaupp, L. (2016). *Die exotisierte Stadt. Kulturpolitik und Musikvermittlung im postmigrantischen Prozess* (Studies in Music, Vol. 1). Hildesheim: Olms.

Gaupp, L. (2020). Epistemologies of diversity and otherness. In L. Gaupp & G. Pelillo-Hestermeyer (Eds.), *Diversity and otherness—Transcultural insights into norms, practices and negotiations.* Berlin: De Gruyter.

Gaupp, L., & Kirchberg, V. (2017). Kulturelle Diversität in den Künsten zwischen Tradition und Zeitgenossenschaft. In L. Hieber (Ed.), *Gesellschaftsepochen und ihre Kunstwelten* (Kunst und Gesellschaft, Vol. 9) (pp. 377–388). Wiesbaden: VS Springer.

Hall, S. (1994). The West and the rest: Discourse and power. In S. Hall & B. Gieben (Eds.), *The formations of modernity* (Introduction to Sociology) (pp. 275–331). Cambridge: Polity Press.

Helin, J., Hernes, T., Hjorth, D., & Holt, R. (2014). *The Oxford handbook of process philosophy and organization studies.* Oxford: Oxford University Press.

Hracs, B. J. (2013). Cultural intermediaries in the digital age: The case of independent musicians and managers in Toronto. *Regional Studies, 49*(3), 461–475. https://doi.org/10.1080/00343404.2012.750425

Husemann, P. (2012). A curator's reality check: Conditions of curating performing arts. In B. von Bismarck, J. Schafaff, & T. Weski (Eds.), *Cultures of the curatorial* (pp. 268–286). Berlin: Sternberg.

Ismaiel-Wendt, J. (2011). *Tracks'n'treks. Populäre Musik und postkoloniale Analyse*. Münster: Unrast.

Kadushin, C. (2012). *Understanding social networks. Theories, concepts, and findings*. New York: Oxford University Press.

Kaup-Hasler, V. (2012). NXT.STP. Documentation 2007–2012. Retrieved January 21, 2019, from https://www.nxtstp.eu/files/NXTSTP_5_years.pdf

Langley, A., & Tsukas, C. K. (Eds.). (2017). *The SAGE handbook of process organization studies*. Los Angeles, CA: Sage.

Latour, B. (2013). 'What's the story?' Organizing as a mode of existence. In D. Robichaud & F. Cooren (Eds.), *Organization and organizing: Materiality, agency and discourse* (pp. 37–51). London: Routledge.

Lind, M. (2012). Performing the curatorial: An introduction. In M. Lind (Ed.), *Performing the curatorial: Within and beyond art* (pp. 9–22). Berlin: Sternberg Press.

Lizé, W. (2016). Artistic work intermediaries as value producers: Agents, managers, tourneurs and the acquisition of symbolic capital in popular music. *Poetics, 59*, 35–49. https://doi.org/10.1016/j.poetic.2016.07.002

Luzina, S. (2015, July 2). Angélica Liddell bei "Foreign Affairs". Die Bühnenmesse der Porno-Queen. Retrieved January 21, 2019, from https://www.tagesspiegel.de/kultur/angelica-liddell-bei-foreign-affairs-die-buehnenmesse-der-porno-queen/11997268.html

O'Neill, P. (2012). *The culture of curating and the curating of culture(s)*. Cambridge, MA: MIT Press.

Peres da Silva, G., & Hondros, K. (Eds.). (2019). *Music practices across borders: (E)Valuating space, diversity and exchange* (Music and Sound Culture). Bielefeld: Transcript.

Raithel, J. (2002). Ethnisch-kulturelle Konfliktpotenziale unter Jugendlichen im (groß)städtischen Raum. Ein Vergleich zwischen deutschen und türkischen Jugendlichen. *Soziale Probleme, 13*(1), 54–79.

Reckwitz, A. (2012). *Die Erfindung der Kreativität. Zum Prozess gesellschaftlicher Ästhetisierung*. Berlin: Suhrkamp.

Reed, M. I. (1992). *The sociology of organizations. Themes, perspectives and prospects* (Studies in Sociology, 1st Publ.). New York: Harvester Wheatsheaf.

Rogoff, I., & von Bismarck, B. (2012). Curating/curatorial: A conversation between Irit Rogoff and Beatrice von Bismarck. In B. von Bismarck, J. Schafaff, & T. Weski (Eds.), *Cultures of the curatorial* (pp. 20–38). Berlin: Sternberg.

Said, E. W. (1991). *Orientalism* (Penguin Books: Penguin History). London: Penguin.

Schatzki, T. R. (1996). *Social practices. A Wittgensteinian approach to human activity and the social.* Cambridge: Cambridge University Press.

Schlagenwerth, M. (2015, Juni 29). Angelíca Liddell. Schreiben ist meine Rache. Retrieved January 21, 2019, from https://www.berliner-zeitung.de/kultur/angel%C3%ADca-liddell%2D%2Dschreiben-ist-meine-rache%2D%2D1299316

Sierz, A. (2001). *In-yer-face theatre: British drama today.* London: Faber and Faber.

Smith Maguire, J., & Matthews, J. (2014). Introduction: Thinking with cultural intermediaries. In J. Smith Maguire & J. Matthews (Eds.), *The cultural intermediaries reader* (S. 1–11). Los Angeles, CA: Sage.

Timm, T. (2011, Mai 5). Die Macht der Geschmacksverstärker, ZEIT online. Kunst. Retrieved December 6, 2012, from https://www.zeit.de/2011/19/Kunst-Kuratoren

von Bismarck, B. (2003). Kuratorisches Handeln. Immaterielle Arbeit zwischen Kunst und Managementmodellen. In M. von Osten (Ed.), *Norm der Abweichung* (Theorie: Gestaltung) (pp. 81–98). Wien: Springer.

von Bismarck, B., Schafaff, J., & Weski, T. (2012). Introduction. In B. von Bismarck, J. Schafaff, & T. Weski (Eds.), *Cultures of the curatorial* (pp. 7–16). Berlin: Sternberg.

von Osten, M. (2003). Einleitung. In M. von Osten (Ed.), *Norm der Abweichung* (Theorie: Gestaltung) (pp. 7–17). Wien: Springer.

Wallerstein, I. (1990). Culture as the ideological battleground of the modern world-system. In M. Featherstone (Ed.), *Global culture: Nationalism, globalization, and modernity* (Theory, Culture & Society) (pp. 31–55). London: Sage Publications.

Westen, M. (2012). How many nations are inside you? On cultural diversity, global art and art museums. In M. T. Horst & G. Schwartz (Eds.), *Changing perspectives. Dealing with globalisation in the presentation and collection of contemporary art* (pp. 76–85). Amsterdam: KIT.

White, H. C. (1992). *Identity and control. A structural theory of social action* (Princeton Paperbacks: Sociology). Princeton, NJ: Princeton University Press.

Willnauer, F. (2007). Musikfestspiele und Festivals. In Deutscher Musikrat (Ed.), *Musik Almanach 2007/08. Daten und Fakten zum Musikleben in Deutschland* (p. 63). Regensburg: Deutscher Musikrat.

Yıldız, E. (2013). Postmigrantische Verortungspraktiken. Ethnische Mythen irritieren. In P. Mecheril (Ed.), *Migrationsforschung als Kritik? Spielräume kritischer Migrationsforschung* (pp. 139–156). Wiesbaden: Springer VS.

7

Challenging Assumptions in Intercultural Collaborations: Perspectives from India and the UK

Ruhi Jhunjhunwala and Amy Walker

The work on this chapter started, in a way, when authors, Ruhi and Amy, met as participants at the inaugural Global Cultural Leadership Programme (GCLP), organised by the EU's Cultural Diplomacy Platform, in Malta in October 2016. The GCLP has a special focus on supporting the role of culture in external relations, as well as examining how culture can contribute to the development of the EU's relationships with its key strategic partners. Previous experiences had made both of us aware of how such programmes can create contexts where participants become cultural ambassadors of an entire country and spokespersons of its politics. This was not the first time either of us had taken on a collective identity. Having managed numerous international arts projects and participated in intercultural exchange programmes, we were used to being the 'Indian' or 'British' partner, navigating the associated stereotypes and

R. Jhunjhunwala (✉)
Bangalore, India

London, UK

A. Walker
London, UK

© The Author(s) 2020
V. Durrer, R. Henze (eds.), *Managing Culture*, Sociology of the Arts,
https://doi.org/10.1007/978-3-030-24646-4_7

prejudices. However, with the first GCLP taking place at a particularly turbulent and fractious moment in global politics, Ruhi found herself in the daunting position of representing a population of over 1 billion and 22 major languages, and Amy struggled to explain the British Brexit vote.

Since this meeting in 2016, we have explored a shared interest in examining how many of the intercultural collaboration and exchange programmes, which seek to enable dialogue and foster mutual understanding and appreciation across cultures, instead frequently perpetuate assumptions and maintain inequitable relationships between partners. Informed by broader academic reading and using examples from our own experience of working on India-UK collaborative arts programmes, this chapter is a collaborative reflection on how cultural diplomacy and international development funding, while crucial to the sector, can reinforce dominant practices affecting both the structural elements of India-UK collaborative arts programming (the allocation of resources, leadership and delivery) and the creative content. We will also consider whether cultural managers and practitioners can work within, navigate and benefit from initiatives and opportunities in these fields whilst challenging international power dynamics and colonial hierarchies. By focusing specifically on the cultural relationship between India and UK, as we have experienced it, this chapter will consider whether cultural diplomacy can enable the production of challenging and experimental artistic work through a process of 'fair cooperation' (Hampel, 2017). Issues relating to the ongoing post-colonial relationship between the two countries will also be highlighted for a better understanding of the context in which these collaborative projects function. Finally, the chapter will consider the role that new generations of cultural managers can play in facilitating innovative forms of artistic production outside of established traditional systems, thus challenging homogenous collective identities and creating spaces for more democratic discourse.

Funding Structures

To examine the impact of cultural diplomacy and international development on collaborations between India and the UK, it is important to have an understanding of the funding opportunities available in both countries. A straightforward economic comparison of governmental per capita spending on the arts and culture was found not to be useful here as there are too many variances between the two countries. A more useful analysis is based on attitudes and priorities expressed in policy and, in particularly, funding priorities around international practice.

Whilst the Department for Digital, Culture, Media and Sport (DCMS) is one of the smallest UK governmental departments, it is growing (DCMS, 2018). Faced with diminishing international influence post-Brexit, its primary objective of promoting a 'global Britain' seems increasingly vital. Conversely, the arts industry is not a priority sector for the Government of India and there is a serious lack of infrastructure to support it. The Ministry of Culture in India does not have a unitary cultural policy and although "the functional spectrum of the Department ranges from creating cultural awareness from the grass root level to the international cultural level" (Ministry of Culture, India, 2018, np); the primary mandate of the Ministry is to maintain and conserve the national heritage of the country, which includes monuments and classical as well as traditional art forms. As a result, over the last decade, funders like Hivos, the Ford Foundation and European cultural bodies, like British Council, the Goethe-Institut and Pro Helvetia, alongside embassies have significantly supported the arts sector in India, especially experimental and contemporary ventures and international collaborations. They have emerged as important contributors to the cultural landscape with the power to shape it, making international development and cultural diplomacy initiatives some of the principal supporters of new artistic work being produced in India.

Returning to the cultural relationship between India and the UK, the two countries have a strong and active tradition of artistic collaboration and exchange, much of which can be traced to their specific political relationship and a shared history. For anyone embarking on a collaborative project that connects India and the UK, there have been additional initiatives in the last few years linked to the 70th anniversary of Indian independence from the UK in 2017. These include funding and partnership opportunities such as the Arts Council England and British Council's collaboration on *Reimagine India*, "a cultural exchange programme designed to develop creative collaborations between art and cultural organisations in England and in India" (Arts Council England, 2018) and *UK/India 2017*, the British Council's programme to celebrate the long-standing relationship between India and the UK. There are also other agencies and bodies in the funding ecology supporting India-UK collaborations as part of a broader mission, such as the Asia-Europe Foundation (ASEF). Still further, many smaller collaborative arts projects and exchanges are supported by charitable foundations frequently originating as family trusts or legacies with a focus on a country or region of origin or interest, such as the Charles Wallace India Trust, the Piramal Art Foundation and Inlaks Shivdasani Foundation.

There is a vibrant two-way scene with increasing audiences for Indian arts in the UK and British arts in India (Thomas, 2018; Das, 2018) and whilst funding sources for these programmes are growing to include private foundations and charitable trusts, the main sources of funding can be divided into: International Development funders, often supporting artists or arts projects within social change programmes; and those active in Cultural Diplomacy, including cultural institutes, embassies and government offices.

International Development

In this chapter, the complex and often contested concept of international development, defined more generally as the process and policies through which living standards of other societies are improved (Diez et al., 2011), refers to funds given as international aid. As described by Stupples (2015), the arts have played an important part in international development programmes since the 1990s, triggered by initiatives like the *UN's World Decade for Cultural Development* (1988–1997). The arts and culture are argued to chime with developmental values such as the right to freedom of expression and are seen by agencies as a way to empower or at least give visibility to underrepresented or marginal groups, promoting tolerance and, more broadly, democracy.

Arts and cultural projects are commonly funded through international development programmes as a tool for communicating a message or disseminating advice—in the vein of theatre workshops promoting health and hygiene among underprivileged communities or educating citizens on their rights. We have also increasingly seen the funding of artistic production (artworks, music, craft products) within cultural entrepreneurship or creative skills development initiatives. However, from our experience, the majority of projects are supported as a way to bring people together to enhance greater mutual understanding, with opportunities for dialogue and debate being created through the process of collaboration on a joint artistic project and—when working bilaterally over longer periods of time—physical exchange.

Cultural Diplomacy

Cultural diplomacy is most commonly understood as "the exchange of ideas, information, art and other aspects of culture among nations and their peoples" (Cummings, 2003, p. 1). However, the extent to which this exchange is for fostering mutual understanding or for gaining influence is less straightforward. Despite its similarity and interchangeable use, we see it as distinct from soft power, which is defined as the ability to influence others through attraction and influence rather than coercion (Nye, 1990). A further useful analysis of these terms can be found in Doeser and Nisbett's report (2017) on the United Nations Office at Geneva (UNOG). Their findings from interviews with diplomats there and the UNOG secretariat indicate that, although the terms are used interchangeably, cultural diplomacy is generally seen as being a more reciprocal process, about 'reaching out', whilst soft power is perceived to be more about influence and coercion, with an emphasis on 'standing out'. Of course, creating visibility for a nation's artistic and cultural products is not necessarily at the detriment of building bridges with others. An important role of cultural diplomacy is the promotion of a national image or images, something that has formed a large part of many of the international cultural projects to which we are often exposed.

Most frequently our own experience of cultural diplomacy in action has been through funding opportunities or initiatives from international, mainly bilateral exchange and collaborative programmes. Here, artists and cultural practitioners have often been brought together to create work, exchange ideas, network and learn from each in order to facilitate greater cultural understanding, build respect and break down barriers. Within broader international relations programmes, such as the GCLP, there can be an added purpose of the initiative being a widely visible indicator of cooperation and partnership between nations. When the countries have a history of conflict, tension or colonial rule, cultural diplomacy can also be a way of retaining, and even celebrating the present, friendly relationship. Alongside the benefits of these initiatives there can also be negative or unintended outcomes, many of which trickle down to become the assumptions and stereotypes that we encounter when working on art and cultural projects and initiatives.

Inherent Inequalities

A common criticism of international development and the giving of 'foreign aid' is that it is inherently paternalistic with (even the most well-intentioned) agencies accused of determining what the recipients need, rather than listening to them. The use of arts and culture in international development programmes is not immune to these accusations, with participants and beneficiaries feeling that they are not consulted in the process, thus creating a situation of dependence rather than empowerment. Cultural diplomacy is frequently a one-way flow of resources that create unbalanced partnerships and hierarchies which, in the context of broader internal relations, can be seen to be enacting hegemonic or imperialistic motivations. As Henze (2016, p. 22) quotes from her interview with a cultural manager from Nigeria, "countries with bigger resources for promotion of their culture and methodology control the global discourse on culture". In any examination of the cultural relationship between the UK and India, their colonial history and post-colonial present cannot be ignored.

Frequently what dictates the organisational structure, or the management processes of the project are assumptions about who has authority over the project based on the source of funds. In the case of India-UK collaborations it is often assumed that, since the UK partner is bringing the money (true in most cases), they also control the project and are accountable for it both artistically and managerially whereas the Indian partner is responsible primarily for logistical support to realise the project. This assumption can be traced back to the paternalistic nature of the funding structure which is then amplified by the colonial history between the two countries. The strained past has the potential to make the Indian partner unwilling to cooperate or be seen as a 'service provider' and the UK partner, in turn, can struggle to assert themselves because of colonial guilt. Even when there is no overt display of power from a partner, the other can slip into a position of anticipatory obedience (Thews & Herke, 2018) creating an unbalanced and often unproductive relationship. Add to this the inevitable cultural conflicts in working styles, methodology and approaches to timeline management, which are not unique to UK-India collaborations, and the collaborative process may be further hindered.

Cultural Stereotypes and Collective Identities

When building bridges between distinct groups, the acknowledgement of difference is part of the process. To make this classification clear, it is tempting to resort to collective identities and cultural stereotypes through the use of easily recognisable images. Whilst this can be valuable and desired in tourism, it is less well received within arts and cultural sectors where its usage is seen as lazy and lacking in creativity especially within contemporary practices.

In India-UK artistic collaborations, there are several tried-and-tested themes, art forms or companies and artists of national repute which have become the go-to choices for collaborations, often establishing a form of canon, not unlike that to which Gaupp refers to in this volume. There is often an implied cultural hierarchy where British 'classics' by writers such as William Shakespeare and Jane Austen are matched and mixed with the traditional and classical dances and music from India or, for a more contemporary working, Bollywood, which comes with its own stereotypes. Whilst work from the UK is often promoted as 'contemporary and cutting-edge', with the big-hitters like the Edinburgh Festivals, Sadler's Wells and Tate Modern promoted extensively overseas, works referencing Indian culture fall back on the age-old motifs and imagery of an exotic and vibrant 'Incredible India' with its mythological epics, Mahabharata and Ramayana. Whether this is due to laziness, lack of awareness or an aversion to tackling current global issues is hard to know. These issues are further explored below from the perspectives of our own experiences of collaborative international work.

Reflections from Practice

In Ruhi's experience of working as a performing arts manager in India for close to a decade, she found innumerable projects coming her way that wanted to 'reimagine India' but incorporated the most obvious elements like Bollywood and/or Indian classical music and dance in the artistic production instead of looking for more innovative or unexpected components. For example, the Kathakali dancers along with the vibrant gypsies of Rajasthan have become the leading cultural icons of India, replicated by media worldwide.

This has been evident recently in the India-UK Year of Culture in 2017, when the Indian High Commission in London organised the 'India@UK, 2017' cultural festival, which promoted many of these same collective identities about India. While the decision to include some experimental and contemporary work by urban practitioners must be noted, the large-scale galas and celebrations showcased Indian traditional dance including Bharatanatyam and Bollywood musicals (of course!), which are the dominant arts forms that are exported. Indian handicrafts were displayed and evenings celebrating 'sacred music' were organised. Even when contemporary work was presented, its description was linked to an ancient traditional form or cultural attribute. While there is absolutely nothing wrong with presenting India's rich cultural heritage at festivals abroad and it is definitely a point of pride, difficulties arise when these art forms become the dominant representatives of the Indian performance tradition. It is worth noting that this approach is not limited to the performing arts. For instance, the announcement for the visit of INS Tarkash, an Indian warship, to the UK in May 2017 (India@UK, 2017) read,

While INS Tarkash is a state-of-the-art stealth frigate, her crew vividly represents every part of India and her rich cultural diversity. Her name is depicted by her insignia—'Tarkash'—a quiver full of arrows, which was an integral part of the battle armour donned by the valiant traditional Indian warriors, who fought the epic battles of Ramayana and Mahabharata.

The question arises whether we are presenting or cultivating the most judicious and befitting image of a country by resorting to the most obvious age-old narratives about it. For a country actively celebrating the emergence of a 'Digital India', not promoting the contemporary and experimental arts being produced there leads to an incomplete and biased representation of the sector.

Similarly, the British Council announced special grants in 2014 to mark the 450th anniversary of Shakespeare's birth and in 2016 under the 'Shakespeare Lives' project for the 400th anniversary of his death. A survey, commissioned by British Council in 2013 and conducted among 5000 young adults in five countries (India, Brazil, Germany, China and the USA), showed that Shakespeare was the UK's greatest cultural icon of all time (Ipsos MORI, 2014). The year 2013 also marked 100 years of Bollywood in India so it is not surprising that Shakespeare's plays and Bollywood were commonplace in most collaborative projects between India and the UK at that time. Thus, while cultural grants celebrating political ties with another nation or linked to commemorative occasions like the ones mentioned above aim to promote the country through cultural diplomacy initiatives, they may instead reinforce stereotypes regarding the nation's collective identity.

Also, as referred to above, many of these projects were conceived and produced by a UK partner who also raised its funds, with the Indian partner involved only in the final phase. As a result, the ability to change or influence the scope of the collaborative project may have been lost. So, we see that alongside the artistic content, the existing funding mechanisms also facilitate the realisation of certain structural hierarchies in practice, thus affecting the status quo of the partners. This point is further explored through the next case study.

Amy worked for eight years as deputy director of Triangle Network, an international network of artists and arts organisations that focuses on cultural exchange, dialogue and professional development, with partner organisations in over 40 countries around the world. When she started in 2008, the overall funding structure of Triangle was very much in line with the one identified in this chapter, with the majority of support for activities taking place outside of the UK coming from the International Development and Cultural Diplomacy sectors. The more significant amounts of funding were meant for regional sub-networks which included the South Asia Network for the Arts (SANA) with partners in Bangladesh, India, Nepal, Pakistan and Sri Lanka; and a hub at Khoj International Artists' Association (Khoj), an arts organisation in Delhi that houses artist studios and a gallery space (Zitzewitz, 2017). SANA was supported by the US-based Ford Foundation from its Knowledge, Creativity and Freedom programme, which had a specific aim "to increase opportunities for cultural and artistic expression for people of all backgrounds" (2004, p. 104). For the SANA grants, the directors of Triangle, based in the UK, were responsible for the monitoring and managing of the resources through the regional hub overseen by the director of Khoj. By funding "a South Asia network of contemporary visual artists and its programme of residencies, workshops and digital communication" (2004, p. 127) Ford Foundation's funds supported artists in the region to travel, experiment, debate and further their practices, and enabled the network partners to improve their digital presences and reach new audiences.

Although not strictly speaking of a collaboration between UK and India, this case study is relevant here because of the way in which the SANA programme was resourced and the relationship it created between the two countries. At the time, many Triangle Network members were informal groups of artists or collectives without a legal constitution, based in countries with limited cultural infrastructure and funding options, making it difficult to raise significant funds for international activities themselves. It was vital for them to be part of something larger that could take on the responsibility of raising and managing resources, which Triangle was able to do as a charity registered in the UK. The Ford Foundation, alongside other international development agencies, was not looking to support UK-based organisations but understood that in order to reach small, independent, civil-society groups in developing countries, it needed to go through a network such as Triangle that met its strict fiscal and legal requirements. Furthermore, in the case of SANA, whilst the Ford Foundation had an office in Delhi, which made for easy communication with Khoj, India's financial law also made it next to impossible for an Indian organisation to distribute funds overseas, making the existence of an administrative centre in the UK even more crucial.

The ultimate outcome was for SANA to be an interdependent network of organisations and artists in South Asia that would tackle the specific lack of regional exchanges and challenge the assumptions within contemporary art practice around the cultural dominance of Europe and North America and the legacy of power relations between the UK and its former colonies in South Asia. However, in reality, an outwardly paternalistic model of practice was reinforced: American funds were given to a UK organisation for dissemination to a regional hub in India, who in turn would disseminate it further within the region. Although the choice of Khoj as the hub was due to it being the most established partner in the region with a solid infrastructure, this resulting model echoed both the global international relations of the time and former colonial ties.

The detection of paternalism in international development policy and practice is hardly a surprise. However, through this example one can see that paternalistic structures often developed through necessity. We felt this factor was important for us to consider, particularly in relation to how it impacted the artists taking part, the arts managers coordinating the activities and the work produced. Although there were examples that could be viewed as 'anticipatory obedience', with partners looking to the UK for reassurance and advice, one of the key roles of the network hub was to support its members. In truth, for many involved there was little knowledge of, or interest in, the funding structure and for those carrying out the reporting, the transparency of the process and the strong and real shared commitment to the goals of the network and the belief in the value of peer-to-peer exchange, experimentation and mutual understanding meant that any inherent hierarchies were viewed pragmatically, as a means to an end rather than a form of control. Whilst the partners involved assumed their stereotypical cultural identities—with the UK sitting in its office holding the purse strings (even if it did not own the purse!) and India acting as a regional middle-man—the structure benefitted hundreds of artists over ten years.

Conclusion

The past few decades have seen our cultural awareness and realities change more radically than ever before, primarily due to easy international travel and advanced global communications. We now inhabit a world where people of different cultures meet and mix freely and more often, creating dynamic spaces for exchange and enabling the arts to be enriched and truly reflecting the societies in which we live. Nevertheless, the big concern that remains is how one views, engages and negotiates the cultural particularities and differences while working on a collaboration. How we negotiate and navigate through the existing systems to make the most of the opportunities available to challenge these assumptions is a crucial responsibility of arts and cultural managers today.

Cultural differences between international partners will always exist, making it impossible to avoid all ensuing conflicts, both artistically and managerially. It is also illogical to try to create homogenous working practices when a core function of collaboration and exchange is to learn from others and celebrate differences, especially through the work that is produced. Instead, we should aspire for significant intercultural sensitivity and a consciousness of context, both of which have the potential to break down the rigid assumptions surrounding us and will significantly impact our selection of project themes, issues, artistic process and subject matter.

Whilst there are various successful guides on "intercultural business behaviour" (see Moll, 2012; Meyer, 2014), which are based on studies exploring how national or cultural aspects influence a person's approach at work, especially their leadership and management styles, this issue needs deeper acknowledgement and critique within arts and cultural management practice (Henze, 2016). In recent times, there has been increased interest in looking at the nature and structure of international partnerships from practitioners, academics and policy makers. For instance, Hampel (2017) examines partnership-based cooperation in cultural policy and cultural management. Starting with the hypothesis that there are no equal collaborations within cultural diplomacy schemes, she discusses "partnership-based practices" through five case studies of

German-Indian cooperation. Rousselin (2017, p. 6) looks at whether genuine horizontal cooperation can ever be possible and if not, can asymmetric cooperation be legitimate if it yields results "and/or generates emancipatory effects". Mandel (2017) presents research on the views of arts and cultural managers from around the world on the effects of internationalisation on their profession as well as current challenges and required competencies and training programmes. The international network for contemporary performing arts (IETM) has also published a 'Fair cooperation toolkit' in 2017 (Van Graan, 2018, p. 4) in order to provide those working in the field with advice and guidance on how to make international collaborations "more equal, meaningful and enriching". All these works aim to offer an insight into different approaches of working on intercultural collaborations because there is no one right or correct way and no thumb-rule for solving any problem. In a way, then, this entire chapter can essentially be summed up with this quote by the Japanese director Tadashi Suzuki who once stated, "international cultural exchange is impossible—therefore we must try" (Bogart, 2007, p. 16).

Arts and cultural managers inhabit a crucial position between funding structures and policies and artists. Acting as facilitators, they are the bridge or link between the two—creating opportunities and facilitating engagements. However, it is important to remember that they are also mediators and moderators, who need to fight the instrumentalisation of culture for political and economic purposes, and as such play a vital role in ensuring that assumptions and stereotypes are not institutionalised.

We would also like to hope that the funding bodies can increasingly provide cultural managers and producers with more freedom to shape the scope of their projects instead of pushing them to follow a prescribed format in order to fulfil the obligations of the grant. With less restrictions, they can develop projects that embody the qualities of a true collaboration, allowing the partners and audience members to engage with each other more meaningfully. As proposed by Vickery (2017, p. 35), greater flexibility could lead to the arts and cultural agencies being trusted as an "informal economy of international deliberations, advocacy and interventionist approaches to culture" ultimately engaging "in their own international cultural politics of 'diplomacy'".

References

Bogart, A. (2007). *And then, you act: Making art in an unpredictable world.* London: Routledge.

British Council. Retrieved on September 20 2018, from https://www.british-council.org/organisation/press/british-council-announces-global-celebration-shakespeare

Cummings, M. C. (2003). *Cultural diplomacy and the United States Government: A survey.* Washington, DC: Center for Arts and Culture.

Das, S. (2018). India should consider cultural exchanges much more diverse than British. *The Wire*, October 15. Retrieved February 7, 2019, from https://thewire.in/the-arts/catherine-david-interview-art

DCMS. (2018). *Annual report and accounts for the year ended 31 march 2018.* London: DCMS.

Doeser, J., & Nisbett, M. (2017). *The art of soft power: A study of cultural diplomacy at the United Nations Office in Geneva.* London: King's College London.

Ford Foundation. (2004). *Annual report 2004.* [Online]. New York: Ford Foundation. Retrieved September 19, 2018, from https://www.fordfound.org/media/1531/ar2004.pdf

Hampel, A. (2017). *Fair cooperation: A new paradigm for cultural diplomacy and arts management* (ENCATC Book Series: Cultural Management and Cultural Policy Exchange, Vol. 3). Brussels, Berlin, Frankfurt, New York and Oxford: P.I.E. Peter Lang.

Henze, R. (2016). How globalization affects cultural management. *Arts Management Quarterly: Quarterly Journal for the global Perspective in Arts and Business, 124,* 19–24.

India@UK. (2017). Retrieved January 7, 2019, from http://indiaatuk2017.com

International Development. (2011). In T. Diez, I. Bode, & A. Fernandes (Eds.), *SAGE key concepts series: Key concepts in international relations.* [Online]. London: Sage. Retrieved January 2, 2019, from https://search-credoreference-com.gold.idm.oclc.org/content/entry/sageukkcinre/international_development/0?institutionId=1872

Ipsos MORI. (2014). *As others see us: Culture, attraction and soft power.* London: British Council. Retrieved from https://www.britishcouncil.org/sites/default/files/as-others-see-us-report-v3.pdf

Mandel, B. (2017). *Arts/cultural management in international contexts.* Hildesheim University/Georg Olms Verlag.

Meyer, E. (2014). *The culture map: Breaking through the invisible boundaries of global business.* PublicAffairs.

Mission Statement: Ministry of Culture India. (2018). Retrieved September 20, 2018, from https://indiaculture.nic.in/

Moll, M. (2012). *The quintessence of intercultural business communication.* Berlin, Heidelberg: Springer Berlin Heidelberg.

Nye, J. S. (1990). *Bound to lead: The changing nature of American power.* New York: Basic Books.

Reimagine India: Arts Council England. (2018). Retrieved September 21, 2018, from https://www.artscouncil.org.uk/funding/reimagine-india

Rousselin, M. (2017). *Can asymmetrical cooperation be legitimised? Habermas, Foucault and Spivak on German-Tunisian Cooperation in higher education* (ifa Edition Culture and Foreign Policy). Stuttgart: ifa.

Stupples, P. (2015). Accounting for art in international development: Insights from artists' initiatives in Central America. In L. MacDowall, M. Badham, E. Blomkamp, & K. Dunphy (Eds.), *Making culture count. New directions in cultural policy research.* London: Palgrave Macmillan.

Thews, A., & Herke, S. (2018). Paternalism in international collaboration: Food for thought for a code of ethics. *Arts Management Quarterly, 129,* 35–38.

Thomas, M. (2018). British museums are full of Indian history. Now, they're finally getting Indian-origin curators. *Quartz,* November 30. [Online]. Retrieved February 5, 2019, from https://qz.com/india/1477396/british-museums-sushma-jansari-on-indians-in-the-arts/

Van Graan, M. (2018). *Beyond curiosity and desire: Towards fairer international collaboration in the arts.* Brussels: IETM, On the Move, DutchCulture.

Vickery, J. (2017). Since internationalism: Diplomacy, ideology, and a political agency for culture. In M. Dragićević-Šešić, L. Rogač Mijatović, & N. Mihaljinac (Eds.), *Cultural diplomacy: Arts, festivals and geopolitics.* Creative Europe Desk Serbia.

Zitzewitz, K. (2017). Infrastructure as form. *Third Text, 31*(2–3), 341–358.

Part III

Education

8

A Call for Reflexivity: Implications of the Internationalisation Agenda for Arts Management Programmes Within Higher Education

Victoria Durrer

The widespread popularity of concepts like 'creativity', evidenced, for instance, in the global cultural policy transfers associated with Richard Florida's creative class (Florida, 2002), have "contributed greatly to the idolisation of the globally mobile, cultural worker" (Luckman, 2013, p. 77). While not wholly new within the history of art (Brockington, 2009), those involved in cultural production are moving across global regions with a new intensity, producing work that mixes forms from different cultures and styles (Isar, 2012; Mosquera, 2010). These factors, coupled with the increasing international interest in the social and economic potential of the arts and cultural industries, have prompted the growth of arts and cultural management programmes in higher education institutes (HEIs) across the globe.

Arts and cultural management education at undergraduate and postgraduate level, aimed at educating individuals to direct, administer and mediate the making and experiencing of creative and aesthetic expres-

V. Durrer (✉)
Queen's University Belfast, Belfast, UK
e-mail: v.durrer@qub.ac.uk

© The Author(s) 2020
V. Durrer, R. Henze (eds.), *Managing Culture*, Sociology of the Arts,
https://doi.org/10.1007/978-3-030-24646-4_8

sions and objects in the fine, visual and performing arts, and with particular (though not sole) attention on the not-for-profit, has become increasingly "booming business" (O'Brien, 2017, p. 525). Recent years have seen the international growth of programmes within the broader context of the internationalisation of higher education (HE) generally (Altbach, 2004). Internationalisation involves government, academic and/or institutional policies, programmes and activities undertaken to manage and take advantage of globalisation (Altbach, 2004, p. 6). In education, it may take place in higher education institutes or other institutions with an educational or training remit or focus.

In attempting to establish themselves as 'world class' and, thus, internationally minded institutions, higher education institutes internationalise in a number of ways. In terms of research, universities and research funding councils encourage work that has international focus or transferability (Altbach, 2004). This chapter focuses on the educational role of higher education, where the process more broadly includes student mobility or international students studying outside their home country, and transnational educational initiatives, such as twin campuses or joint programmes.

Where practice and professional status once dominated the professional development and standing of practitioners, educational programmes have emerged as a significant site where privilege, routines, codes of practice and hierarchies are established, broken and/or maintained (DiMaggio, 1987; Suteu, 2006; Tatli & Özbilgin, 2012). These processes are both institutional and social, taking place through the teaching and learning practices facilitated by the institutional context of higher education, the design of programme curriculum and the delivery of teaching by individual educators. Additionally, how students receive and engage in those processes are significant factors for socialisation into the profession. As a result, the global growth of programmes and the mobility of students within programmes make education an increasingly important yet under-researched and under-interrogated realm where arts and cultural managers are socialised into the assumptions, traditions and norms of the profession on an international scale.

The growing global reach of these socialisation processes raises questions as to how internationalised arts and cultural management education may facilitate connections between different peoples, nations and cultures, but equally serve as a mechanism for facilitating global cultural inequalities and hegemony (Henze, 2017; Jacobsen, 2015; Shome, 2009). As producers of cultural forms, arts and cultural managers working in the fine, visual and performing arts engage with creative and aesthetic expressions—arts and cultural objects, exhibitions and performances—which are inherently reflective of broader social as well as personal cultural ideas, stereotypes, knowledge and values. Work by Saha (2013) argues for deeper critical engagement with the role of higher education, including attention to teaching and learning practice, as a key site

> where…structural challenges within the [cultural industries] relating to [the politics of representation] and issues of access and equality can…be highlighted as well as… partially resolved. (p. 11)

Yet, there is very little critical examination of programme development, curriculum design and teaching and learning practices, which have emerged alongside, or even as a result of internationalisation (see Nisbett, this volume).

This chapter begins with an exploration of the rationale for and the processes of the emergence of higher education in arts and cultural management internationally. The term 'arts management' will be used for brevity, but it refers to both arts and cultural management as well as arts and/or cultural administration. While their focus may differ within different national and local contexts, they are all broadly focused on the activity described above. Particular attention is given to the internationalisation of programmes and their role in the international politics of representation, in which arts management practice is implicated. Illustrations from educational practice are given through brief attention to the diversity of arts management classrooms in higher education and issues around the internationalisation of programme content. Drawing from a literature review of work from higher education, arts and cultural management, cultural policy, sociology and postcolonial studies, the chapter raises ethical concerns for arts management educators working within this increasingly internationalised context. It concludes by suggesting ways to facilitate greater reflexivity in teaching and learning practice as well as to enhance greater study of the processes and implications of the internationalisation of arts and cultural management education.

Arts and Cultural Management Education: A Global Landscape

There is a growing body of reports and research that detail the international growth of arts and cultural management education (Evrard & Colbert, 2000; Laughlin, 2017; Suteu, 2006). This development has taken place particularly in North America, Europe and Anglophone countries, and South East and East Asia with some, but lesser, growth within countries in Middle East and African Nations (MENA), Latin and South America as well as parts of Central and Eastern Europe (Boylan, 2000; Suteu, 2006; Paquette & Redaelli, 2015; Dragićević-Šešić, 2015; Mandel & Allmanritter, 2016; Costa, 2017; Edelman & Coy, 2017; Durrer, 2018a; O'Connor, Gu, & Vickery 2019; Hernández-Acosta, 2013). As a result, "higher education arts and cultural management programmes have…become mainstream" (Figueira & Fullman, 2016, p. 154).

New programmes in arts and cultural management education, particularly at postgraduate taught level have emerged with greater frequency in Europe since the 1980s and 1990s and parts of Asia since the millennium. Boylan (2000) has detailed the emergence of arts and cultural management training centres and undergraduate and postgraduate level university-based programmes across the globe. While countries in Middle East and African Nations and parts of Central and Eastern Europe have seen less growth (Mandel & Allmanritter, 2016), Dragićević-Šešić's (2003) survey for UNESCO has captured offering across Europe, the Russian Federation, the Caucasus and Central Asia. Eastern Europe, in particular, saw the first MA programme in Serbia (Belgarde Art Academy) in the 1980s, followed by Poland, Hungary, Bulgaria, Latvia and Lithuania after the fall of Communism (Suteu, 2006, p. 83). While looking at the creative and cultural industries more broadly, work referenced in a special issue by O'Connor et al. (2019) expands on this literature, exploring the implications of this growth on creative and cultural practices.

There is a somewhat shared rationale for this educational growth across the globe. In the United States, Laughlin (2017) provides details on the emergence of university programmes in the 1960s and the growing recognition of a need for university training among those in the profession, as well as those funding the sector more broadly. Similar routes were taken elsewhere. Within Europe, the development of arts and cultural management as a discipline of higher education study is a result of what Suteu (2006, p. 30) refers to as a "boom…in the cultural apparatus" of Western Europe in a post-World War II response to the role of culture as a "crucial condition for insuring stability in a newly peaceful Europe". The outgrowth of the Arts Council movement from the UK at this time to other Commonwealth countries (Canada, New Zealand, Australia) as well as in the Republic of Ireland and the United States had an important influence on the establishment of the practice and its subsequent teaching in those areas (Chong, 2002; Upchurch, 2016).

According to Dragićević-Šešić (2015), the fall of the Berlin wall saw recognition of the social, political and cultural importance of arts managers in parts of Western and Eastern Europe at local, national and international levels. Additional catalysts included changes in leisure time and the means for cultural consumption as well as a call for the democratisation of culture in places like France and a broader "drive towards alternative cultural movements" emerging in the 1960s (Suteu, 2006, p. 30). Further growth of urbanisation and an increase in middle classes across the globe has seen art become more of a commodity, no longer dependent upon wealthy patronage, equally impacting the relationship of cultural institutions to the public (Singh, 2018) and no doubt the development of training in that field. The increasing importance of the concepts of managerialism and New Public Management and the drive for efficiency and effectiveness they have promoted in public services have also impacted the development of educational programmes in the United States and the UK (DiMaggio, 1987; Paquette & Redaelli, 2015), practices which have spread globally through the internationalisation of higher education.

State bureaucrats and policymakers have been involved in the development of many arts management and cultural policy training programmes within nations. Suteu (2006), Dragićević-Šešić (2015) and Dragićević-Šešić and Mihaljinac (this volume) recognise the significant roles that UNESCO and the Council of Europe have both played in the development of arts, cultural policy and arts and cultural management training worldwide. As noted in an earlier study (Durrer, 2018a, p. 68),

> the UNESCO Chairs Programme has led to the evolution of a number of higher education programmes in places such as Serbia, Lithuania and Spain. Work by the Council of Europe helped initiate the establishment of the European Network of Cultural Administration Training Centres in 1992 as well as a number of networks for professional development and training. (Suteu, 1999, 2006)

In the US, The National Endowment for the Arts joined others in calling for the development of "formal arts administration courses" in the 1960s (National Endowment for the Arts, 1965, p. 25; Laughlin, 2017). This relationship to funding bodies is also seen in England where Arts Council England established a partnership with City University in London in the late 1960s/early 1970s to launch what is widely recognised as the first higher educational programme in arts administration there (Sternal, 2007; See also Durrer, 2018a, p. 82, n2).

In addition to the emergence of arts and cultural management programmes within specific nations, information gathered from the Arts and Humanities Research Council funded network, *Brokering Intercultural Exchange*, demonstrates that over the course of its development, arts and cultural management education has undergone a kind of internationalisation (Durrer, 2018b). Within arts and cultural management specifically, this internationalisation has taken place in different ways. Suteu (2006, pp. 85–87, 103–130) identifies two main types of education: those that exist in higher education institutes and those within the profession itself. Viewed as professional development, examples include short-term training programmes like Clore Leadership in the UK and Ireland as well as initiatives led by diplomatic cultural institutes.

Though not within the scope of this chapter, it is important to recognise the role of these professional development programmes within international diplomatic cultural institutes such as Goethe or the British Council (explored in greater detail in this volume by Dragićević-Šešić & Mihaljinac). Still, these programmes also extend to higher education. The Goethe Institut, for instance, has recently developed a partnership with Leuphana to establish an international, online distance learning *Arts and Cultural Management Masters* in the English language (Leuphana University, 2018). Internationalisation has also occurred within higher education through the validation of programmes by longer standing ones, such as the relationship between Goldsmiths, University of London and LaSalle College of Arts' undergraduate programmes (LaSalle College of Arts, 2012), and recruitment of international students onto arts management programmes.

While there is less known about the mobility of students in arts management specifically, there has been increased global mobility of students in the arts within higher education more generally (Booth, Ophuysen, & Koleva, 2004) and some change within arts management education specifically. European art schools have experienced an increase in the amount of students from Southeast Asia and the United States (Booth et al., 2004). The impact of Brexit withstanding, data collected from the UK Higher Education Statistics Agency (HESA) shows that within UK arts management programmes specifically, there is a growing nonUK contingent in total on the courses from 40% in the academic year 2005/2006 to near 60% in 2009/2010 to near 60% in 2015/2016 (HESA, 2017).[1] Mobility may be short term, through study abroad programmes or longer term for the duration of an entire course of degree study and it may be based on institutional partnerships which see institutes of higher education making agreements for the mobility of students or based on individual student choice (Booth et al., 2004).

Forms of internationalisation are also seen in the increase in programmes focused on international exchange activities in arts and cultural management. For instance, Fisher and Karpodini-Dimitriadi (2007) have considered courses in transnational cultural cooperation projects. The *Cultural Diplomacy Programme*, initiated by the Service for Foreign Policy Instruments of the European Commission in 2016 to "carry out activities enhancing the EU's cultural engagement with third countries and their citizens" (Cultural Diplomacy Platform, 2018), holds a Global Leadership Programme aimed at capacity building and collaborative peer-to-peer learning and network building between managers from EU member states and those in Brazil, Canada, China, Japan, India, Mexico, Russia, South Africa, South Korea and the United States (see Jhunjhunwala & Walker, this volume). The Master of Management in International Arts Management is delivered through a partnership of four universities (HEC Montréal, Canada; Southern Methodist University, USA; SDA Bocconi School of Management, Italy; and The Universidad de los Andes, Columbia). The programme is specifically focused at those who are either currently engaging or wishing to engage in arts management practices in heritage, performing arts or cultural industries (film, publishing, sound recording, radio and television) that take place within international contexts (MMIAM, 2018).

Arts management networks are also playing a role in this internationalisation through the exchange of approaches to curriculum design and teaching and learning practices, both within and across global regions. Acknowledged as "significant pillars" of education, the *Association of Arts Administration Educators* (AAAE) initiated in 1979 in the United States and focused largely on North America (see Laughlin, 2017); The *European League of Institutes of the Arts* (ELIA); and the *European Network on Cultural Management and Policy* (ENCATC) emerged in the latter part of the twentieth century (Brkić & Bereson, 2016, p. 1). Since 2011, a number of new networks in both education and policy have emerged in Asia impacting arts and cultural management study across the region: The *Asia Pacific Network for Cultural Education Research* (ANCER), initiated in Singapore in 2011; The *Asian League of Institutes of the Arts* (ALIA) in South Korea in 2012; *Strategic Management in the Arts for Theatre* (SMART) in India in 2015; the *Taiwan Association of Cultural Policy Studies* (TAPCS) in 2015; and the *Greater Mekong Subregion Hub for Cultural Change Makers* in Cambodia in 2016 (Brkić & Bereson, 2016).

These international networks themselves are further internationalising. Beginning in the 1990s, AAAE and ENCATC have not only embraced members from beyond their geographic region (Edelman & Coy, 2017) but also recently established partnerships with ANCER and TAPCS in

2016–2017 (Brkić & Bereson, 2016). In 2017, the partnership between AAAE, ENCATC and TAPCS realised the launch of a *Brussels Manifesto* for arts management, cultural management and cultural policy education. The document details their shared values and a desire to facilitate greater exchange, "collaboration and sharing of resources (including pedagogies for teaching and research) between and beyond [their] networks" (AAAE, ENCATC, & TAPCS, 2017, p. 1). The document further recognises the importance of maintaining a "critical balance [between] local needs with global challenges" in education and practice (AAAE et al., 2017, p. 1). This balance includes championing

> international competencies, [which involve appreciation of]… context specificities and…respect [for] the diversities of [one another's] respective cultures. (AAAE et al., 2017, p. 1)

The benefits of internationalisation to pedagogical and teaching approaches within institutions and amongst educators in the arts are purported to encourage

> cultural and social enrichment, inspir[e] an open climate in the academy, and [support] diversity in teaching methods, multiculturalism, enhancement of cultural awareness and enhancement of [institutional] reputation. (Booth et al., 2004, p. 28)

Yet, while such developments may highlight a more "global embrace and approach", they may equally forewarn new mechanisms of global cultural hegemony (Brkić & Bereson, 2016, p. 1).

The international expansion of arts and cultural management training and education places HEIs and educators within a "global environment of the arts" (Booth et al., 2004, p. 19). However, like the development of public cultural policies and the founding of many (particularly publicly funded or state initiated) cultural institutions, this internationalisation is a "product of historical forces" inscribed with the dynamics of geopolitical and economic power undetachable from notions of colonial expansion (Hesmondalgh & Saha, 2013, p. 186; Bennett, 1995; Durrer, Henze, & Roß, 2016). The knowledge regarding arts management practice is largely dominated by values and traditions from geopolitically and economically dominant countries in the Global North and West (Milena Dragićević-Šešić & Nina Mihaljinac, this volume). As a result, the internationalisation of arts management education implies a 'cultural hierarchisation' (Bhaba, 2012) and has strong implications in the politics of representation at a global scale. This politics is explored in further detail below.

Arts and Cultural Management Education Content

The proposition of teaching arts and cultural management becomes somewhat daunting when first considering the scope of what one is actually teaching about: the 'management' of cultural forms. Determining what it means to 'manage' cultural forms is debated, but there is general agreement that it involves a marriage of applied management skills, critical understanding of wider social, political and economic contexts, and some knowledge of, or interest in, the arts. The rise of the 'managerial imperatives' of Anglo-American models and changing requirements for efficiency and effectiveness in public sector accountability for state funding of arts and culture therein, has had a direct impact on the training and development of arts managers in the United States, the UK and its commonwealth countries, and continental Europe. A number of programmes, particularly in North America, have aligned with business or management schools within higher education (Chong, 2002, 3; Suteu, 2006). In fact, Marginson (2010a, p. 139) explains the spread of managerialism has been an important "vehicle for the partial fashioning of the knowledge economy along Anglo-American lines".

Practices in Great Britain and the United States have, thus, been highly influential in curriculum development across the globe (Henze, 2017; Mandel & Allmanritter, 2016; Suteu, 2006). While over ten years old, Suteu's (2006, pp. 86–87, 103–130) classification of dominant approaches to curriculum design and their associated 'basic composition' in European curriculum is an incredibly useful introduction into thinking about arts and cultural management curriculum. Programmes in the United States and Europe typically emphasise what are often seen as 'transferrable' and applied skills in funding, managing and disseminating arts and cultural products (Durrer, 2018a). Such courses provide a broad overview of skills, issues and theoretical underpinnings of arts and cultural management.

Competencies required are argued to be a balance between managerial and sector or artform specific concerns as well as what Suteu (2006) refers to as the capacity to read context and meaning:

> mastering needs at local level, having strategic vision, [the] ability to network and relate to other socio-economic domains and seize global dynamics. (p. 126; see also Brkić, 2009)

Additionally, being able to work in both international and inter- as well as multi-cultural contexts, being entrepreneurial and innovative, and possessing the capacity to read, respond to and critique cultural policy are also important skills (Dewey & Rich, 2003; Dewey & Wyszomirski, 2004; Suteu, 2006; Varbanova, 2012). The internationalisation of HE programmes and thus the growing international cultural diversity of the classroom would seem to present an opportunity here (Booth et al., 2004; Luckman, 2013), yet one not without its challenges (Nisbett, this volume). These points will be further explored below.

Many programmes, particularly across Europe, include the presence of practitioners in educational programming, through work placement or work-based learning and guest talks from industry professionals (Blumenreich, 2012). Arts and cultural management practitioners are significant contributors to higher education programmes and curriculum development, especially within the UK (Carty, this volume). Within cultural work more generally, they are argued to be particularly suited to introducing and socialising students for the conditions and realities of cultural work (Ashton, 2013). This relationship between education and practice is particularly pertinent because much of the arts and cultural sector places a high value on on-the-job learning, professional networks and individual personalities as key factors for achieving employment (Suteu, 2006; Varbanova, 2012; Ashton, 2013). HE programmes may capitalise on this point by promoting themselves as sources of networking as well as learning. Tacit, local knowledge can become an issue amongst students in highly internationalised programmes (Chan, 2011), creating an imbalance between students who have familiarity with the arts and cultural sector local to the university and those international students who do not.

University internationalisation strategies as well as the irregular nature of the job market, the socio-political frameworks and creative/artistic developments within specific arts and cultural sectors mean that HE training in arts and cultural management tends to be generalist. Generalist approaches are argued to allow graduates greater flexibility in responding to the job market as well as territorial and cultural contexts in ways that specialising may prevent (Varbanova, 2012; Suteu, 2006, p. 51). While specificity often comes through work-based learning, generalisation in programme design is critiqued as being haphazard in development, lacking long-term vision for arts and cultural management education (Ebewo & Sirayi, 2009; Figueira & Fullman, 2016). This lack of directed specificity, grounded in the awareness and sensitivity to the varying considerations involved in inter- and/or transcultural exchange between the cultural logics of different sites (for instance, region, nation, county and/or neighbourhood) or diverse peoples (for instance, diverse nationalities, races, ethnicities and/or religions), inevitably impacts how individuals are socialised into the profession and what knowledge, language, values and traditions that may come to be challenged or perpetuated in the management of art and culture, as a result.

The Politics of Teaching the Management of Art and Culture

While an emphasis on applied skills in arts and cultural management implies that culture is an "objective phenomenon" (Yeganeh & Zhan, 2006, p. 362), the practice of management is actually one that involves the creation, representation and dissemination of cultural meanings (Hall, 1997c, p. 25).

According to Stuart Hall (1997a),

cultural meanings…organise and regulate social practices, influence our conduct and consequently have real, practical effects…it is participants in a culture who give meaning to people, objectives and events…it is by our use of things and what we say, think and feel about them—how we represent them—that we give them a meaning. (p. 3)

In its practice of directing, administering and mediating arts and cultural expressions, arts management is "a thoroughly cultural process" (Hesmondalgh & Saha, 2013, p. 188), which "intersects with issues of culture and identity" (Luckman, 2013, p. 70). Arts management practice itself is "primarily symbolic, expressive, and informative …[placing] emphasis on communicating ideas, knowledge, values, beliefs" (Hesmondalgh & Saha, 2013, p. 187). The applied aspects of practice that are seen to be a crucial part of management curriculum, such as devising missions and visions, strategic planning, marketing, practical management and human resources, become a "regime of representation" (Hall, 1997b, p. 259). These practices facilitate a representational context from, or in which, individuals (professional colleagues, consumers, public or audience) further receive or interpret cultural meanings.

Furthermore, the naming of arts exhibitions, the advertising created for theatre productions and audience development initiatives (for instance) all attribute value and meaning. They exercise symbolic power, engaging one's "feelings, attitudes and emotions…at deeper levels than we can explain in a simple, common-sense way" (Hall, 1997b, p. 226). In light of the now international association of arts and culture with urban regeneration, economic development and tourism as well as social cohesion, civic engagement, educational attainment, peace and reconciliation, and the protection of cultural diversity and expression and promotion of sustainable development (Durrer, 2018a), this 'regime' has widespread implications for how we, as a society, approach, relate to and understand ourselves and others.

While global exchange is becoming far more complex and can no longer be reduced to a notion of the centre and periphery or the "West and the rest", (Featherstone, 1995; Singh, 2018), the internationalisation of arts management education sees the flow of knowledge, values, assumptions and traditions as still typically based in Global North and West experiences, serving as a means of soft power (see Dragićević-Šešić & Mihaljinac as well as Jhunjhunwala & Walker, this volume). Higher education typically represents the dominant cultural and educational values of a country (Figueira & Fullman, 2016, p. 157). Further, formal education is a means by which 'power specialists' are determined. Featherstone (1995, p. 3) refers to these individuals as those who "produce and mobilise culture" and who are actors who determine what "particular cultural forms gain…in autonomy and prestige."

Altbach (2004, p. 12) argues that students studying abroad become socialised by the representative systems they experience, returning home after the completion of their studies as

> carriers of an international academic culture…that reflects the norms and values of…major metropolitan universities. (p. 12)

As a result, geopolitically dominant representations of culture and associated forms of arts and cultural management practice can become normalised irrespective of their appropriateness or transferability to different socio-cultural and political contexts (Suteu, 2006). Citing Henze (2017), Dragićević-Šešić and Mihaljinac (this volume) explain that, particularly

> in postcolonial contexts, such exchanges [in education have typically been conducted] in culturally unaware or insensitive ways, with 'patronising' educational programmes in arts and cultural management that often lack consideration for the circumstances, experiences and expertise of local practices.

The discourse regarding the 'management' of art and culture in higher education may, thus, be informed by the specificities of societies with imperialist histories and cultural practices.

The approaches of internationalisation within arts and cultural management education outlined above are both mechanisms for the commodification and capitalisation of education (O'Connor et al., 2019) as well as means for the greater diversity of what Freire (1970) referred to as 'cultural voice': "the ability of…people to name [or represent] their world" (Singh, 2018, p. 95). Freire maintained that education was not neutral. Rather, it is either for "domestication or for freedom…conditioning or deconditioning" (Veiga, 1977, p. 9). Power exists not just in "economic exploitation…but also in exercise of symbolic power through representational practices" (Hall, 1997c, p. 259), such as work in arts and cultural management. So, the marketisation and standardisation of management practice that is taking place through its internationalisation in higher education may present opportunities for global habituation or cultural hegemony of geopolitically dominant practices on the part of those engaging in education. However, it also presents opportunities for meaningful and mutual exchange of ideas, the development of trans- or international relationships and greater empathy and understanding among ethnicities, cultures and nations (Marginson & Sawir, 2011).

Similarly, Figueira and Fullman (2016, p. 157) describe HE's normative and potentially culturally imperialist role in society, yet equally acknowledge that HE has an intercultural role—neither of which is fully understood and certainly not within the context of arts and cultural management education. This neglect not only concerns our understanding of how curriculum design and teaching practice impacts students. It is also about how the very presence of internationally diverse groups of students, the varying pedagogical histories and cultures they, and educators, bring to the classroom and how they receive teaching, as well as experience learning, may conversely impact on curriculum design and teaching practice (Warren, 2011). The implications, challenges and opportunities this internationalisation presents will be explored in further detail below, through the areas of classroom diversity and programme content.

Diversity in the Classroom

Internationalisation in arts management education results in greater international cultural diversity of students and educators into the classroom, which brings with it an array of different pedagogical cultures, languages and frames for understanding culture. We learn from practice-based research that practitioners who engage in international exchange experience dialogue and exposure to 'otherness' in ways that promote awareness of "alternative cultural values" (Rösler, 2015, p. 471). Such awareness is further claimed by practitioners to 'profoundly shape' their training and practice, leading to what is perceived as positive cultural change within artistic, institutional and political spheres (Rowntree, Neal, & Fenton, 2010, p. 2). The significance of this awareness to practice is not only reserved for exchanges between nations but also within, as practitioners and publics of different cultural, national and ethnic backgrounds come together (Henze, 2017, p. 16).

As a result, competing in a sector that is now not only constituted by a global labour market, bolstered by internationalised education, but also one that is deeply socio-economically and politically intertwined means that creative and cultural industry "students in highly diverse classrooms should be at a tremendous advantage", according to Luckman (2013, p. 77). Drawing particular attention to students in "countries who receive far more students than they send overseas (such as the US, Australia, New Zealand and the UK)", Luckman's (2013, p. 77) point raises questions as to 'who' might be at the advantage she perceives. For individuals, particularly those "raised in post-colonial contexts", there is great familiarity with often unavoidable and "different routes of the 'international'" (Shome, 2009, pp. 701–702; see also Joseph, 2008). So, one is left to wonder if these opportunities are not meant to further advantage students from geopolitically powerful nations.

In fact, there is much evidence that students who are viewed as 'international' or 'other' to the institution or discipline in question are disadvantaged. As such, students in internationalised classrooms are, perhaps even unintentionally, considered in binary ways as "us/other or local/international" (Joseph, 2008, p. 32; Marginson, 2010b). Due to how their pedagogical cultural perspectives often differ from a host university, international students are typically positioned as being at a learning deficit (Lumby & Foskett, 2016). Nisbett's empirical study (this volume) sheds light on Luckman's research, which shows that the opportunity for cross-cultural skills development "offered by…multi-national classrooms is not yet being fully realised in cultural-work related degrees in English speaking nations" (Luckman, 2013, pp. 77–78). Their work as well as others within HE studies in Anglophone countries demonstrate that often-minimal interaction takes place between international and local students either within or outside the classroom (Marginson & Sawir, 2011; Trice, 2003). There is growing acknowledgement of our lack of understanding of how this interaction may or may not be taking place within arts management programmes specifically, nor regarding the roles of educators in the process (Cuyler, 2017; Nisbett, this volume). This point here is not about further operationalising international students but more about highly regarding the potential for learning that mixed classrooms bring. This diversity could help us to more critically consider the realities of how globalisation and cultural, ethnic and national diversity impact the values and everyday practices of arts managers, and collectively so.

A further point of note is that international cultural diversity is not the only diversity present in arts management education. Postgraduate students arrive to study from a range of life stages, experiences and needs. Some are returning to academia for professional development after years of working in the field and others are progressing directly from undergraduate study with little to no professional experience. Many have come from a variety of disciplinary backgrounds: for example, arts and humanities, management, social sciences and law. This professional diversity is equally present amongst educators, with some academics having previously worked as practitioners and some practising professionals involved in programme development and delivery (Ashton, 2013; Carty, this volume). Taken together, this range of experiences means that there are a variety of values underpinning what is meant by 'managing culture' and what constitutes 'valid' knowledge in addition to teaching and learning traditions. This variety brings richness as well as challenges to the teaching and learning experience. Yet, despite the daily negotiation it involves in curriculum development and in teaching and learning practice, it is seldom explored or interrogated (Chan, 2011; Nisbett, this volume).

Internationalising Programme Content

The difficulties presented above relate to how we understand and undertake a process of 'internationalising' our programmes and curricula. Now a critical area of study in higher education (Kehm & Teichler, 2007), it has received really no attention in arts and cultural management education. As Joseph (2008, p. 31) points out more broadly and Shome (2009) and Nisbett (this volume) indicate in relation to studies in the cultural field, strategies to address the greater international classroom diversity and to upset the Global North Western dominance of theoretical positionings for culture typically involve minor accommodations in "curriculum, pedagogical and assessment practices". These accommodations often include 'added-on' international case studies and readings (Joseph, 2008, p. 31; Lumby & Foskett, 2016). Yet, how much these additions are respectful and mindful of the specific, local and cultural logics in which they are situated remains to be understood. Deeper interrogation of "cultural differences and knowledge hierarchies" at play not only within education but also within specific disciplines is lacking (Joseph, 2008, 31; Lumby & Foskett, 2016).

Furthermore, Shome (2009, pp. 694, 696) points out that even with the best of intentions amongst scholars who recognise the need for expanding our disciplinary understanding towards more "diverse global, and especially non-western, contexts", there is still a "parochial", reliance, particularly in cultural studies, on usual suspects (see also Abbas & Erni, 2005; Shohat & Stam, 2005). A canon, as it were, that consists of Raymond Williams and Pierre Bourdieu among others. As a result, the very positioning of a discipline of study, like arts and cultural management, remains arrested in a particular viewpoint, value system and way of thinking. It is admittedly difficult to challenge this positioning, particularly from the viewpoint of educators trained by, and now working within and from, this frame of reference. It is further questionable as to how doing anything more than superficially addressing reading lists might actually be possible, as we are all limited by our own frames of reference to some extent (Haigh, 2009).

Ethical Concerns

One way to begin addressing these challenges is to more directly and openly embrace the classroom environment in higher education as a place of learning for educators, as well as students. Educational practices are the 'everyday ways' in which a dominant ideology of a discipline is cemented or challenged, not only for students but educators as well (Murji, 2018). Its inter-, multi- and trans-disciplinary nature means that arts management education is already adept at interacting with and between different knowledge and value systems (Paquette & Redaelli, 2015). Internationalisation in higher education now presents all of us an opportunity to explore that strength anew.

Saha (2013) calls attention to the role of education in facilitating greater, critical pedagogical engagement with how the systems and the agency of practitioners in cultural work reinforce or challenge cultural stereotypes and hegemony in cultural work. The work by Ashton and Noonan (2013) in which Saha's argument is presented gives attention to teaching and learning practice as a key site for this interrogation. However, while the studies presented within that edited collection are important for furthering awareness of the relationship of education to practice, they tend to emphasise what education can do *for* practice, rather than putting the critical lens on education as a practice itself.

Curriculum design and teaching and learning practices are underpinned by cultural, social, political, economic, site-specific and historical circumstances as well as the personal dispositions of educators, all of which coalesce towards socialising students to "certain routinised ways, of understanding [and] knowing how" to be arts managers and 'do' arts management (Reckwitz, 2002, p. 250). Greater examination of these developments in educational practice will assist us in understanding education as a site of social, cultural and political representation and meaning-making, thus enhancing our ability to not only understand the role of educators and teachers in that process, but teaching and learning practice as well.

Within their examination of the internationalisation of higher education in the cultural and creative industries more broadly, O'Connor et al. (2019) indicate that educators need to see their work as "ethical-political…but also pedagogical and personal". In her critique of curriculum internationalisation, Joseph (2008) argues that the

> core tenet of international education and internationalising the curriculum…[is]…willingness to destabilise our own understandings of ways of

being and knowing and to interrogate the power dimensions and notion of difference in the contexts we work and live in. (p. 34)

and it is argued here, that we, as educators, help create. In relation to HE, Bliming (1998, in Holzweiss & Walker, 2016, p. 429) explains that ethical decision making "is a series of compromises between personal values, institutional values, and situational needs". How ethics is acted out often relies on intuition, rather than professional training (Holzweiss & Walker, 2016).

In arguing for reflexive approaches in the practice and teaching of public administration management, Cunliffe and Jun (2005) point a way forward to a more ethical educational practice that embraces the personal. They explain,

Reflexivity…goes beyond calculative problem solving toward exploring tensions and recognising the ephemeral nature of our identities and our social experience. It also draws on social constructionist assumptions to question and explore how we contribute to the construction of social and organisational realities, how we relate with others, and how we construct our ways of being in the world. By doing so, we can become more creative, responsive, and open to different ways of thinking and acting. (p. 228)

Being self- and critically reflexive about arts and cultural management education in relation to the politics of representation involves considering the interplay of "epistemological and ontological frameworks [with] knowledge construction, curriculum and pedagogy" and the origins or histories of each (Joseph, 2008, p. 38). As indicated by Hall (1997a, 1997b, 1997c), Singh (2018), Isar (2012) and Featherstone (1995), these histories are personal, social, and geopolitically and economically informed.

Reflexivity puts an interrogation of one's underlying personal assumptions about teaching and learning as well as arts and culture at the heart of interrogating the politics of arts and cultural management education. It is not just about 'reflecting' on one's teaching practice. It is also about positioning oneself and one's practice as active in the shaping of the wider institutional, political, social, cultural, economic, global/local frames, in which pedagogy, curriculum and teaching and learning activities are situated (Giroux, 2001 in Joseph, 2008, p. 33).

Taking a Critical and Self-Reflexive Approach to Teaching

There are a number of ways in which educators may engage in such reflexion within arts and cultural management. As demonstrated by Warren (2011), autoethnographic, critical ethnographic and performance approaches to understanding teaching and learning are useful. They illuminate teaching practice itself as a "vital site for investigation" (p. 140). Warren (2011) points out the importance of understanding one's own pedagogical history, specifically reviewing and examining how one arrived at the arts management classroom, what individuals and moments have assisted in shaping one's understanding of what 'teaching' means, and how that is enacted in practice.

In addition to considering the values one places on the notion of education and the concept of 'teacher', one might equally consider the history behind how one arrived at involvement in the subject of arts and cultural management. This line of inquiry fosters understanding and interrogation of one's own traditions, assumptions and belief systems regarding the subject as well as the means by which it is taught. Gaining an understanding of students' pedagogical histories would be equally valuable. Sharing these experiences with students might go some way towards a shared awareness, even if a different understanding, of "how what we believe got to be that way" (Warren, 2011, p. 140). While such processes may still be "oriented towards a Western consciousness, framework, and ethos" (Shome, 2009, p. 696), they may nevertheless build awareness of how difference and power occur in arts and cultural management education. Thus, building greater understanding of how certain forms of knowledge, values and skills come to be (and may not eventually be) privileged over others in the shaping of the profession.

Critical ethnography of teaching and learning practice is another way to facilitate reflexivity. There is a shared disquiet amongst educators and students as to how arts and cultural management education seems to fall short of "accommodat[ing]… cultural difference in practice" (Nisbett, this volume; Durrer, 2018b). Addressing this concern more explicitly through critical ethnographic studies of one another's teaching and learning practices might assist in revealing some of the well-intentioned, yet ineffective ways in which we strive to address internationalisation (Joseph, 2008; Warren, 2011). Further, empirical studies on internationalisation within specific disciplines are needed, like that carried out by Nisbett (this volume) and those by O'Connor et al. (2019).

In addition to conceptual acts of understanding the world or knowing how to do something, reflexivity involves "awareness of [the] physical and social selves in the acts of knowledge construction" (Nguyen & Larson, 2015, p. 333; Reckwitz, 2002). This includes considering the spatial circumstances of our classrooms, the physical relationship of students to one another and to educators, as well as how we facilitate students engaging physically (as well as mentally) in the experience of arts management. How we physically conduct a lecture or facilitate group work, such as through role play (Sutherland, 2013), and how we arrange a classroom communicates hierarchies of value (Jamieson, 2003). Thinking about the body in teaching and learning also includes curriculum elements that facilitate students in the act of 'doing' arts management, as well as reflecting on that 'doing'. The presence of work placements on programmes is one example. Such an awareness will extend understanding of how programme subjects, theoretical frames, curriculum and content reinforce, challenge and shape ideas of representation and meaning-making.

Conclusion

This chapter has pointed out a need for more research on the internationalisation of higher education in arts and cultural management and, thus, into the role this education plays within the politics of representation. It argues that fuller consideration of the practice of educators and the teaching and learning processes they facilitate in HE is required in order to understand how ideas, values and practices of representation are perpetuated, spread and/or challenged. A number of gaps in our understanding have been highlighted. These include a need for more critical examination of programme development, curriculum design and teaching and learning practices and particularly within internationalised contexts.

Further study might begin in a number of ways. Perhaps more straightforwardly, audits of curriculum—what is taught, why and how—would give insight into what is currently being taught and, thus, perceived to be of legitimated value to the profession. While these have been carried out previously and are referenced above, they stand in isolation. Complementary ethnographic studies of these teaching and learning environments situated within specific national, but importantly local contexts are needed to deepen the meaning of this data. Systematic comparative study of programme audits, situated within national and local contexts, would illuminate shared and differing values in educational practice for arts and cultural management as well as an understanding of any situated logics in arts and cultural management practice. This analysis would also allow for a more thorough and fruitful interrogation of the questions of transferability raised by others (Dragićević-Šešić & Mihaljinac, this volume; Suteu, 2006).

Surveys as well as ethnographic studies of teaching and learning experiences from the perspective of both students and teachers would provide understanding of the socio-cultural reality of the learning environment and its implications for the professionalisation and standardisation of practice on a global scale. Equally, understanding individuals' pedagogical histories and cultures as well as the expectations and motivations for engaging in arts and cultural management education would shed light on how our personal beliefs, life histories and philosophies shape or challenge the standardisation of the profession by way of education.

This investigation should not be reserved for what might be arguably referred to as objective, critical observation, but should also involve processes that facilitate greater self- as well as critically reflexive practices amongst educators (academic and practitioner) and with students (Cunliffe, 2002). Reflexive teaching and learning approaches will assist in illuminating the personal and systemic assumptions, values and conventions that underlie the growing international field of arts and cultural management, giving firmer ground from which to explore the ethical and social roles of the discipline more deeply (Cunliffe & Jun, 2005).

Research across higher education training (Holweiss & Walker) and training in public administration (Cunliffe & Jun, 2005) and creative and cultural industries, specifically (Nisbett, this volume; O'Connor et al., 2019), indicates there is not only a desire but also practical ways forward for these types of ethical, reflexive practices in arts management education.

Note

1. The author wishes to thank Dr. Peter Campbell, University of Liverpool, for assisting in the analysis of this data.

References

AAAE, ENCATC, & TAPCS. (2017). *The Brussels manifesto on arts management, cultural management and policy education.* Retrieved June 21, 2018, from https://www.encatc.org/media/2907-brusselsmanifestofinal.pdf

Abbas, A., & Erni, J. (2005). Introduction: Internationalising cultural studies. In A. Abbas & J. Erni (Eds.), *Internationalising cultural studies* (pp. 1–12). Malden, MA: Blackwell Publishing.

Altbach, P. (2004). Globalisation and the university: Myths and realities in an unequal world. *Tertiary Education Management, 10*(1), 3–25.

Ashton, D. (2013). Industry practitioners in higher education: Values, identities and cultural work. In D. Ashton & C. Noonan (Eds.), *Cultural work and higher education* (pp. 172–194). Basingstoke: Palgrave Macmillan.

Ashton, D., & Noonan, C. (2013). Cultural work and higher education. In D. Ashton & C. Noonan (Eds.), *Cultural work and higher education* (pp. 1–21). Basingstoke: Palgrave Macmillan.

Bennett, T. (1995). *The birth of the museum: History, theory, politics.* London: Routledge.

Bhaba, H. (2012). *The location of culture.* Abingdon: Routledge.

Bliming, G. (1998). Navigating the changing climate of moral and ethical issues in student affairs. In D. L. Cooper & J. M. Lancaster (Eds.), *Beyond law and policy: Reaffirming the role of student affairs* (New Directions for Student Services, 82) (pp. 65–75). San Francisco, CA: Jossey Bass.

Blumenreich, U. (2012). Higher education in the field of cultural mediation and the labour market for cultural mediation. In *International Conference on Cultural Policy Research*, Barcelona.

Booth. J., Ophuysen, T., & Koleva, P. (2004). *Bringing international mobility in the arts to the forefront: Exploring student and teacher mobility in the arts.* Amsterdam: ELIA. Retrieved July 1, 2016, from http://www.elia-artschools.org

Boylan, P. (2000). *Resources for training in the management and administration of cultural institutions, a pilot study for UNESCO.* London: City University London.

Brkić, A. (2009). Teaching arts management: Where did we lose the core ideas? *The Journal of Arts Management, Law, and Society, 38*(4), 270–280.

Brkić, A., & Bereson, R. (2016). *Cultural networks and quantum reality: Rise of cultural education networks in Asia.* Paper presented to International Conference on Cultural Policy Research, Seoul Korea, 7 July. Retrieved August 21, 2016, from http://www.iccpr2016.sm.ac.kr

Brockington, G. (2009). Introduction: Internationalism and the arts. In G. Brockington (Ed.), *Internationalism and the arts in Britain and Europe at the Fin de Siècle* (pp. 1–24). Bern: Peter Lang.

Carty, H. (this volume). Intercultural exchange: A personal perspective from the outsider inside. In V. Durrer & R. Henze (Eds.), *Managing culture: Reflecting on exchange in our global times* (pp. 259–268). Basingstoke: Palgrave Macmillan.

Chan, B. (2011). Postgraduate transnational education in non-business subjects: Can it fit conceptualizations of curriculum internationalisation? *Journal of Studies in International Education, 15*(3), 279–298.

Chong, D. (2002). *Arts management.* Abingdon: Routledge.

Costa, L. (2017). Training for cultural production and management in Brazil. *The Journal of Arts Management, Law, and Society.* https://doi.org/10.1080/10632921.2017.1366378

Cultural Diplomacy Platform. (2018). *Who we are.* Retrieved October 1, 2018, from https://www.cultureinexternalrelations.eu/about-us-2/

Cunliffe, A. L. (2002). Reflexive dialogical practice in management learning. *Management Learning, 33*(1), 35–61.

Cunliffe, A., & Jun, J. (2005). The need for reflexivity in public administration. *Administration & Society, 37*(2), 225–242.

Cuyler, A. C. (2017). A survey of arts management educators' teaching on diversity issues. *The Journal of Arts Management, Law, and Society, 47*(3), 192–202.

Dewey, P., & Rich, D. (2003). Developing arts management skills in transitional democracies. *International Journal of Arts Management, 5*(2), 15–18.

Dewey, P., & Wyszomirski, M. J. (2004). International issues in cultural policy and administration: A conceptual framework for higher education. In *The Third International Conference on Cultural Policy Research*. Retrieved February 8, 2019, from http://neumann.hec.ca/iccpr/PDF_Texts/Dewey_Wyszomirski.pdf

DiMaggio, P. (1987). *Managers of the arts: The careers and opinions of administrators of U.S. resident theatres, art museums, orchestras, and community arts agencies*. Washington, DC: Seven Locks Press.

Dragićević-Šešić, M. (2003). Survey on institutions and centres providing training for cultural development professionals in Eastern Europe, Central Asia and the Caucus Region. In ENCATC (Ed.) *Training in cultural policy and management: International Directory of training centres* (pp. 6–14). Brussels: UNESCO/ENCATC. Retrieved April 7, 2016, from http://unesdoc.unesco.org/images/0013/001305/130572e.pdf

Dragićević-Šešić, M. (2015). Capacity-building programmes: Keeping institutional memory and regional collective consciousness alive. In P. Dietachmair & M. Ilić, (Eds.), *Another Europe: 15 years of capacity building with cultural initiatives in the EU neighbourhood*, (pp. 101–117). Amsterdam: EU Cultural Foundation. Retrieved May 18, 2016, from http://www.culturalfoundation.eu/library/another_europe

Dragićević-Šešić, M., & Mihaljinac, N. (this volume). Cultural management training within cultural diplomacy agendas in the MENA region. In V. Durrer & R. Henze (Eds.), *Managing culture: Reflecting on exchange in our global times* (pp. 205–231). Basingstoke: Palgrave Macmillan.

Durrer, V. (2018a). The relationship between cultural policy and arts management. In V. Durrer, D. Obrien, & T. Miller (Eds.), *The Routledge handbook to global cultural policy* (pp. 64–85). Abingdon: Routledge.

Durrer, V. (2018b). Learning about intercultural relations in arts and cultural management higher education. Retrieved February 6, 2019, from https://managingculture.net/2017/07/24/learning-about-intercultural-relations-in-arts-and-cultural-management-higher-education/

Durrer, V., Henze, R., & Roß, I. (2016). Arts managers as intercultural brokers. *Arts Management Quarterly, 124*, 25–30.

Ebewo, P., & Sirayi, M. (2009). The concept of arts/cultural management: A critical reflection. *The Journal of Arts Management, Law, and Society, 38*(4), 281–295.

Edelman, D., & Coy, K. (2017). Emerging international networks in arts and culture research and education. In F. Imperiale & M. Vecco (Eds.), *Click, Connect and Collaborate! New directions in sustaining cultural networks,*

ENCATC conference proceedings (pp. 119–128). Brussels: ENCATC. Retrieved February 8, 2019, from https://www.encatc.org/media/2852-encatc_congress_proceedings_2017.pdf

Evrard, Y., & Colbert, F. (2000). Arts management: A new discipline entering the millennium. *International Journal of Arts Management, 2*(2), 4–13.

Featherstone, M. (1995). *Undoing culture: Globalisation, postmodernism and identity.* London: Sage.

Figueira, C., & Fullman, A. (2016). The role of higher education in the professionalisation of education of future leaders in international/external cultural relations. In F. Imperiale & M. Vecco (Eds.), *Cultural management education in risk societies—Towards a paradigm and policy shift?!, ENCATC conference proceedings* (pp. 149–167). Brussels: ENCATC. Retrieved February 8, 2019, from https://www.encatc.org/media/1487-encatc_ac_book_2016.pdf

Fisher, R., & Karpodini-Dimitriadi, E. (Eds.). (2007). *Training in transnational cultural co-operation projects: Reflections and challenges on validation and certification.* Amsterdam: Boekmanstichting. Retrieved February 8, 2019, from http://www.vania-project.eu

Florida, R. (2002). *The rise of the creative class: And how it's transforming work, leisure, community and everyday life.* New York: Basic Books.

Freire, P. (1970). *Pedagogy of the oppressed.* New York: Continuum.

Giroux, H. (2001). *Theory and resistance in education: Towards a pedagogy for the opposition* (Rev. ed.). Westport, CT: Bergin & Garvey.

Haigh, M. (2009). Fostering cross-cultural empathy with non-Western curricular structures. *Journal of Studies in International Education, 13*(2), 271–284.

Hall, S. (1997a). Introduction. In S. Hall (Ed.), *Representation: Cultural representations and signifying practices* (pp. 1–11). London: Sage.

Hall, S. (1997b). The spectacle of the 'other'. In S. Hall (Ed.), *Representation: Cultural representations and signifying practices* (pp. 223–290). London: Sage.

Hall, S. (1997c). The local and the global: Globalisation and ethnicity. In A. King (Ed.), *Culture, globalisation and the world system* (pp. 19–39). Minneapolis: University of Minnesota Press.

Henze, R. (2017). *Introduction to international arts management.* Wiesbaden: Springer.

Hernández-Acosta, J. (2013). Differences in cultural policy and its implications for arts management: Case of Puerto Rico. *The Journal of Arts Management, Law, and Society, 43*(3), 125–138.

HESA. (2017). *Data set: The number of postgraduate taught students on courses with specific key words at UK HE providers 2005/6, 2009/10 and 2015/16 by HE provider.* London: HESA.

Hesmondalgh, D., & Saha, A. (2013). Race, ethnicity and cultural production. *Popular Communication, 11*(3), 179–195.

Holzweiss, P., & Walker, D. (2016). Ethics in higher education: Using collective experiences to enhance new professional training. *Journal of Student Affairs Research and Practice, 53*(4), 429–443.

Isar, Y. (2012). *Shifting economic power: New horizons for cultural exchange in our multi-polar world.* Zalzburg Global Seminar, White Paper Theme 2, Salzburg, Vol. 8, Session 490. Retrieved October 10, 2016, from https://www.salzburgglobal.org/fileadmin/user_upload/Documents/2010-2019/2012/490/whitepaper3_490.pdf

Jacobsen, U. C. (2015). Cosmopolitan sensitivities, vulnerability, and Global Englishes. *Language and Intercultural Communication, 15*(4), 459–474.

Jamieson, P. (2003). Designing more effective on-campus teaching and learning spaces: A role for academic developers. *International Journal of Academic Development, 8*(1–2), 119–133.

Joseph, C. (2008). Difference, subjectivities and power: (De) colonizing practices in internationalizing the curriculum. *Intercultural Education, 19*(1), 29–39.

Jhunjhunwala, R., & Walker, A. (this volume). Challenging assumptions in intercultural collaborations: Perspectives from India and the UK. In V. Durrer & R. Henze (Eds.), *Managing culture: Reflecting on exchange in our global times* (pp. 155–169). Basingstoke: Palgrave Macmillan.

Kehm, B. M., & Teichler, U. (2007). Research on internationalisation in higher education. *Journal of Studies in International Education, 11*(3–4), 260–273.

LaSalle College of Arts. (2012). LaSalle College of Arts partners with world-renowned Goldsmiths, University of London. Retrieved September 11, 2018, from http://www.lasalle.edu.sg/news/lasalle-college-of-the-arts-partners-with-world-renowned-goldsmiths-university-of-london/

Laughlin, S. (2017). Defining and transforming education: Association of arts administration educators. *The Journal of Arts Management, Law, and Society, 47*(1), 82–87.

Leuphana University. (2018). Master arts and cultural management. Master Arts. Retrieved September 11, 2018, from https://www.leuphana.de/en/professional-school/masters-studies/arts-and-cultural-management.html/

Luckman, S. (2013). Precariously mobile: Tension between the local and the global in higher education. In D. Ashton & C. Noonan (Eds.), *Cultural work and higher education* (pp. 69–86). Basingstoke: Palgrave Macmillan.

Lumby, J., & Foskett, N. (2016). Internationalisation and culture in higher education. *Educational Management and Leadership, 44*(1), 95–111.

Mandel, B., & Allmanritter, V. (2016) Internationalisation in the professional field of arts management—Effects, challenges, future goals and tasks for arts and cultural managers in international contexts. In F. Imperiale & M. Vecco (Eds.), *Cultural management education in risk societies—Towards a paradigm and policy shift?!, ENCATC conference proceedings* (pp. 262–276). Brussels: ENCATC. Retrieved February 8, 2019, from https://www.encatc.org/media/1487-encatc_ac_book_2016.pdf

Marginson, S. (2010a). Space, mobility and synchrony in the age of the knowledge economy. In S. Marginson, P. Murphy, & M. Peters (Eds.), *Global creation: Space, mobility and synchrony in the age of the knowledge economy* (pp. 117–149). New York: Peter Lang Publishing.

Marginson, S. (2010b). Making space in higher education. In S. Marginson, P. Murphy, & M. Peters (Eds.), *Global creation: Space, mobility and synchrony in the age of the knowledge economy* (pp. 150–200). New York: Peter Lang Publishing, Inc.

Marginson, S., & Sawir, E. (2011). *Ideas for intercultural education*. Basingstoke: Palgrave Macmillan.

MMIAM. (2018). Master of Management in International Arts Management. Retrieved October 2018, from https://www.master-in-international-arts-management.com/

Mosquera, G. (2010). Walking with the devil: Art, culture and internationalisation. In K. Anheier & Y. Isar (Eds.), *Cultural expression, creativity and innovation* (The Cultures and Globalisation Series, 3) (pp. 47–56). London: Sage.

Murji, K. (2018, July). *Race, multiculture and higher education*. Talk presented at Intercultural Relations in Higher Education, AHRC Brokering Intercultural Exchange Seminar 3, Zurich University of the Arts.

National Endowment for the Arts. (1965). *The first annual report of the National Council on the Arts 1964–1965*. Retrieved October 1, 2018, from https://www.arts.gov/sites/default/files/NEA-Annual-Report-1964-1965.pdf

Nguyen, D., & Larson, J. (2015). Don't forget about the body: Exploring the curricular possibilities of embodied pedagogy. *Innovative Higher Education, 40*(4), 331–344.

Nisbett, M. (this volume). 'Silence is golden': Cultural collision in the classroom. In V. Durrer & R. Henze (Eds.), *Managing culture: Reflecting on exchange in our global times* (pp. 233–258). Basingstoke: Palgrave Macmillan.

O'Brien, D. (2017). Culture as a vocation: Sociology of career choices in cultural management. *International Journal of Cultural Policy, 23*(4), 525–526.

O'Connor, J., Gu, X., & Vickery, J. (2019). Teaching the cultural and creative industries: An international perspective. *Arts and Humanities in Higher Education, 18*(2–3), 93–98.

Paquette, J., & Redaelli, E. (2015). *Arts management and cultural policy research.* Basingstoke: Palgrave Macmillan.

Reckwitz, A. (2002). Toward a theory of social practices: A development in culturalist theorizing. *European Journal of Social Theory, 5*(2), 243–263.

Rösler, B. (2015). The case of Asialink's arts residency program: Towards a critical cosmopolitan approach to cultural diplomacy. *International Journal of Cultural Policy, 21*(4), 463–477.

Rowntree, J., Neal, L., & Fenton, R. (2010). *International cultural leadership: Reflections, competencies and interviews.* London: Cultural Leadership Programme. Retrieved February 11, 2016, from http://creativeconomy.britishcouncil.org/media/uploads/files/International_Cultural_Leadership_report.pdf

Saha, A. (2013). The cultural industries in a critical multicultural pedagogy. In D. Ashton & C. Noonan (Eds.), *Cultural work and higher education* (pp. 214–231). Basingstoke: Palgrave Macmillan.

Shohat, E., & Stam, R. (2005). De-eurocentricizing cultural studies: Some proposals. In A. Abbas & J. Erni (Eds.), *Internationalising cultural studies* (pp. 481–498). Malden, MA: Blackwell Publishing.

Shome, R. (2009). Post-colonial reflections on the 'internationalisation' of cultural studies. *Cultural Studies, 23*(5–6), 694–719.

Singh, J. (2018). Regulating cultural goods and identities across borders. In V. Durrer, D. Obrien, & T. Miller (Eds.), *The Routledge handbook to global cultural policy* (pp. 89–101). Abingdon: Routledge.

Sternal, M. (2007). Cultural policy and cultural management related training: Challenges for higher education in Europe. *The Journal of Arts Management, Law, and Society, 37*(1), 65–78.

Suteu, C. (1999). *Networking culture: The role of European cultural networks.* Strasbourg: Council of Europe Publishing.

Suteu, C. (2006). *Another brick in the wall: A critical review of cultural management education in Europe.* Amsterdam: Boekman.

Sutherland, A. (2013). The role of theatre and embodied knowledge in addressing race in South African higher education. *Studies in Higher Education, 38*(5), 728–740.

Tatli, A., & Özbilgin, M. (2012). Surprising intersectionalities of inequality and privilege: The case of the arts and cultural sector. *Equality, Diversity and Inclusion: An International Journal, 31*(3), 249–265.

Trice, A. (2003). Faculty perceptions of graduate international students: The benefits and challenges. *Journal of Studies in International Education, 7*(4), 379–403.

Upchurch, A. (2016). *The origins of the arts council movement. Philanthropy and policy.* Basingstoke: Palgrave Macmillan.

Varbanova, L. (2012). *Strategic management in the arts.* Abingdon: Routledge.

Veiga, J. (1977). Preface. In P. Freire (author), *Cultural action for freedom* (pp. 7–12). New York: Penguin Books (1970).

Warren, J. (2011). Reflexive teaching: Toward critical autoethnographic practices of/in/on pedagogy. *Cultural Studies? Critical Methodologies, 11*(2), 139–144.

Yeganeh, H., & Zhan, S. (2006). Conceptual foundations of cultural management research. *International Journal of Cross Cultural Management, 6*(3), 361–376.

9

Cultural Management Training Within Cultural Diplomacy Agendas in the MENA Region

Milena Dragićević-Šešić and Nina Mihaljinac

Introduction

Throughout history, the concept of cultural development has been imposed by foreign agents using different pretexts and reasoning, from UNESCO cultural actions to economic international aid programmes. Since the period of decolonisation down to the present era, the internationalist discourse of progress and modernisation has come together with programmes of former colonising powers (Berre & Høyum, 2015). The discourse of cultural management has been a part of this, as Shome (2012, p. 202) indicates when writing that the "west has staged itself as universally modern through relations of colonialism" and it is trying to maintain this role. By promoting allegedly universal professional norms, various international organisations whose missions are embedded in Western ideologies and institutions, such as the European Union, UNESCO, the UN and foreign cultural centres, use diverse international cultural actions as 'soft power' (Nye, 2004) tools to secure the continua-

M. Dragićević-Šešić (✉) • N. Mihaljinac
University of Arts in Belgrade, Belgrade, Serbia

© The Author(s) 2020
V. Durrer, R. Henze (eds.), *Managing Culture*, Sociology of the Arts,
https://doi.org/10.1007/978-3-030-24646-4_9

tion of their international presence and global impact. The term 'soft power' refers to the process of seeking to influence and change in a dissimulating way the public opinion of one country in another country. Capacity-building programmes dedicated to cultural professionals are a major part of such initiatives, the goals of which are to encourage non-Western cultural professionals to 'modernise' their cultural systems by adopting and implementing Western operational modes and concepts. In the Western neoliberal framework, cultural entrepreneurship is that of the goals which are most promoted.

Since there is a significant difference in local and Western visions, needs and interests, these programmes are rarely completely accepted in Global South communities, which is why Western organisations often struggle to find better modes of international operation. This chapter is based on one such initiative. It investigates the reasons for the low impact of capacity-building programmes in non-Western countries, drawing especially on the following study "*Mapping the training experiences in cultural management in Middle East and North Africa (MENA) region*", which was funded by the European Union Med Culture programme in 2015 (Dragićević-Šešić, Mihaljinac, & El Amine Moumine, 2016). The most important conclusion of this research is that foreign trainers, when imposing schemes in cultural management as 'universal practices', and without knowing the local context, questioning their own position, or taking account of possible clashes with the values, interests and aspirations of local cultural operators, are in reality giving more weight to arguments that critique the spread of neo-colonialization and globalisation through Western aid.

This research created a space for discovering a multitude of voices among cultural professionals who come from the Middle East and North Africa (MENA) countries, and consequently led to the creation of a platform for critical debate on Western technical assistance missions (TAMs). As a result, this chapter aims to connect the findings of empirical research on Western TAMs in MENA countries (and generally speaking, in the Global South) with theories that deal with issues of postcolonialism and post-development.

Firstly, the methodological and theoretical approaches, as well as key concepts, are presented (cultural management, international cooperation, soft power, postcolonialism, post-development theory, geopolitics of emotion, TAM, capacity-building). Secondly, findings regarding the training experiences in cultural management in the Middle East and North Africa region are described. Finally, the evaluation of international TAMs given by participants and trainers is explained. In addition to promoting critical reflections and the questioning of TAMs as soft power tools, the chapter outlines some directions for redefining international cultural relations. The most important one refers to the equal cooperation between the Global North and South (van Graan 2016).

Context and Methodological Framework

This paper analyses the empirical data collected within the study entitled, *"Mapping the training experiences in cultural management in Middle East and North Africa (MENA) region"*. This was conducted in 2015, mainly from the point of view of postcolonial and post-development theories.

The empirical research carried out is based on theories of cultural management and cultural diplomacy. The goal has been to identify and provide comprehensive information on cultural management training programmes (both formal and informal) which is currently available in eight MENA countries: Israel, Palestine, Jordan, Lebanon, Egypt, Algeria, Tunisia and Morocco. The study employed the following methods: 81 interviews with local cultural professionals, university professors and local, regional and EU-level trainers of cultural management in MENA countries—Algeria (3), Egypt (9), Lebanon (14, of which 3 persons come from Syria), Morocco (19), Tunisia (7), Palestine (7), Israel (11), Jordan (3) and Europe (8). The majority of those interviewed (70%) were cultural professionals—artists, curators, activists and leaders of cultural organisations, while 30% were university professors and trainers. Other approaches included an analysis of training formats and curricula; desk research and literature review; observation of several training programmes as case studies and comparative analysis of the impact of training programmes developed by European Union National Institutes for Culture (EUNIC) and other EU programmes (MED culture), foreign cultural centres and the European Cultural Foundation (ECF).

During the research, an important question regarding Global North TAMs organised in these countries was raised: is the TAM's actual (and hidden) purpose to promote capitalist values (i.e. individualism, creativity, innovation and market-orientation), so that cultural professionals from so-called 'underdeveloped' countries adopt and further promote them, thus creating an environment favourable to a wide spread of market logic? It is well known that international corporations use human and natural resources in these countries in order to reduce costs and develop productivity. Thus, a further and significant research question was raised: what is, or what could be, the role of Global North TAMs in these processes?

Results from our research are here analysed from the point of view of postcolonial and post-development theories, with the argument that the majority of international TAMs primarily serve as a means of Global South *soft power* (Nye, 2004). Being part of a constellation of actions aimed at influencing social and public opinion, seamlessly affecting local cultures, identities, values and differing senses of self, these missions support the concept of a superior West with a role to spread modernity "into less 'backward' parts of the world" (Shome, 2012, p. 203). In other words, these actions support a kind of *orientalisation* (Said, 1978) of the Global South and thereby create an environment for the development of a 'culture of humiliation', which is described in a study entitled *Geopolitics of Emotions* (Moïsi, 2010).

According to Moïsi (2010), a 'culture of humiliation' is exemplified by the Arab-Islamic world on account of its historical decline (explained further below) and political humiliation. Humiliation means impotence, the loss of a sense of control over one's own life. Fear in the West stems from 'the other' and, paradoxically, the more the West needs 'the others'—as part of the workforce—the more it rejects them. Not only that, the Western World is also no longer a main actor of globalisation and is slowly losing its dynamism. The paternalistic perspective on Global South countries, especially those from the MENA region, arises from this Western culture of fear, which is now intensifying during the present-day period of fear of terrorism and immigration. Therefore, the West is trying to preserve its identity and its global role of trendsetting and modernity. This is why a binarily constructed attachment to traditions (which necessarily renders something anti-modern or non-modern) on the one hand, and the aspiration of progress on the other hand, is normalised by Western modernity (Shome, 2012). As stated by Turner (1978, p. 8), the notion persists that "in contrast to Western society, Islamic civilisation is static and locked within its sacred customs, its formal moral code, and its religious law", providing the justification of Western interventions which are aimed at development assistance. This construction is repeated and asserted in the majority of Western TAMs.

This position is confirmed by the UNESCO Convention on the *Protection and Promotion of the Diversity of Cultural Expressions* (UNESCO, 2005, Article 1, (i)), which states,

> to strengthen international cooperation and solidarity in a spirit of partnership with a view, in particular, to enhancing the capacities of developing countries in order to protect and promote the diversity of cultural expressions.

One of the purposes of the international arts and cultural exchanges organised under the UNESCO 'cooperation for development' is to foster empathy and understanding among diverse cultures and help develop 'underdeveloped' countries. Yet, those exchanges still largely flow from economic and former colonial powers (above all EU former colonial powers such as France, the UK, Spain and Germany, with the exception of Nordic countries that entered the world-scene relatively recently), and as such they are far away from 'fair cooperation' (Hampel, 2017). The mere notions of development and developing countries have become more and more disputed. According to post-development criticism, the way the concept of development is understood today is rooted in a colonial discourse that constructs the (Global) West and the North as 'advanced' and 'progressive', and the (Global) South and East as 'backward' and 'primitive' (Escobar, 1995; Esteva, Babones, & Babcicky, 2013; Sachs, 1992). Furthermore,

> the dominant paradigm of knowledge associated with theories of development and modernisation is unable to provide satisfactory answers to problems such as poverty, unemployment and environmental degradation of

the 'Third World' countries. Until recently, development was treated as a linear progression. Therefore, 'Third World' countries, the knowledge paradigm indicated, can only be transformed into modern developed countries by the application of modern technology and capitalist relations in production. (Ranaweera Banda, 2004, p. 98)

Research, Education and Cultural Policies: State of the Arts in the MENA Region

Although there are cultural management researchers in the region, Arab management thought is characterised by discontinuity, lack of focus and identity problems (Ali, 1995). These factors have numerous implications, especially related to the lack of strategic managerial thinking and the development of specific areas of non-profit management (culture, education, public health, etc.). Ali's (1995) key conclusion is that Arab countries do not have their own management theory and authentic practice, which is also why there is a need to stimulate cultural management both as a type of research to be embedded in the local socio-political and cultural context and as a practice. From 2008, cultural policy research and analysis has been introduced in the region, supported by the European Cultural Foundation through the *Al Mawred Al Thaqafy regional Culture Resource Centre* (Boekmanstudies, 2010). However, it is only since 2010 that national cultural policy groups have been created within civil society to investigate and discuss instruments and measures of cultural policies. (Dragićević-Šešić, 2015a; Ettijahat, ECF, & Al Mawred, 2013). Furthermore, with only a few exceptions, parliaments rarely debate cultural issues.

Obstacles within educational and cultural policies are partially related to unstable and harsh situations in the region (wars in Syria; terroristic acts in Lebanon, Tunisia, Egypt; military rule in Egypt; migrations and refugees; the Israeli-Palestinian conflict, etc.). Governments across MENA countries do not support the arts primarily because of their critical potential towards religion, state and governance, social injustice (for instance, in Israel, a new law was recently introduced envisaging that projects in culture financed by the Ministry should be 'loyal to the state'), or because the arts are seen as a part of a Western (colonising) culture (Algeria, Morocco, Jordan, etc.). As a result, there are explicit cultural policies which mostly support public cultural infrastructure and traditional and safe cultural formats. As a consequence of this, the public cultural system is somehow inert, being characterised by rigid structures and lack of autonomy. Some cultural activities are funded by the Ministry of Education or other ministries, but the majority of funds are also going to selected traditional forms of expressions. The large number of applications that are coming from art collectives and non-governmental organisations (NGOs) every year to the Arab Fund for Arts and Culture operating from Beirut (founded in the framework of Alliance of Arab Foundations, established in Geneva; Arab Culture Fund, 2007), show that there is a need for promotion of contemporary arts. In spite of efforts to engage governments in funding, up to now the Fund is operating with finances coming from the Global North.

For this reason, which can be named as a 'fright from culture' or a 'colonisation of culture', governments have not supported the development of art production disciplines and cultural management programmes in university systems in ways that have commonly occurred elsewhere globally. Thus, there is not necessarily a large body or network of cultural professionals engaging in what may be understood as typical arts management practice, such as realising artistic, cultural and activist projects and engaging audiences. Furthermore, there is a lack of systemic artistic education in primary and secondary schools (which naturally differs from country to country; e.g. the artistic education is lacking in Morocco, but exists in Tunisia). As a consequence, this is a challenge for audience development. As stated in a research interview, culture is seen as a "luxury", or as a Western product, both by authorities and by a large part of the population.

When it comes to cultural markets, a major contribution to the development of creative industries comes through international mechanisms (e.g. through the Arab Fund), which combines the political influence and economic interest of Western industries who typically find inexpensive labour forces in those countries. Also, this contribution is mainly dedicated to civil society organisations. It could be said that the interest of domestic private agents to work in the creative industries has risen in the region since 2010, especially due to the activities of international organisations and their political, humanitarian and cultural diplomacy agendas (e.g. the genre of documentary film is supported as a tool for the promotion of human rights and democracy). Still, in spite of the gained cultural management skills, a new generation of artists and cultural managers cannot apply these skills in most of the MENA countries, since cultural markets do not exist (Lebanon is an exception to a certain degree). Only some domains of cultural industries, for example film or music festivals, are state-funded via other ministries rather than the Ministry of Culture, and this fragmentation of funding is characteristic of the split between 'arts' and 'cultural industries', non-profit and profitable sectors. Thus, artistic production cannot be self-sustainable, and nor can cultural organisations.

Civic associations have different roles in MENA countries. In Maghreb, for example, there is a tradition of youth and citizen art associations (without political and social engagement); in other countries such as Egypt, there are currently no possibilities to register a civil society association, and therefore many of them have started working as limited companies (Boekmanstudies, 2010). Shortly after the Arab spring, especially in Tunisia and Egypt, civil associations in arts and culture have emerged, but new political processes have endangered this newly gained freedom (ENCPG, 2012), forcing many of them to emigrate to Lebanon (e.g. Al Mawred, Action For Hope).

State of the Arts in Education and Continuous Professional Development

Research in the MENA region emphasises common and numerous training needs. Therefore, the research funded by the MED Culture programme, which offered the empirical basis for this chapter, indicated, as stated by the interviewees, that all knowledge and skills listed in the questionnaire, such as project/event management and art production, PR and marketing/communication skills, audience development, are important and underdeveloped (see: Annex B in Dragićević-Šešić et al., 2016).

Nevertheless, most of the research participants highlighted skills related to cultural policies, advocacy and legislation as well as fundraising, project proposal writing and audience development.

Within the framework of the MED Culture research, it was important to see how higher education (universities and institutes) responds to those demands. The lack of higher education programmes in cultural management and other related professions in MENA countries currently perpetuate the low status of professionalism in the cultural domain there, enabling the justification of international capacity-building transfer and influences. Higher education can play a key role in raising the status of the profession—but only those occupations that are 'studied' and researched within higher education can achieve status in society, knowledge, abilities and skills, thus delivering the perceived quality of products and services and contributing to the quality of life and deeper social changes. Higher education is an important factor in diminishing or perpetuating social inequalities (depending on the accessibility and (non) offered equal opportunities). This point was especially emphasised in the study entitled *Feasibility Research on Establishing an MA programme in Cultural Policy and Cultural Management in the Arab Region* (Al Mawred, 2014).

The University sector and public universities in the MENA region are presently under the direct control of state educational policies and governance. They have very limited budgetary, managerial and pedagogical independence. In many cases, like in Tunisia, they are directly managed by the government, which means that their autonomy in terms of launching new programmes is extremely limited. Besides this, private and foreign universities are market oriented, and their freedom is limited by market demands. While the number of private universities has significantly risen after the Arab spring, as has been explained by one cultural policy expert in the region, educational programming has not matched this growth.

Still, there are noted curricular differences between cultural management programmes in the region, depending on the cultural context, cultural policies and international relations. In Tunisia and Morocco, as well as in Lebanon within French-speaking universities, there are numerous bachelor and master programmes linked to socio-cultural mediation.[1] In other countries, education for cultural professions is mostly related to heritage, archaeology and conservation (Egypt) or to art practices (theatre practice in Morocco). However, Lebanon and Israel have developed some types of courses that are dedicated to new concepts such as curatorship and creative industries connected to cultural economy, as well as building managerial capacities in domains such as cultural tourism, event and heritage management. In Egyptian and Palestinian universities, there are few emerging initiatives in cultural management. Algeria and Jordan have not introduced any relevant programmes for cultural development professions, and there is no mention of cultural management even as an elective subject (EUNIC, 2013).

Academics teaching at cultural management programmes have established relationships with foreign colleagues, and in a few cases, they have developed institutional collaboration (mostly in cultural mediation and arts). Among those initiatives are: Institut Superieur d`Animation de la Jeunesse (ISAJ) Tunisia, joint Master programmes: Universities of Lyon II with Creteil; and St Joseph University of Beirut with University of Marseille, France. Existing cultural mediation courses do not attract a large number of students in MENA countries because cultural professions have lost their prestige. At the same time, cultural management programmes are based in different disciplinary departments, such as the law, linguistics, literature, economy, arts and sociology, among others. Thus, curricula are largely based on those disciplines that often lack knowledge and skills important for cultural management practice. For example, the *Master de mediation culturelle* in Beirut has many subjects related to linguistics and Lebanese art and literature, since those subjects are studied in that department, while topics such as project management appear very late in the programme, and financial management, contracting or marketing not at all. Each interviewed professor underlined the fact that monodisciplinary limitations prevent the real development of cultural management curriculum.

Another deficiency is the absence of centres for continuous professional development within universities. Any such centres, which could be devoted to cultural managers, marketing experts, curators and public administrators, have to date not been identified. However, in Tunisia, one Institute, ISAJ, is intending to develop an Incubator named *The*

Centre of Entrepreneurship. In Morocco, Ibn Tofail University has organised a continuous professional development department, which holds programmes in accountancy, management, audits and marketing. On the other hand, continuous professional education appears in the region only by independent international organisations. As L. Friedman and D. Ronen, university professors from Israel, explain in an interview,

> Numerous obstacles in education, training and capacity building have been identified. Freedom and lack of autonomy of the university and public cultural system were underlined as the crucial problem, as well as authorisation (accreditation). Lack of human resources for teaching and training is of specific importance for the development of university accredited courses, as there are no people qualified to hold courses in cultural management. (Dragićević-Šešić et al., 2016, p. 46)

When it comes to employability, it seems that academics are primarily focused on educating students for jobs in the public cultural, educational or scientific realms. Jobs in the public sector are highly dependent on ruling party power (*Akademia*, 2013). While the 'entrepreneurial' approach exists in business and management schools, there are only a few courses dedicated to art and culture entrepreneurialism. The relationship towards the private sector also differs between Lebanese programmes, which prepare students for art entrepreneurship, and programmes in North Africa, which are geared mostly towards public sector cultural work. Only recently have citizen associations promoting entrepreneurship started to emerge. For example, the *Association 'Process' Tunisia* organises competitions for students and young designers to design objects for everyday use, linking winners with supporting enterprises.

As there are not enough university programmes or training courses in cultural management, the majority of practitioners have learned the practice hands-on, through trial and error rather than through formal education. Therefore, foreign humanitarian, political and cultural organisations as well as diplomats active in those countries no doubt saw a huge opportunity for intervention and proposed different kinds of training formats and schemes, both on national and regional levels, but according to their own aims. Unfortunately, due to the aforementioned reasons and as is indicated from research interviews, universities are currently incapable of becoming active partners in this process, and thus they are unable to appropriate those programmes and adapt them to local context and needs. As a result, the majority of TAMs are still held in foreign cultural centres in cooperation with international partners.

Of note is the case of the Arab-English Master programme in Cultural Policy and Management, that was developed, based on a feasibility study, by University Hasan II in Casablanca together with the University of Hildesheim and the University of Arts in Belgrade, and UK experts engaged by the British Council. It took four years between the first call for students and their selection (2015) and the actual launching of the programme (autumn 2018). This period of delay (2015–2018) was not used to enlarge the number of Arab academics involved, or to engage those that could be prepared for future academic engagement. Out of a selected twelve students, only six are currently attending the programme (as delays led others to different opportunities, and few could not obtain a Moroccan visa). This first attempt to create the first pan-Arab Master programme in Cultural Management ended with an engagement of Arab professors for general subject areas such as history, sociology and history of art, while key topics of cultural management are held by professors of Global North with the assistance of local practitioners for the workshops. There is a hope that, among those, future trainers and professors are one day going to be raised from within the region itself.

TAM and Their Impact: Conflictual Agendas?

The research presented here classifies international training programmes in three groups: national, international and civil society. The first group relates to cultural diplomacy bilateral programmes, which are mostly characterised by specific political (foreign policy) agendas of each state. The second group relates to international (humanitarian) developmental aid, which is inspired by UN and UNESCO declarations and conventions such as the 2005 UNESCO Convention and UN Millennium development goals (United Nations, 2000) and Sustainable Development

Goals: The United Nations Development Programme (UNDP, 2015). The third group consists of very different regional and international European civil society actors, which are located in between political, humanitarian and inherently cultural agendas.

Cultural Diplomacy (Bilateral) Programmes

Soft power is more and more embedded in governmental foreign policy actions, using art and culture as a diplomatic tool. Both artistic exchange (touring, art residencies, artist mobility, cultural professionals and cultural goods) and capacity-building programmes dedicated to cultural professionals are part of the investments aimed at supporting foreign policy goals through the selection of what the country which initiates the training deems to be priority countries, artistic fields and methods of intervention. The effectiveness of cultural management capacity-building programmes in establishing long-term ties with beneficiary countries is more efficient than other forms of cultural diplomacy (i.e. artistic collaboration and exchange), which are one-time events usually offered to the same local elites. Thus, numerous European foreign institutes have developed bilateral cultural management training programmes in MENA countries that aim to train future cultural operators who will be devoted to collaboration with their countries and who will present their positive—artistic, cultural, social—image in the cultural realm in MENA countries. At the same time, through these workshops and training opportunities, countries can promote their political culture and values such as democracy, the importance of civil society, gender equality and freedom of expression. This rationale is very visible in the analysis of TAM target groups (members of civil society, women, youth) and the chosen themes of workshops (e.g. intercultural dialogue, women in arts). A strong indication of how economic and other interests are cloaked behind alleged international aid or cooperation programmes is by their donation of software and transfer of technological know-how, so that Global South countries become dependent buyers of Global North products. Capacity-building programmes within bilateral developmental aid are often not explicitly considered as part of cultural diplomacy, with reasoning typically emphasising humanitarian rhetoric, empathy and solidarity.

Among the European countries that present cultural management training programmes, the most active one is Germany (predominantly through its Goethe institutes) that offers further professionalisation to MENA cultural operators through a six-week training programme in Germany (visits of German cultural organisations and workshops in cultural policy, project management, team management, finances and budgeting, fundraising, marketing and communications). There are several important Goethe Institute activities: MOOC, free online courses as developed with Leuphana University, Lüneburg (this is not limited to MENA but professionals from MENA can apply) and the Moving MENA Mobility Fund for cultural professionals and artists to attend important events. Another programme, entitled 'KULTURAKADEMIE', was devoted (till 2015) to experienced cultural professionals in order for them to gain similar knowledge and skills. After attending the programme, participants had the opportunity to undertake an internship in Germany or to apply for project grants. At the same time, the German UNESCO Commission has developed the regional programme named CONNEXXIONS (2011–2018), which is more related to cultural capacity-building for civil society actors and professionals (linked to the German transformation partnership) and the SOUTHMEDCV (in partnership with Interarts Barcelona, BAC arts Tunisia, Gudran Egypt, NCCA Jordan and Kayyal Puppet Theatre in Lebanon), in order to strengthen the capacity of cultural operators to cooperate with other sectors.

Another two programmes entitled *Training for cultural managers in the Arab world* and *Basic courses in cultural management* are also presently being used as a systematic MENA action. There are also some ad hoc yet specific programmes by Goethe institutes in the region, such as the Goethe Institute in Alexandria, which organise the training of trainers (ToT).

The British Council has also been active in running internationally oriented programmes, for example, *Cultural Leadership International* and *Future Leaders Connect—The global network for emerging policy leaders*. The British Council sporadically organises other cultural management training initiatives such as the *Cultural Skills* programme in *Entrepreneurship and Innovation in the Arts*, or a training programme developed by The British Council Israel, the Negev Development Authority, The Arab Culture Association and *Nesta* Foundation for Innovation. Through all those programmes, the British Council promotes the UK as the world leader in the field of creative industries:

> There will be substantial benefits from close co-operation, including in areas such as science, education and culture, and the creative industries. The UK's decision to withdraw from the EU places more importance on the role of the British Council in developing even stronger ties between the UK and countries around the world where the UK will be seeking to develop stronger trade relationships. This work will support long-term growth and development globally, and complement the government's ambition for a truly global Britain. (British Council, 2017, p. 12)

Other foreign institutes (the French institute, the Flemish institute, the Cervantes Institute and the Swedish International Development Cooperation Agency—SIDA) are likewise organising capacity-building programmes, but they do so only occasionally, since cultural management training is not a priority within their cultural diplomacy policy (Al Mawred, 2014). For example, *The Creative Force Programme* is managed by SIDA in the framework of the *Swedish Results Strategy for Special Initiatives for Human Rights and Democratisation, 2014–2017* (SIDA, 2014). This programme supports collaborative initiatives that contribute to strengthening democratisation and freedom of expression through capacity-building activities. The USA is present in the region as well: the USA Embassy offers scholarships for cultural management in Israel; USAID and Friedrich Ebert Stiftung, a German foundation closely linked to the Social Democratic Party, have established a Vocational training centre in Jordan; the John F. Kennedy Centre for the Performing Arts offers skills building for arts managers through the Institute for Arts Management and training for professionals around the world in the form of a ten-month fellowship; and a Youth empowerment development association (YUDA, Grassfield, USA) has organised Arts Management Training in Ramallah, Palestine and other workshops that are primarily dedicated to empowering woman and youth.

International Developmental Aid—EU and EU Countries, UN, UNESCO

Cultural training after the Arab Spring was often part of programmes for civil society development and the fight for democracy. The EU has been developing numerous programmes regarding cultural cooperation in the Mediterranean region. Diversified ad hoc projects devoted to cultural management and fundraising target two clearly distinct groups: well-known cultural professionals and the youth sector that is interested in developing cultural activist projects. Major training projects are delivered by the Anna Lindh foundation, EUNIC and the newly established MED Culture organisation, which is strictly devoted to the MENA region.

The Anna Lindh Foundation's *Dawrak Programme* brings cultural professionals together from across the Mediterranean to improve mutual respect between cultures and to support civil society. In coordination with the Goethe Institute, the foundation runs the largest network of civil society organisations involved in the promotion of intercultural dialogue across Europe and the Mediterranean, called CIN—Cultural Innovators Network. The main rationale of this enterprise has been to build and "promote mechanisms for democratic, inclusive discourse, exchange of working experiences, acceptance of innovative approaches, and mutual consultation and cooperation" (Cultural Innovators Network, 2018).

EUNIC has launched a EUNIC MENA Project addressing democratic empowerment, cultural policy and the creative economy. The aim has been to support the creative sector in the MENA region in redefining cultural policies that will respond to the changing socio-political context, demonstrate the potential of the creative industries, increase and reshape the scope of cultural exchanges and strengthen the competitiveness of the sector. The main project activity has been the *Dead Sea Forum*, which offered the actors of cultural and civil societies the opportunity to meet and create a cross-border network. The EUNIC Pilot was developed afterwards and consisted of two training sessions implemented by a training team of the Marcel Hicter Association from Brussels. As one positive dimension of the training, the participants mentioned various training methods, gaining new skills, information and knowledge, networking and forming partnerships, all of which touch on the main critiques of the Europe-MENA balance, in which they stressed the excessive emphasis on the European perspective and on theoretical information (Klesse, 2015).

The regional EU-funded programme Med Culture, 2014–2018, which featured as a part of the regional programme, *Media and Culture for Development in the Southern Mediterranean*, was launched with the aim of creating and sustaining institutional and social environments propitious to culture as a stimulus and defendant for freedom of expression and sustainable development, reinforcing the capacities of the public and private cultural sectors (Klesse, 2015). The *Houna a Shabab* programme organised by the Med Culture group in the period 2015–2017 includes a regional conference on creativity and culture for development, national focus group meetings in respective countries and capacity development activities on cultural management and policy issues.

European civil society, motivated with cultural and political agendas, has developed actions to enhance collaboration across the Mediterranean region. Mobility, freedom of the circulation of artists and cultural goods are essential motives for their engagement. To achieve this goal, the capacities of professionals on both sides of the Mediterranean have to be raised through partnership training projects (e.g. Roberto Cimetta Fund's *Upline, Meliopee* programme, EFA *Ateliers for Young Festival* managers and Tamasi Tot programmes). Amongst all the European civil society initiatives, the European Cultural Foundation from Amsterdam has emerged as the most ambitious initiator of Euro-Arab cooperation, enhancing measures that are bringing continuous longitudinal changes. ECF was the first to enter the region (2004) in the domain of capacity-building for arts and culture, developing a contract with a pan-Arabic organisation, Al Mawred Al Thaqafy, a unique regional resource and training centre. This contract envisaged a comprehensive training programme aimed at avoiding pitfalls from previous Western projects that included one-way knowledge transfer between North-South. ECF and Al Mawred launched the first *Training of Trainers* programme in the Arab region. The purpose was to enable professionals with local knowledge and practice to become the first generation of trainers who would be able to hold training in Arabic, to codify practice-based local knowledge, appropriating the know-how that came from the Global North and to further transfer these "new" cultural management skills in the Arabic region. The main training activities addressed difficult questions: how to research local cultural policies, how to engage with communities and stake-holders and it included other skills deemed necessary for strategic management, such as planning, fundraising, evaluation, audience development and PR. This programme plays an especially important role in the region (Ammar Kessab, expert).

The ECF also launched the *Tandem Shaml* programme in 2012, a cultural management exchange programme between EU and MENA countries (Dietachmair & Ilić, 2015). It enables different organisations to find a matching partner and gives them the opportunity to develop projects together. So far this programme has enabled 200 organisations from 28 countries, out of which 14 came from the MENA region, to be trained to cooperate with organisations from the EU and other European countries, including Turkey and Serbia.

UN conventions and resolutions are an important source of 'inspiration' for capacity-building programmes developed within EU and UNESCO agendas, promoting human rights, freedom of expression and artistic freedom. UNESCO is recognised in the region as an organisation that protects and promotes tangible and intangible heritage. Visibility and importance of world heritage lists overshadow other UNESCO activities, such as trainings for understanding and reporting the 2005 Convention. Several UNESCO projects, such as *MedLiHer* (UNESCO, 2012) and *Renc Euromed* (Euroculture, 2004), are important for promoting cultural management and heritage protection in the MENA region. Most UNESCO activities have a strictly cultural agenda as their main aim, but, since they are one of other UN organisations, their programmes also have a political agenda in promoting human rights and artistic freedom.

Assessment of International TAMs by Local Professionals and Trainers

All these trainings have been assessed by both practitioners and trainers and results have raised some concerns. First of all, the construction of the MENA region within the Global North political discourse was criticised.

In fact, many cultural practitioners from the region do not see themselves as part of the same cultural and political context.

It was commonly stated that the knowledge gained cannot be directly implemented. Participants consider the majority of training programmes offered by foreign actors as relevant and needed, as they bring new theoretical knowledge and insights (such as cultural policy and cultural development issues), but they see practical elements, specifically financial management, legislation, risk management and HR, as irrelevant. Even the trainers from the Global North have pointed out the communication and content adequacy problems:

> Local and international trainers often do not know each other. Their mutual introduction and exchange of knowledge and information is not `structured enough or intentional, but rather a consequence of a chance. (Goran Tomka, expert-trainer, Serbia)

The majority of training is offering only basic skills, which are inadequate for experienced professionals who are in "need of professional advancement" (Huda Odeh, local professional, Palestine). Paradoxically, training programmes are accessible and well known mainly to established professionals. Yet, the content is dedicated to beginners and young practitioners. This disjoint is why there is a clear suggestion that diverse voices should be included in the development of training programmes, linking numerous local and international partners in designing comprehensive long-term educational structures with clear pathways and opportunities for follow-up training.

It was also underlined that "trainings are not satisfactory or sufficient" and that "training offer is sporadic and non-diversified". As stated by Dr. Alia Arra Sougly, who took part in our study,

> one time workshops accomplish a limited amount of change. This horizontal approach by international organizations goes contrary to sustainable developmental needs of longitudinal impact.

It is obvious that most of the critiques coming from the MENA region address superficiality and lack real collaborative practices in designing capacity-building programmes with top-down approaches dominating TAMs implementation. Our study has stressed that new emphasis is needed in both content (e.g. cultural policy, global context discussions and international relations) and in the forms of TAMs, especially to foster critical and strategic thinking when addressing mid-career professionals. Issues and training related to entrepreneurial skills are less urgently needed as they are currently not sensitive to the MENA context and socio-political relations there.

On the other hand, Al Mawred programmes (ToT in 2005, CP in 2008, NCP research groups in 2011, *Abarra* in 2012, and finally *Tandem Shaml*) have shown the extent to which capacity-building programmes could be locally and regionally relevant if designed and developed on local knowledge and potentials. Sustainable results will come only if training programmes envisage the endorsement of local cultural community, trainers and lecturers.

Capacity-Building Programmes as a Soft Power Tool

In the new 'geopolitics of emotion' (Moïsi, 2010), Global South countries that are living in a 'culture of humiliation' are offered expertise and tools belonging to Global North systems and contexts. As Van Graan (2018, p. 73) indicates, the means for the role of culture may change over time:

> Yesterday, it was culture and development, then intercultural dialogue and cultural diplomacy, then creative and cultural industries, and tomorrow it will be climate change and the arts, etc.

Still, when it comes to the field of culture, tools and expertise that are being transferred from the North belong to the corpus of cultural management (which implies governance of public, civil and private organizations, both from the cultural heritage and contemporary arts). Cultural management programmes are aimed at 'modernization' of public systems and giving tools for the survival of civil and private organisations in a neoliberal system. Consequently, they do not support critical thinking, nor do they provide new opportunities for shaping local authentic cultural systems, such as the challenges seen in training on project and strategic management, marketing, fundraising, business administration, cultural entrepreneurship, cultural leadership and human resources.

This trend of promoting managerial skills in culture is based in the international developmental discourse and is officially related to fights against poverty (UN, 2000; UNDP, 2015). Although there are attempts to reduce the negative impacts of the commodification of arts and culture (UNESCO, 2005), the tools developed for this cause have been inadequate as they are based mostly on knowledge transfer and not on the support of the production of local knowledge systems. The neoliberal discourse of creative industries has become dominant in the cultural sphere. Thus, the concepts of creativity, innovation, strategies, job market, employment and value-chain have formed a new vocabulary for international programmes (European Commission, 2014; UNESCO, 2010).

Since 2000, numerous culture cooperation programmes have been designed for MENA countries. These include public officials' dialogue on cultural policy issues, engagement of foreign professionals, development of the strategic and management capacities of public cultural institutions, involvement of artists and civil society actors in intercultural dialogue projects, capacity-building and information dissemination (Dragićević-Šešić et al., 2016). The purpose of capacity-building within 'beneficiary' countries is usually twofold: within the frame of cultural diplomacy, training is mostly linked to stimulating cultural activism as a part of a democratic political struggle. For example, the *Abarra Programme* could only gather donors from MENA countries that participated in the Arab Spring, excluding cultural operators from Morocco, Algeria and other areas (Dragićević-Šešić, 2015b). When it comes to training initiated by international organisations, such as UNESCO, the focus is on raising skills such as marketing, fundraising and project management, which are needed for the development of cultural industries (UNESCO, 2005).

Capacity-building programmes as a part of cultural diplomacy represent a very effective method of reaching foreign policy goals, by bridging two countries closely together, changing the image of the country (if linked with colonialism or war conflicts), and finally by widening the market for their products. In a postcolonial context, they are typically carried out in culturally unaware or insensitive ways, with 'patronizing' programmes that often lack a considered approach to the circumstances, experiences and expertise of local practices (Henze, 2017). These approaches have always influenced local communities, values and behaviours in their specific cultural fields, in different ways, by creating an "interplay between broad structural changes and the adaptive strategies of threatened local groups and communities" (Khalaf, 2001, p. 9).

Thus, rather than responding to specific local conditions, cultural logics and training needs, cultural management (including entrepreneurialism and leadership training programmes) often serve as a means of soft power, creating a state of "uneasiness in culture" (Freud, 1930, pp. 57–146) among trained cultural professionals. Furthermore, they facilitate greater divisions in the cultural realm: those who are trained feel ill at ease with the Western knowledge they acquire, while the others who do not participate in training programmes feel even more alienated (Dragićević-Šešić et al., 2016). Our position is that skills and knowledge in the field of cultural management cannot be transferred without discussing and understanding the cultural policy context and state of the arts in these cultural practices (local knowledge). Furthermore, such training processes need to be safeguarded from attempts of promotion of the Global North. In the Global South, we tend to embrace policy themes emanating from the Global North because of the resources attached to these. This means that none of the training programmes should be developed without proper local research. Involvement of local researchers and trainers would clearly make a difference within the training content from one country to another. Even if it counts as a type of 'world' research (like the recent British Council research of training skills), it cannot be implemented without changes in every country, as many questions would be inappropriate or understood completely differently in different contexts.

Conclusion

In this chapter, we tried to understand the reasons for the proliferation of ad hoc and short arts and cultural management training programmes offered to MENA countries. We considered how these programmes are situated in between political, humanitarian and cultural diplomacy agendas. The research has shown that, in spite of the diversity offered, the impact of capacity-building training programmes was low due to the following factors. For one, methods are being taught as transferrable without acknowledgement and responsiveness to specific local conditions, socio-cultural and political contexts or local needs. Secondly, training programmes are often developed without proper local partners. As a result, they are not likely to contribute to the evaluation and development of local knowledge in the long term.

Despite these problems, training has been justified among donors mostly by way of economic arguments: by the support they give to professionals to be able to raise funds, widen markets, achieve sustainability of their organizations, raise employment in creative sectors and by their contribution to the GDP of their countries. An additional issue is that these arguments remain favourable to public authorities of Western countries, even if they do not resonate in environments that lack transparent cultural policies and market mechanisms. Cultural policy and management training experts, who often lack knowledge and insights related to the cultural domain in MENA countries and are seemingly unable to take account of nationally specific cultural policies, legislation and financing systems (Dragićević-Šešić 2010), are currently designing capacity-building formats and training that mostly enhance technical skills that may be only partially applicable, and mostly when Arabic cultural operators appear on international collaborative funding schemes, such as the ones indicated by Jhunjhunwala and Walker (this volume). There is, thus, a crucial issue that must be discussed within organisations involved in Global North technical assistance and aid—namely, the importance of critical reflection and articulation of the professional position of educators and trainers working in the framework of Western TAMs. When neoliberal developmental discourse impregnates foreign policies, is it possible for the trainers and educators to take a critical position towards these policies, and to fully respect local knowledge and context when they are operative? Most TAMs as a part of developmental aid programmes and soft power tools are using a new vocabulary and propagating a neoliberal approach to cultural development. These tend to be envisioned through statements which allege that creative industries are creating jobs, bringing economic values, multiplying social effects, raising social capital and promoting copyright-based industries. However, these points do not fully translate to MENA countries, where the nature of the job market in the cultural sphere is extremely precarious and there are no active employment policies in any of the MENA countries that relate to the cultural realm except in a few domains, like film and music industry.

Finally, a question remains as to who is ultimately profiting from these raised competences. MENA cultural managers might be able to communicate with their Global North colleagues, but they have become importers more than exporters of cultural values and goods. Does this contribute to cultural development or more to an economy of spectacle, mass tourism, events and entertainment? Is the art market with its speculative 'transfers' the real aim of this education? Such questions further raise the importance of training and education in the MENA region that focuses on critical reflections, equal partnerships, local practices, inspiring and motivating self-generated visions, networking and governance models.

Note

1. Cultural mediation is a term that has integrated socio-cultural animation in French cultural policy and practice; it refers to a wide scope of activities which are mostly related to different forms of raising accessibility, participation, interpretation and the promotion of artistic and cultural practices.

References

Akademia (University Magazine). n. 24/2013. Manouba University, Tunisia, p. 17.
Al Mawred. (2014). *Feasibility research on establishing an MA programme in cultural policy and cultural management in the Arab region.* Cairo: Al Mawred.

Ali, A. (1995). Cultural discontinuity and Arab management thought. *International Studies of Management and Organisations, 25*(3), 7–123. Abington: Taylor & Francis.

Arab Culture Fund. (2007). Retrieved August 31, 2018, from https://www.arabculturefund.org/

Berre, N., & Høyum, F. N. (2015). Forms of Freedom. African independence and Nordic models. The National Museum of Art, Architecture and Design, Norway. Retrieved January 13, 2017, from http://nasjonalmuseet.no/Forms +of+Freedom.+African+Independence+and+Nordic+Models.b7C_ wlfG5o.ips

Boekmanstudies. (2010). *Cultural policies in Algeria, Egypt, Jordan, Lebanon, Morocco, Palestine, Syria and Tunisia: An introduction*. Amsterdam: Culture Resource (Al Mawred Al Thaqafy), the European Cultural Foundation, Boekmanstudies.

British Council. (2017). *Corporate Plan 2017–20*. Retrieved April 21, 2017, from https://www.britishcouncil.org/sites/default/files/corporate-plan-2017-20.pdf

Cultural Innovators Network. (2018). *Who we are*. Retrieved February 21, 2019, from http://culturalinnovators.org/about-us/

Dietachmair, P., & Ilić, M. (2015). Another Europe, capacity building programmes in the EU neighbourhood, 1999–2014. In *European Cultural Foundation: Tandem—Cultural managers exchange* (pp. 162–173). Amsterdam: European Cultural Foundation.

Dragićević-Šešić, M. (2010). Opening horizons: The need for integrated cultural policies in the Arab world. In *Cultural policies in Algeria, Egypt, Jordan, Lebanon, Morocco, Palestine, Syria and Tunisia, an introduction* (pp. 227–261). Amsterdam: Boekmanstudies.

Dragićević-Šešić, M. (2015a). Arabic spring and the work of cultural policy groups—A bottom-up cultural policy. *Journal of the Institute of Theatre, Film, Radio and Television, n. 28*, 217–242. Belgrade: Institute of Faculty of Dramatic Arts.

Dragićević-Šešić, M. (2015b). *The Abarra program evaluation: Executive summary*. Amsterdam: Al Mawred and European Cultural Foundation.

Dragićević-Šešić, M., Mihaljinac, N., & El Amine Moumine, M. (2016). *Thematic study: Higher education and training in cultural management and cultural policies in Southern Mediterranean countries*. Brussels: Med-Culture Programme. Retrieved March 15, 2018, from https://www.medculture.eu/library/thematic-studies/higher-education-and-training-cultural-management-and-cultural-policies

ENCPG. (2012). The Egyptian National Cultural Policy Group 2012—Proposal for a general framework for a new cultural policy in Egypt. The People's Assembly Culture, Media and Tourism Committee.

Escobar, A. (1995). *Encountering development: The making and unmaking of the third world*. Princeton, NJ: Princeton University Press.

Esteva, G., Babones, S., & Babcicky, P. (2013). *The future of development: A radical manifesto*. Bristol: Policy Press.

Ettijahat, ECF, & Al Mawred. (2013). Current developments of cultural policies in the Arab Region. Retrieved March 15, 2019, from http://mawred.org/wordpress1/wp-content/uploads/2013/10/Cultural-Policies-3rd-Report-Jan.-2013-to-June-30.-2013.pdf

EUNIC. (2013). Pan-Arab postgraduate qualification in cultural management—A feasibility study. Retrieved August 31, 2018, from http://egypt.eunic-online.eu/?q=content/pan-arab-postgraduate-qualification-cultural-management-feasibility-study-eunic-egypt

Euroculture. (2004). Rencontres européenes et méditerranéens. Retrieved June 12, 2018, from https://euroculture.wordpress.com/que-fait-on/education-artistique/

European Commission. (2014). *The creative Europe programme*. Retrieved June 12, 2018, from https://ec.europa.eu/programmes/creative-europe/node_en

Freud, S. (1930). *Civilization and its discontents* (pp. 57–146). SE, Volume XXI. London: Hogarth.

Hampel, A. (2017). *Fair cooperation*. Bruxelles: PIE Peter Lang.

Henze, R. (2017). *Introduction to international arts management*. Wiesbaden: Springer VS.

Khalaf, S. (2001). *Cultural resistance: Global and local encounters in the Middle East*. London: Saqi Books.

Klesse, A. (2015). *Evaluation report: The MENA/European training in culture and creative sector management 2014/2015*. Brussels: Marcel Hicter.

Moïsi, D. (2010). *Geopolitics of emotion: How cultures of fear, humiliation, and hope are reshaping the world*. New York: Anchor Books.

Nye, J. (2004). *Soft power: The means to success in world politics*. Retrieved December 25, 2018, from https://www.belfercenter.org/sites/default/files/legacy/files/joe_nye_wielding_soft_power.pdf

Ranaweera Banda, R. M. (2004). Development discourse and the third world. Retrieved March 17, 2017, from http://www.ruh.ac.lk/research/academic_sessions/2004_mergepdf/98-103.PDF

Sachs, W. (1992). *The development reader. A guide to knowledge and power*. London: Zed Books.

Said, E. (1978). *Orientalism*. New York: Pantheon.

Shome, R. (2012). Introduction. In *Asian modernities: Culture, politics and media* (pp. 199–214). London: Sage.

SIDA. (2014). Results strategy for special initiatives for human rights and democratisation for the period 2014–2017. Retrieved December 25, 2018, from https://si.se/app/uploads/2017/10/results-strategy-for-special-initia-tives-20142017.pdf

Turner, B. (1978). *Marx and the end of orientalism*. New York: Routledge.

UNESCO. (2005). *Convention on the protection and promotion of the diversity of cultural expressions*. Paris: UNESCO.

UNESCO. (2010). *International fund for cultural diversity*. Retrieved June 12, 2018, from https://en.unesco.org/creativity/ifcd

UNESCO. (2012). *Mediterranean Living Heritage (MedLiHer)*. Retrieved June 12, 2018, from https://ich.unesco.org/en/medliher

United Nations. (2000). United Nations millennium declaration. Retrieved December 25, 2018, from http://www.un.org/millennium/declaration/ares552e.pdf

United Nations Development Programme (UNDP). (2015). Retrieved December 25, 2018, from https://www.undp.org/content/dam/undp/library/corporate/brochure/SDGs_Booklet_Web_En.pdf

Van Graan, M. (2016). Theatre, theatre festivals and cultural diplomacy. In M. Dragićević-Šešić (Ed.), *Cultural diplomacy: Arts, festivals and geopolitics* (pp. 185–192). Belgrade: Creative Europe Desk Serbia and Faculty of Dramatic Arts.

Van Graan, M. (2018). The EBBS and flows of arts and culture policy: The South-Africa experience. In M. Dragićević-Šešić & J. Vickery (Eds.), *Cultural policy and populism. Cultural policy yearbook 2017–18* (pp. 68–74). Istanbul: Iletisim.

10

'Silence is Golden': Cultural Collision in the Classroom

Melissa Nisbett

Introduction

British universities are key players in the global education marketplace. Since the 1990s, the UK has seen a rapid rise in the internationalisation of the higher education sector, alongside much of the Western world. China, in particular, presents unparalleled opportunities for market growth. Despite Chinese universities encouraging inward mobility by offering scholarships, courses in English and lower tuition fees (Stokes, 2017), Chinese learners continue to travel abroad. The numbers of Chinese students in the UK far outstrips any other nationality. The Higher Education Statistics Agency reports show that 95,090 Chinese learners studied in the UK in 2016–2017 (HESA, n.d.), which demonstrated a 14% rise since 2013. There have not been significant increases in numbers from any other country. According to former government minister David Willetts, British universities offer a 'service' like any other

M. Nisbett (✉)
King's College London, London, UK
e-mail: Melissa.nisbett@kcl.ac.uk

© The Author(s) 2020
V. Durrer, R. Henze (eds.), *Managing Culture*, Sociology of the Arts,
https://doi.org/10.1007/978-3-030-24646-4_10

sector and this service accounts for the second largest export to China after the motor industry (BBC, 2015).

Despite my university being the fifth largest recruiter of international students in the UK (HESA, n.d.) and Chinese learners forming the largest group of international students, it currently holds only 1.5% of the market share and plans to expand this over the next five years. Each year, I work with a new cohort of 200 postgraduate students from over 50 countries. There is a normative belief within my department and institution that diversity enhances the quality and richness of the teaching and learning experience. Indeed part of our reputation, popularity and appeal rests on this assumption. At the same time, research has consistently shown that increased internationalisation presents a range of pedagogical challenges, especially in relation to Chinese students. These concerns are well documented and challenges include classroom marginalization and clashing learning styles (see Gu & Maley, 2008; Knight, 2011; Parris-Kidd & Barnett, 2011; Stanley, 2011; Zhou, Topping, & Jindal-Snape, 2011). A recent survey undertaken by the Higher Education Policy Institute revealed that only 36% of domestic students felt that they benefitted from studying alongside international students. A further 32% were neutral and 32% didn't see any benefits (Stokes, 2017). So despite the ideological aspirations around diversity, not to mention the economic targets from international recruitment, research continues to show that internationalisation can lead to tensions in the classroom. This chapter explores the impact of international diversity on educational experience and understanding.

Whilst I have witnessed and experienced the challenges of internationalisation first-hand, I had little understanding of their origins, constituent parts or driving forces. This lack of knowledge led me to develop a research project to explore the impact of internationally based cultural diversity on teaching and learning, and how it played out in the context of the classroom on a postgraduate cultural industries programme. Through exploring the student and staff experience, it was hoped that diversity could be better understood and even harnessed as a teaching resource.

I set up a project team consisting of a small group of postgraduate students. I was particularly struck by a comment that one of the students made during our initial discussions. She was surprised that whilst there seemed to be widespread recognition of the pedagogical challenges created by internationalisation, they were largely unspoken about by both staff and students:

It's ironic that we are on the cultural industries masters, yet there is a taboo when it comes to talking about culture and ethnicity.

After four months of data collection and analysis, the research revealed that both staff and students had unwittingly contributed to these difficulties: staff through their teaching and pastoral care duties, and students through their behaviours and attitudes inside and outside of the classroom. The research showed that we were all implicated not only in the dynamics that created these tensions but also in the collective lack of understanding required to address such challenges. This chapter tells the story of the research, shares a selection of empirical data, engages with the relevant literatures and offers some learning points.

Methodology

Whilst there are many aspects to 'diversity', this project concentrated on nationality. Although the importance of intersectionality[1] was noted, the size of the project and its budgetary restrictions meant that the research had to be tightly framed and the scope kept narrow. The research involved 15 semi-structured, qualitative interviews. A purposeful sampling technique was used to select ten students and five academics for interview. The scholars had a breadth of experience, from newcomers to those who had been at the university for over a decade. The students who participated in the research were from Russia, Chile, Germany, Spain, the United States of America, China (x2), Hungary, Britain and Japan. They were all based in London and studying on a 12-month long cultural industries postgraduate programme. They were chosen on the basis of their nationalities in order to provide geographical spread and cultural breadth, and as students who had already showed an interest in issues of internationalisation. A further five students were selected to assist me in collecting and analysing the data. They were from China, Vietnam, France, the United States and India. They were paid for their labour and were chosen via an application process. I actively invited the students to become my peers. The rationale for this was twofold. As this was the first research that they had conducted, this project contributed to their intellectual development and formed a useful learning experience for their dissertations that would begin several months later. Secondly, I wanted students to be involved because they are implicated in classroom dynamics. I was keen to hear their views and interpretations of the data and how these insights were informed by their classroom experience. This helped me to see things that I would not have been able to otherwise (Warren, 2011). There was a genuine sense of exchange and of learning together and from each other. Whilst this project was not conducted as a formal autoethnography, there was a great deal of 'reflexive accounting' (Altheide & Johnson, 1994, p. 585), where my role as a teacher was at the centre of the sense making process. I constantly reflected upon my teaching philosophy, my observations of others' pedagogic practice and my own experience in the classroom. Like Warren in his pursuit of a 'reflexive pedagogy' (2011, p. 140), this project was very much an exercise in self-reflection and self-awareness, which saw the classroom as 'a productive site for critical investigation' (2011, p. 141) that was 'open to critical dialogue' (2011, p. 141). This tendency was encouraged amongst the whole research team.

We decided as a team that our Chinese and Vietnamese researchers would interview the Asian participants, as we felt that our interviewees may open up more and that the interviewers would be familiar with particular cultural codes that others may miss or misinterpret. Whilst this project did not set out to be a study of Chinese learners, the experience of the Chinese students and the feelings towards them by other students dominated the research. As will become clear from this chapter, the Chinese students became a central strand of the research. This emphasis was perhaps to be expected since 45% of our cohort is Chinese. I am based within a culture and creative industries department, and the creative sectors in China are growing at a rate unseen anywhere else in the world. *The Economist* (2013) reported that 451 new museums opened across China in 2012 alone, compared to 20–40 museums built annually in the USA from 1998 to 2008. Qualified and trained professionals are urgently required. As my Chinese students have explained to me, post-graduate degrees in China take three years to complete and cost the equivalent of studying for a one-year programme in London, so doing a degree at a prestigious institution in the UK is not only highly desirable but entirely feasible, especially in light of a thriving Chinese economy with a growing middle class.

We used thematic analysis as a means to analyse the data, which involves identifying recurring themes and patterns, and analysing them in their context (Braun & Clarke, 2006). Also known as 'qualitative content analysis', thematic analysis derives from Grounded Theory (Glaser & Strauss, 1967), which means that theory is constructed through an engagement with the data and through an inductive approach, and not posited or hypothesised in advance of the data collection. For a comprehensive description of the method, see Braun and Clarke (2006). In the following sections, I examine the themes that emerged from the data, and bring in the literature to explore these in more depth.

Data, Analysis and Discussion

Cultural Difference

A key theme that emerged from the interviews focused on the lack of participation in seminars by Chinese students. All of our interviewees raised this and the conversations were often contentious. The Chinese students felt the need to explain the reasons for the lack of participation and even justify it. They were frequently apologetic in tone, in contrast to the non-Asian participants, who expressed irritation. For example, a European student remarked 'if you don't participate, everybody is disadvantaged'. Although there are some issues around confidence, particularly in relation to language ability, there is also an underlying factor at the root of this, which centres on cultural difference. Chinese students come from a markedly different educational background, which does not feature seminars or a culture of open debate. Chinese students see their tutors as the definitive source of knowledge. They are not encouraged to interrogate, critique or challenge what they learn, as is commonplace in the UK. I teach on courses where students are expected to independently explore and appraise topics, and engage with questions that do not have clear-cut answers. In contrast, the focus in China is on memorisation and learning by rote, which is connected to Confucianism. It is seen as an important process of deep learning, which involves practice, review and reflection. It is a technique that is used in conjunction with a range of other strategies (Li & Cutting, 2011; Watkins & Biggs, 1996) as a prelude to deeper understanding, rather than an end in itself (Kennedy, 2002). In the UK, this is often mistakenly viewed simplistically as shallow, superficial and even 'foolish' (Luk & Lin, 2007, p. 17), as merely remembering without learning. This attitude captures what Cortazzi and Jin identify as different 'cultures of learning', which are

> *taken-for-granted frameworks of expectations, values, attitudes and beliefs about what constitutes good learning.* (1996, p. 169)

These frameworks include how to teach and learn, whether and how to ask questions, and so on. It is these differing approaches that result in what Griffiths, Winstanley, and Gabriel (2005) term 'learning shock', which is an emotional experience tied to learning that can cause anxiety, confusion, disorientation and frustration. Like culture shock, it results from the removal of familiar cues, cultural norms and expectations, and requires a process of adjustment and adaptation in order to understand a new environment.

So participation in class is not straightforward. The Asian interviewees discussed their reluctance to participate in class, and were aware of the other students' frustrations. This extract is taken from an interview between our Chinese researcher and a Japanese student:

> Interviewee: *Western students have a critical thinking style … they are trained for discussion or debate … because their education system requires them to be more expressive … to express their own opinion … this is the way they run things, but in my country it's not … standing out is not a good thing …*
> Interviewer: *The philosophy … I understand. The person who stands out will be treated as the target …*

Interviewee: *A target, or people think of them as annoying …*
Interviewer: *Or showing off …*
Interviewee: *Showing off or selfish or something like that …*

One of the Chinese participants captured this perfectly: '*in China, silence is golden*'. Both of the Chinese interviewees discussed this further:

I can't think while talking like the others … I need my own space, my own time, quietly, to read and to think.
    I don't participate … because … sometimes when I want to speak, I just can't interrupt others … when they're talking … I don't think it's responsible to just speak it out if something occurs to me … I hope to get other information and analyse it and when I have my own conclusion … then I'm able to introduce it to others … Most people who do not participate are Chinese and it's related to the culture.

In Confucian heritage, a mastery over the material is emphasised and silence is highly valued (Lees, 2013). Both students and staff did not understand that there was an active decision not to participate, which was related to cultural preference. Non-Asian students saw the lack of participation in seminars as wholly negative. It prompted a variety of responses, from confusion to condescension.

In the seminars, the Chinese students don't participate. Is it that they just don't care? Why not? Is it possible to do anything to make them care? But then who should do it? Not me, I am a student, but I care and I want to make it work.
    I don't really blame the East Asians. In general we feel indifferent to people who don't engage. I don't develop any form of xenophobic feelings. It's sad.

These comments are not unusual. I have a vivid memory of a Canadian student who came to see me a few years ago, to tell me, in frustration, that '*we've decided that if they're not going to speak, then we're not going to make them speak!*' Ironically, she was studying an introductory module exploring the central question 'what is culture?' Similarly, in some recent student feedback, I observed the following comment:

A prevailing part of the classroom community is Chinese people and many of them either pretend they don't speak English or don't want to contribute to the discussion. It made this module less useful.

Non-participation was repeatedly mistaken for a lack of engagement, willingness or interest. Implicit within this is also the perception that students who participate the most, such as those from North America or Europe, make a bigger contribution. This replicates Lo's findings (2019), where the quiet behaviour of Chinese students in Canada was deemed unintelligent. This cultural relativism is unfortunately not uncommon. We operate within our own cultural frame of reference. In my experience, even within postgraduate courses at top universities, students can be strikingly unaware of their own cultural biases. We can be fairly ethnocentric in our views, often seeing our culturally influenced assumptions, values, beliefs and attitudes as 'normal', even superior. Ironically, the classroom is the perfect place to explore such assumptions. Students often come to learn that they are the products of their own culture, which can come as a shock, and that no culture is inherently better or worse than any other or should come to dominate.

To add further complexity, some staff members also saw this as a straightforward intellectual problem:

We need to have students who are equally prepared, equally able in terms of language and motivation, so that a seminar is a seminar, rather than me trying to play catch up … It's an unnecessary challenge for teaching … We have such an ability range in our classrooms that you can't presume that there is an 'equal' because there isn't … and, of course, if you teach the lowest common denominator, you overlook the best … I try to get around it as best I can but I'm leaving some of the better students behind because I'm having to make sure that the worst ones 'get it'.

As with any cohort, there is inevitably variation within academic ability, but the lack of seminar participation in this case was misunderstood as being simply about aptitude. As the interview data and literature reveal, this is not merely a case of some students 'getting it' and others not, or a lack of preparation, interest or motivation. All of this points to a lack of 'intercultural understanding', which is defined as having the knowledge, appreciation, attitudes, skills and behaviours to 'interact effectively and appropriately with people from other cultures' (Perry & Southwell, 2011, p. 455).

This situation was further exacerbated by differences in cultural capital (Bourdieu, 1984) between the Chinese and non-Chinese students. Our Vietnamese researcher discussed the global media restrictions that prevent Chinese students from being able to access particular Western academic materials in advance. In contrast, the European and North American students tend to be more familiar with the continental critical theory that forms the backbone of the taught programmes in which many international students come to study, often having encountered it at undergraduate level. Lo's research (2019) looks at cultural capital more closely. Pierre Bourdieu's project on the tastes and preferences of the French bourgeoisie (1984) has been criticised for focusing on class whilst overlooking gender and ethnicity, and thus neglecting intersectionality. Lo extends Bourdieu's theory to 'race', coining the term 'white capital' to explain white cultural norms in the classroom and how 'whiteness' comes to dominate. For Lo, whiteness is a form of power that is privileged within everyday interactions and reproduced in unconscious, unspoken, subtle and intangible ways, which sets a normative standard for patterns of behaviour. 'Whiteness' is automatically perceived as a 'normative and universal condition' (Rich, 1979 in Moon, 1998, p. 178) so the attendant power dynamics remain unrecognised (Frankenburg, 1993 in Moon, 1998), in turn, bolstering the position of white students in the classroom, as 'white behaviour' implicitly indicates intelligence and further marginalises Chinese students.

Integration and Cohesion

Naturally, the issues discussed so far have an impact on socialisation, integration and cohesion amongst the students. The majority of the interviewees discussed the lack of integration between Chinese students and other nationalities, even integration with other Asian students. There seemed to be a mutual rejection, which is difficult to articulate without appearing to essentialise. As with the issue of classroom interaction, the Chinese students were well aware of this. One Chinese learner explained her pragmatic reasons for not socialising:

> *I don't care about socialising ... we don't live together, we don't have class together. I can't see any reason that we would just hang out ... in China, I obey the natural process ... it's more natural to speak Chinese ... it's not natural to speak English.*

Our Vietnamese researcher suggested that because of the geographical distance between China and Europe/North America, and its historical isolation, there is an assumption that you will never see your classmates again, which can have an impact on cultivating friendships. Another Chinese participant confirmed this:

> *Even if you feel a connection with these people in London, you would hardly have a chance to meet them again in the future ... it hurts, actually, because you see people going by ... but what's the point of wasting time making friends ... there's no point ... we might never meet foreign friends again.*

For some Chinese students, there is enough diversity within China itself to experience a genuine cultural exchange during postgraduate study in another country:

> *Even if we are all from China, we come from different parts, so we're still going to think differently ... China is so big and people from the north and the south have totally different ideas.*

In addition, forming connections with those we see as being like ourselves is a natural response to experiencing another culture. Yet this can be at odds with the impulse of many academics, who, with the best intentions, encourage students to interact outside their national groups. This reveals a limited understanding and says more about their own approach, values and cultural norms around the foregrounding of independence in a purely intellectual sense.

Bochner (1977, p. 292) argues that bonds between students from the same country are vitally important and should not be 'administratively interfered with, regulated against, obstructed, or sneered at'.. Yet this is at odds with a normative bias in the literature, especially within earlier work. Adler (1975, p. 17), for example, describes the tendency for students to gravitate towards others of their own culture as 'regressive'. Whilst I haven't witnessed attempts to prevent the formation of these relationships, I have observed colleagues criticising the impulse of students who seek out others from the same country. This perhaps demonstrates a limited 'intercultural competence' amongst academic staff, which Byram, Nichols, and Stevens (2001) describe as the

> ability to interact with 'others', to accept other perspectives and perceptions of the world, to mediate between different perspectives, to be conscious of their evaluations of difference. (p. 5)

As teachers, we need a better understanding of these emotional and cultural complexities, as well as a more developed intercultural competence. Lewthwaite (1996) found that the greatest block for international students to adapt to their new cultures was a lack of intercultural communicative competence. There is a need for both students and staff to develop this skill, regardless of nationality. Yet for the European, South American and North American students, the responsibility seemed to be firmly placed with the Chinese students, who were solely blamed for the poor integration. As with the seminar participation, the Chinese students were seen to be at the root of the problem, as this interview extract reveals:

Asian people tend to be quiet but I don't think it's language difficulties and not even the fact that they're shy … they don't want to participate and sometimes when you are put with a group of Chinese people, you're excluded, they don't interact with you … they don't help. I didn't have a very good experience. You're excluded and they start talking Chinese … of course it's more comfortable for them but it's not helping the interaction.

This lack of integration is discussed in the literature, although it is presented benignly and from the opposite perspective, with the Chinese learners providing vital support to each other (see Zhou et al., 2011). As with the interviewee's comments, this viewpoint fails to get at the cultural complexity and doesn't tackle the issue of division. I am all too familiar with scanning the classroom and seeing students sitting in their national groups, as are my colleagues, one of whom told the following anecdote:

> *A European white student comes into the classroom … there were three groups of students. One group consisted of white students and two groups consisted of Chinese and other Asian students. The non-European, non-white groups were closer to the door. But she looked at the classroom and then went around the other two groups to the white group. The people in the two other groups saw it … it was very obvious. That was disappointing, but that was her choice.*

Another colleague spoke of her ethical dilemma when three European students requested to move to another seminar group because they were the only non-Chinese students. They were unhappy that they were in seminar groups dominated by Chinese students in the previous term and had been the only ones to participate in discussions, and were dissatisfied with the lack of critical debate.

Many interviewees felt the Chinese culture was not globally inclusive, even though most had not fully grasped the underlying cultural difference. Chinese students were also compared with Korean, Japanese and Taiwanese learners, who were perceived to be more sociable and outgoing, more participatory in class, more academically critical and less inward-looking. Whilst this ethnic stereotyping and essentialism is problematic, these accounts nevertheless provide an insight into students' perceptions.

The need to cleave to one's own culture and/or the rejection of the new culture is a plausible and rational response to learning and/or culture shock, especially if the new culture is deemed to be at odds with the 'host' culture, as in the case of this study. According to one of Gu's participants (2005), successful study in the UK requires Chinese students to 'enjoy loneliness', which is a saddening indictment of the British Higher Education sector.

Cultural Adaptation

This leads to the question of what can be done in order to create a more satisfying learning experience for all. How can greater participation, integration and understanding be encouraged and cultivated? Should tutors adapt their pedagogical approach to suit these different cultures? And what might that look like in a cohort where over 50 countries are represented? Should the Chinese learners adapt, since they are choosing to study in the UK? Should the non-Chinese students adapt, since they are the minority in the department? Should all students adapt, since they come to London for a multicultural experience and such diversity reflects an increasingly intercultural workforce and globalised world more broadly?

There is an impulse within my department for academics to be more inclusive and attempt to adapt, but there is no consensus around best practice. For example, one popular strategy for encouraging Chinese students to participate has been to ask the class to reflect upon and share their personal experience, in reference to the topic being discussed. One colleague remarked:

Because I'm aware of diversity and want to encourage everybody to speak … and feel that they're entitled to speak, I encourage people to talk about their perspective … It puts students in the position of being expert in their home culture. It allows them to feel confident in what they're saying and it is educational for others … Some of it will include insightful analysis. Some of it will not. I'm loathe to shut people down, particularly if they don't talk very much. I'd rather people said <u>something</u>, even if it wasn't the most sparkling and enlightening comment … I want them to feel that they are making a valuable contribution to the class discussion. I'm also aware that by being inclusive, I'm in some ways 'othering' … it's a thin line between encouraging inclusion and exoticising.

Many colleagues have adopted this approach, yet it is not without problems. Whilst it is a well-intentioned gesture, it can lead to superficial conversations. Moreover, it can prove unpopular with other students, as it can lead to seminars centring on personal anecdotes, which diverts attention away from theoretical discussions:

> *It's fine to share experiences of your national background, but this should be five or ten minutes … I don't give a shit about twenty different national examples … I was not interested in sharing my experience because it felt redundant … the fifteenth national personal experience on top of the fourteen other experiences!*

One of the Chinese participants shared a similar opinion on this. She was not interested in hearing the personal experiences of her classmates because 'it's not something that I can use in my studies'. So these students disregard what is intended to be an inclusive gesture.

Some of the literature argues that students from a culture different to that of their institution should adjust and adapt to their new situation, and that this should take precedence over a developmental shift for everyone (Oberg, 1960; Adler, 1975; Furnham, 2004). So according to these accounts, it is the Chinese students who should adapt as they assimilate into the dominant culture as set by the organisation. Gu and Maley's work (2008) suggests that whilst the Chinese students struggle culturally, they are willing to change and they can succeed in adopting a different way of life and process of learning. Hall's (1976, p. 42) notion of 'hidden cultures' states:

> these habitual responses, these ways of interacting, gradually sink below the surface of the mind and … control from the depths. The hidden controls are … experienced as though they were innate … What makes it doubly hard to differentiate the innate from the acquired is the fact that, as people grow up, everyone around them shares the same patterns.

In other words, particular behaviours are embedded and become habitual through repetition over time (see Oberg, 1960 for a similar account). Whilst Gu and Maley (2008) challenge the view that culture is innate, their work neglects the structural factors within the classroom, such as the power dynamics described in this article. In line with the literature more generally, they do not get at the precise details of what happens when international students adapt in order to learn and live in the UK. Moreover, if people succumb to a process of cultural inculcation that accrues and deepens over years, then dismantling these beliefs and patterns of behaviour presumably happens over time? Yet it is presented in the literature simply as learning another way of being and doing. This process would need to happen quickly and efficiently within a typical British 12-month postgraduate programme.

Whilst some Chinese learners may seek to better understand British culture, the average British academic, in turn, tends to know very little about Chinese culture and, in my experience, can show scant interest, curiosity or willingness to learn. I find this especially troubling in a department that studies culture and society. It seems ironic to teach students about culture and cultural difference theoretically but fail to accommodate its manifestation in practice. In addition, some colleagues, especially those with longer careers and who are more experienced, view the internationalisation of higher education as a further neoliberal assault, which is detrimental to the education sector and must be resisted. Adaptation is simply seen as capitulation.

Whilst there is a normative assumption throughout the university that integration should and will take place, there is little discussion of its practical or ethical dimensions. The literature is inconsistent on the impact of the transitions made by Chinese students. Whilst the earlier publications tell a positive narrative around personal journeys of transformation (see, e.g. Adler, 1975; Anderson, 1994; Byrnes, 1965), more recently, there have been descriptions of the stress and anxiety caused by overseas study (Cushner & Karim, 2004; Gu, 2012). Gu, Schweisfurth and Day (2008) see the process of transition as a part of natural growth and maturity, and that Chinese students have two sets of values: one for the UK and another for China. This suggests a dual identity that can be summoned or performed at will, yet there is scant detail on this notion of duality and no body of evidence. There is also an assumption across this literature that everyone should aspire to experience this type of personal transformation (Tishman, Jay, & Perkins, 1993). Boyle and Boice (1998, p. 87) straightforwardly refer to this as 'cultural learning', whilst others emphasise the development of new skills, such as critical thinking, independence, flexibility and open-mindedness (Adler, 1975; Gu et al., 2008; Gu, 2012). Even those who acknowledge difficulties along the way see these as part of a transformative learning experience that is wholly positive (Griffiths et al., 2005). Whilst phrases such as 'reborn' (Anderson, 1994, p. 321), 'personal expansion' (Murphy-Lejeune, 2003, p. 113) and 'rebirth' (Gu, 2011, p. 223) are repeatedly used, remarkably little detail is provided on the actual process and there is a dearth of empirical data on the students' perspectives.

Gu's research suggests, then, that culture is not deterministic in this sense, but it is something that can change and be learned. Presumably, this interpretation also means that it can be unlearned. Griffiths et al. see the process as 'the undoing of earlier learning' (2005, p. 275), similarly expressed by Anderson as 'making the familiar unfamiliar' (1994, p. 297). Yet within institutions, there seems to be no recognition of this 'undoing', 'unlearning' or 'unfamiliarising'. There is very little guidance from my university, and conversations amongst academics are confined to interested minorities who personally struggle with the pedagogical challenges. Although it remains unspoken, the Chinese students are expected to adapt, to do so quickly and largely on their own, in line with the self-directed and independent learning that is expected and encouraged in a top British university. Yet according to Griffiths et al. (2005), this is a process that involves the radical reconstruction of identity, which includes elements of crisis, despair and paralysis in the classroom. They see the learning process as going beyond cognition, encompassing an emotional, as well as an intellectual, response. If we accept that we can change our cultural norms and, as Anderson (1994, p. 297) states, this is a process of 'accepting the unfamiliar, accepting the uprooting and alien values, and the loss of loved objects and people', then it follows that this is a complex and difficult procedure. This is not merely a process of dropping one learning style and picking up another, as is assumed both in the literature and amongst colleagues within my university. We are seeking a rapid retraining of the brain, which involves replacing an everyday set of behaviours, values and actions with another that may be alien, contrasting or even in opposition—a far cry from Hall's (1976) long and slow process of habitual patterning.

For many postgraduate students, this could mean temporarily or permanently adopting different values to replace those that have been learnt for the first twenty years of their lives. We are implicitly asking for profound change at the deepest level—a complex process of psychological and sociocultural readjustment that may be difficult, unsettling, disorientating and uncomfortable. Institutional support is obviously crucial, yet this is an aspect of learning that I have never heard discussed or even mentioned at a managerial level. Furthermore, it raises the question of how easy or difficult it might be to learn new cultural reference points at the same time as unlearning and possibly abandoning old ones in a short period of time. If students are forced to confront and shift their cultural and social norms, ideas and behaviours, and they largely rely on themselves to thrive, there must be great determination, flexibility and resilience at play. More nuanced accounts of this complexity both theoretically and empirically, and from the perspective of both the students and institutions is needed, instead of the glossy version provided in the literature, where the summative result eclipses the formative process.

Institutions are implicitly assuming and expecting that 'acculturation' takes place. Kim and Abreu (2001) describe this as 'the process of adapting to the norms of the dominant group' (cited in Kim & Omizo, 2006, p. 246), as opposed to 'enculturation', the process of retaining the norms of the 'indigenous' group (Kim & Omizo, 2006). There has been some progress within the discipline of psychology in relation to how we understand these terms. Berry, Kim, Power, Young, and Bajaki (1989) theorised four distinct states:

1. *Integration*: individuals are proficient in the culture of both the dominant and indigenous group. Acculturation and enculturation ('biculturalism') take place.
2. *Assimilation*: individuals assimilate the culture of the dominant group but reject the indigenous culture. Acculturation occurs but enculturation does not.
3. *Separation*: individuals are not interested in the dominant group's culture. They seek to maintain and perpetuate their original culture. Enculturation is present, but not acculturation.

4. *Marginalization*: individuals have no interest in either dominant or indigenous cultures. No acculturation or enculturation.

Research within psychology posits 'integration' as the best possible scenario (Berry et al., 1989; Gonzales, Knight, Birman, & Sirolli, 2004; Kim & Omizo, 2006), as there is enhanced psychological wellbeing and greater cognitive function amongst those with a high level of engagement with two cultures. Kim and Omizo (2006) tested this amongst Asian American students and positively correlated integration with increased individual and collective self-esteem, cognitive flexibility and self-efficacy (a belief in one's own competency).

Although it provides a useful starting point, Berry et al.'s model is limited. It assumes that cultures are neutral and benign, and that there is no conflict between two distinct cultures. What if the dominant culture is at odds with the indigenous culture? The data in this research project certainly signals some incompatibility. The authors also imply that individuals can simply choose whether or not to integrate, assimilate or separate. This raises questions of agency, especially in an environment like higher education where there are inherent power dynamics already at play. More generally, as with the intercultural relations literature, the acculturation literature from psychology lacks operational detail on the actual processes of change within cultural reformulation, and the emotional and psychological dimensions of these transitions. Implicit within acculturation is a diminution of the significance of one's heritage, yet enculturation is formulated on the basis of a persistent cultural identity.

It is also worth considering what might happen upon completion of the degree. Our Chinese students typically return to their home country to gain employment in the burgeoning creative industries, but also due to cultural and social expectations. Born during the time when China operated its one child policy (which was revoked in 2015), young Chinese students are expected to return home to support ageing parents. Honouring parents is a central tenet within Confucian ideology. This can be very different to our other international students, who often feel frustrated and restricted by the British post-study work visa regulations, which ensure that many students have to leave the country within a few months of finishing their studies. So for Chinese students, there is a rapid process of acculturation, where enculturation may or may not take place, which, after twelve months, they are then required to relearn and assimilate back into their original cultures, in a sort of reverse culture shock. This requires a cultural dexterity that is currently unaccounted for in the literature. Further empirical research is required to properly understand the complexities of this transitional process and the longer-term implications.

The question also remains regarding how to develop an intercultural competence. Byram et al. (2001) explain that this requires knowledge of different cultures and social processes; skills such as comparison, interpretation and interaction; and the cultivation of particular values and attitudes including curiosity and openness. This does not sound unreasonable but the question of *how* is left open. Kramsch (1993) refers to a 'third place', where differing cultures can be observed, which is similarly described by Byram (1997) as the ability to 'decentre'. Forsman (2005) discusses a twofold process of decentring from your own taken-for-granted-ness, before reconstructing someone else's frame of reference. Byram et al.'s edited collection (2001) helpfully features numerous projects designed to engender intercultural competence including the exploration of values, prejudices and stereotypes through fictional literature, tandem learning and the analysis of cultural material from particular countries such as newspapers, poems and music. These innovative teaching approaches require creativity, imagination and effort. The authors see teachers as 'facilitators', yet this assumes that tutors have already obtained the prerequisite intercultural sensibility. Most lecturers have little or no training in how to teach overseas students and there tends to be limited, if any, institutional provision. Moreover, most Chinese students have never had to adjust to an unfamiliar learning style and teaching environment before. It is no surprise that this creates encounters ripe for 'misunderstanding, stress and failure' (Gu & Maley, 2008, p. 227).

Conclusions

This study explored how cultural diversity was understood and experienced both inside and outside of the classroom by staff and students on a creative industries programme at King's College London. The research revealed a number of issues around educational experience and background, cultural capital, philosophical outlook and social integration, all of which pointed to cultural difference. There were considerable misunderstandings by both students and staff. For example, the lack of participation in seminars by Chinese students was the result of an active philosophical choice and cultural preference, underpinned by a thoughtful process of internal decision-making, as students felt caught between two disparate cultures of learning and were thrust into a situation in which they were encouraged to behave in a way that they deemed inappropriate (Parris-Kidd & Barnett, 2011). For academic staff, it can be difficult to distinguish between students that choose not to participate and those unable to participate. The large cohort intensifies this, as academics only become familiar with a small proportion of students. The idea that students would actively consider and choose not to participate was an anathema to the majority of participants. The reluctance to participate in class was misinterpreted as a lack of motivation, effort, interest, willingness or intellectual ability. It was interpreted as poor academic performance. This paints a limited picture of intercultural understanding.

London's multiculturalism and vibrant cultural scene is a key selling point of our department, which centres on the study of culture. Yet in reality, students experienced discomfort caused by a lack of understanding of cultural difference. This led to some intolerance, even resentment. There was an unspoken assumption that if you are in a British institution, you should immediately and automatically subscribe to British educational norms. This research revealed the tensions that result when these norms are perceived to have been violated, for example, by not participating in class discussions. Particular behaviours were unconsciously judged and deemed unacceptable, rather than questioned, grappled with and attempts made to understand. The Chinese student body was singled out as the source of frustration. These assumptions were often unspoken because they were not even recognised. This is a sad irony for a group of people whose interests centre on culture. As a department that offers programmes on the study of culture, we attract and recruit students on this basis, yet there is a limited intercultural understanding at our core.

Within the research, diversity was viewed as a problem and a source of compromise, rather than, in the words of Griffiths et al., as 'gifts and benefits' (2005, p. 293). One colleague explained:

> *It's really tough … it's always imperfect … we're always striving to do better but we're always very aware of where we fall short … If I focus on encouraging one type of discourse and behaviour, it inevitably pushes out another … It's simply not possible to meet all of the students' needs and expectations … We do our best … a lot of the time we're aiming for the best compromise possible … we can't reach an ideal scenario because of the diversity.*

Rather than fully understanding the fundamentals, staff sometimes misdirected their efforts and overcompensated by becoming excessively focused on being inclusive within the confines of the classroom. Diversity is yet to be properly understood, although its importance is acknowledged and genuine attempts are made to cater for and respond to it. In addition, these ongoing negative experiences may actually be erecting barriers to intercultural understanding, rather than dismantling them, as argued by Stanley (2011).

The literature on this topic repeatedly falls short. Whilst the challenges are recognised, they are presented benignly as opportunities for students to attain individual transformation and personal growth. This obscures the reality of what is a difficult process of adjustment. The literature calls for acculturation, potentially disregarding the cultural, social and emotional experience, and places sole responsibility on the students. It also assumes that they will have the necessary cognitive and emotional tools to undergo this largely self-directed process.

This study has shown that staff and students need to develop the knowledge, skills, values and attitudes required to 'decentre'. However, this is something that will take time and needs to be driven by a willingness to change. None of this can be taken for granted. A process of adaptation that is intercultural and integrative is required, in which staff and students can engage with empathy, curiosity and respect, rather than the Chinese students hastily learning the new rules as best they can.

Arguably, it is important for academics to achieve this in order to then foster it within their students. However, responsibility cannot rest solely with academics. Although colleagues share their experiences, there is little formal discussion at an institutional level, despite the challenges being symptoms of increased internationalisation and the continued exploitation of overseas markets. Most universities push for greater internationalisation, yet fail to provide support (or even recognise) the resulting classroom difficulties. Responsibility must rest with institutions, rather than falling on the shoulders of conscientious scholars who care about student welfare, their own pedagogy and the classroom experience, and who navigate these challenges as best they can.

Acknowledgements Thanks go to the Faculty of Arts & Humanities and the Department of Culture, Media and Creative Industries at King's College London for providing the budget for this project. Thank you to the anonymous colleagues and students who participated as interviewees in this study, as well as the students that assisted me with this research: Rashmi Dhanwani, Sebastien Donnadieu, Linh Huynh (Zeo), Lara Longo and Ruiyan Zhu. Final thanks go to Victoria Durrer and Raphaela Henze for their invitation to join the Arts and Humanities Research Council (AHRC) funded international network, *Brokering Intercultural Exchange* (www.manaingculture.net), which explores the role of pedagogy within intercultural understanding and for their editorial work on this chapter.

Note

1. Intersectionality refers to the relationship and interaction between various social and cultural categories that inevitably and unavoidably impact on each other such as gender, sexuality and social class.

References

Adler, P. (1975). The transitional experience: An alternative view of culture shock. *Journal of Humanistic Psychology, 15*(4), 13–23.

Altheide, D. L., & Johnson, J. M. (1994). Criteria for assessing interpretive validity in qualitative research. In N. K. Denzin & Y. S. Lincoln (Eds.), *Handbook of qualitative research* (pp. 485–499). Thousand Oaks, CA: Sage Publications.

Anderson, L. E. (1994). A new look at an old construct: Cross-cultural adaptation. *International Journal of Intercultural Relations, 18*(3), 293–328.

BBC Radio 4. (2015, August 31). *Today Programme*, 6–9 am.

Berry, J. W., Kim, U., Power, S., Young, M., & Bajaki, M. (1989). Acculturation attitudes in plural societies. *Applied Psychology, 38*(2), 185–206.

Bochner, S. (1977). Friendship patterns of overseas students: A functional model. *International Journal of Psychology, 12*(4), 277–294.

Bourdieu, P. (1984). *Distinction*. London: Routledge.

Boyle, P., & Boice, B. (1998). Best practices for enculturation: Collegiality, mentoring, and structure. In M. S. Anderson (Ed.), *The experience of being in graduate school: An exploration. New directions in higher education* (pp. 87–94). San Francisco: Jossey-Bass.

Braun, V., & Clarke, V. (2006). Using *thematic analysis* in psychology. *Qualitative Research in Psychology, 3*(2), 77–101.

Byram, M. (Ed.). (1997). *Face to face: Learning language and culture through visits and exchanges*. London: CILT.

Byram, M., Nichols, A., & Stevens, D. (Eds.). (2001). *Developing intercultural competence in practice*. Clevedon: Multilingual Matters Limited.

Byrnes, F. C. (1965). *Americans in technical assistance: A study of attitudes and responses to their role abroad*. New York: Praeger.

Cortazzi, M., & Jin, L. (1996). Cultures of learning: Language classrooms in China. In H. Coleman (Ed.), *Society and language classroom* (pp. 169–203). Cambridge: Cambridge University Press.

Cushner, K., & Karim, A. (2004). Study abroad at the university level. In D. Landis, J. Bennett, & M. Bennet (Eds.), *Handbook of intercultural training* (pp. 289–308). Thousand Oaks, CA: Sage.

Forsman, L. (2005). The basis for being able to respect the Other. *IATEFL ISSUES* (International Association of Teachers of English as a Foreign Language), February–March, pp. 4–5.

Frankenburg, R. (1993). *White women, race matters: The social construction of whiteness*. Minneapolis: University of Minnesota Press.

Furnham, A. (2004). Foreign students' education and culture shock. *The Psychologist, 17*(1), 16–19.

Glaser, B. G., & Strauss, A. L. (1967). *The discovery of grounded theory: Strategies for qualitative research*. New York: Aldine.

Gonzales, N. A., Knight, G. P., Birman, D., & Sirolli, A. A. (2004). Acculturation and enculturation among Latino youths. In K. I. Maton, C. J. Schellenbach, B. J. Leadbeater, & A. L. Solarz (Eds.), *Investing in children, youth, families, and communities: Strengths-based research and policy* (pp. 285–302). Washington, DC: American Psychological Association.

Griffiths, D. S., Winstanley, D., & Gabriel, Y. (2005). Learning shock: The trauma of return to formal learning. *Management Learning, 36*(3), 275–297.

Gu, Q. (2005). 'Enjoy loneliness': Understanding voices of the Chinese learner. *Humanising Language Teaching, 7*(6). Retrieved September 26, 2016, from http://www.hltmag.co.uk/nov05/mart01.htm

Gu, Q. (2011). An emotional journey of change. In L. Jin & M. Cortazzi (Eds.), *Researching Chinese learners: Skills, perceptions and intercultural adaptations* (pp. 212–232). Basingstoke: Palgrave Macmillan.

Gu, Q. (2012). The impact of study abroad on the student self. *University World News Global Edition*. Issue 206. Retrieved September 6, 2016, from https://www.nottingham.ac.uk/educationresearchprojects/documents/impactchinesereturnees/university-world-news-2012-jan-29.pdf

Gu, Q., & Maley, A. (2008). Changing places: A study of Chinese students in the UK. *Language and Intercultural Communication, 8*(4), 224–245.

Gu, Q., Schweisfurth, M., & Day, C. (2008). *A comparative study of international students' intercultural experiences*. Full Research Report ESRC End of Award Report, RES-000-22-1943. Swindon: ESRC.

Hall, E. (1976). *Beyond culture*. New York: Anchor Books.

Higher Education Statistics Agency. (n.d.). Retrieved July 15, 2018, from https://www.hesa.ac.uk/data-and-analysis

Kennedy, P. (2002). Learning cultures and learning styles: Myth-understandings about adult (Hong Kong) Chinese learners. *International Journal of Lifelong Education, 21*(5), 430–445.

Kim, B. S. K., & Abreu, J. M. (2001). Acculturation measurement: Theory, current instruments and future directions. In J. G. Ponterotto, J. M. Casas, L. A. Suzuki, & C. M. Alexander (Eds.), *Handbook of multicultural counseling* (pp. 394–424). Thousand Oaks, CA: Sage.

Kim, B. S. K., & Omizo, M. M. (2006). Behavioral acculturation and enculturation and psychological functioning among Asian American college students. *Cultural Diversity and Ethnic Minority Psychology, 12*(2), 245–258.

Knight, J. (2011). Education hubs: A fad, a brand, an innovation? *Journal of Studies in International Education, 15*(3), 221–240.

Kramsch, C. (1993). *Context and culture in language teaching.* Oxford: Oxford University Press.

Lees, H. (2013). Silence as a pedagogical tool. *Times Higher Education.* Retrieved August 23, 2016, from https://www.timeshighereducation.com/comment/opinion/silence-as-a-pedagogical-tool/2006621.article

Lewthwaite, M. (1996). A study of international students' perspectives on cross-cultural adaptation. *International Journal for the Advancement of Counselling, 19*(2), 167–185.

Li, X., & Cutting, J. (2011). Rote learning in Chinese culture: Reflecting active Confucian-based memory strategies. In L. Jin & M. Cortazzi (Eds.), *Researching Chinese learners: Skills, perceptions and intercultural adaptations* (pp. 21–42). Basingstoke: Palgrave Macmillan.

Lo, S. W. (2019). White capital: Whiteness meets Bourdieu. In L. Michael & S. Schulz (Eds.), *Unsettling whiteness* (pp. 163–173). Oxford: Inter-Disciplinary Press.

Luk, J., & Lin, A. (2007). *Classroom interactions as cross-cultural encounters.* London: Lawrence Erlbaum Associates.

Moon, D. (1998). White enculturation and bourgeois ideology: The discursive production of "good (white) girls". In T. K. Nakayama & J. N. Martin (Eds.), *Whiteness: The communication of social identity* (pp. 177–197). Thousand Oaks, CA: Sage.

Murphy-Lejeune, E. (2003). An experience of interculturality: Student travellers abroad. In G. Alred, M. Byram, & M. Fleming (Eds.), *Intercultural experience and education* (pp. 101–113). Clevedon: Multilingual Matters.

Oberg, K. (1960). Culture shock: Adjustment to new cultural environments. *Practical Anthropology, 7*(4), 177–182.

Parris-Kidd, H., & Barnett, J. (2011). Cultures of learning and student participation: Chinese learners in a multicultural English class in Australia. In L. Jin & M. Cortazzi (Eds.), *Researching Chinese learners: Skills, perceptions and intercultural adaptations* (pp. 169–187). Basingstoke: Palgrave Macmillan.

Perry, L. B., & Southwell, L. (2011). Developing intercultural understanding and skills: Models and approaches. *Intercultural Education, 22*(6), 453–466.

Rich, A. (1979). *On lies, secrets, and silence*. New York: Norton.

Stanley, P. (2011). Meeting in the middle? Intercultural adaptation in tertiary oral English in China. In L. Jin & M. Cortazzi (Eds.), *Researching Chinese learners: Skills, perceptions and intercultural adaptations* (pp. 93–118). Basingstoke: Palgrave Macmillan.

Stokes, R. (2017, September 18). How can universities help international students feel at home? *The Guardian*. Retrieved July 13, 2018, from https://www.theguardian.com/higher-education-network/2017/sep/18/how-can-universities-help-international-students-feel-at-home

Tishman, S., Jay, E., & Perkins, D. N. (1993). Teaching thinking dispositions: From transmission to enculturation. *Theory into Practice, 32*(3), 147–153.

Warren, J. T. (2011). Reflexive teaching: Toward critical autoethnographic practices of/in/on pedagogy. *Cultural Studies? Critical Methodologies, 11*(2), 139–144.

Watkins, D. A., & Biggs, J. B. (Eds.). (1996). *The Chinese learner: Cultural, contextual and psychological influences*. Hong Kong: University of Hong Kong.

Zhou, Y., Topping, K., & Jindal-Snape, D. (2011). Chinese postgraduate students and their UK tutors. In L. Jin & M. Cortazzi (Eds.), *Researching Chinese learners: Skills, perceptions and intercultural adaptations* (pp. 233–249). Basingstoke: Palgrave Macmillan.

No Author. (2013, December 21). Mad about museums. *The Economist*. Retrieved September 14, 2016, from http://www.economist.com/news/special-report/21591710-china-building-thousands-new-museums-how-will-it-fill-them-mad-about-museums

11

Intercultural Exchange: A Personal Perspective from the Outsider Inside

Hilary S. Carty

Introduction

In probing issues of cultural diversity and intercultural exchange, this chapter draws on my perspective as a practitioner—a 'doer' as much as a thinker, an activist as much as an academic. My core subjects are cultural management, leadership and the Creative Industries, and I have been fortunate to lecture in Austria, Germany, Holland and the UK. Being of Caribbean descent, this discussion starts with an exploration of some of the challenges of being culturally different within the academic arena, particularly when working in Western Europe, where the significantly mono-cultural classrooms contrast starkly with my home town of London and its diverse population. I investigate whether there is sufficient breadth and depth of intercultural experience being delivered through existing university exchange programmes. Finally, I explore what, beyond the practice itself, are the underlying aspirations for such encounters? What, ultimately, are we seeking to achieve? Is it enough to replicate the status

H. S. Carty (✉)
Clore Leadership Programme, London, UK

© The Author(s) 2020
V. Durrer, R. Henze (eds.), *Managing Culture*, Sociology of the Arts,
https://doi.org/10.1007/978-3-030-24646-4_11

quo within our cultural institutions and within society—or should we be stimulating action for change?

Context

As curiosity, travel and twenty-first century migration create new and dynamic social encounters, explorations of creativity and cultural expression are reflecting ever more unusual and unexpected cultural juxtapositions. Likewise, the curriculum of cultural management has moved from the core tenets of arts and venue management and now embraces the subjects of intercultural exchange, its purpose, its manifestations, its impact and its outcomes—outcomes on culture, on place, people and on practice.

As an educator of cultural management, it is critical to secure both the experience and appreciation of cultural exchange within the core curriculum. As an educator whose cultural origin often differs from the students in the lecture theatre, the experience of presenting—and unwittingly representing—can be charged with unusual dynamics, underlying curiosity and unspoken expectations. From time to time, the interaction is, in itself, an intercultural exchange.

The perspective of the educator in that context is one that I am keen to explore. The student asks questions, ponders out loud and seeks answers to issues, beliefs and uncertainties. But what of the educator her/himself? What is necessary to maintain that gaze, deliver content and context, when in addition to the expected lecture room dynamic, your own cultural background becomes part of the educational curiosity?

In a global environment that is changing at a bewildering pace, the continuing health of the cultural sector, and of cultural learning, will be dependent on its capacity to acknowledge, address and respond to a maelstrom of external drivers now impacting cultural practice, including globalisation, changing demographics and new communities of influence. We are witnessing political, social and economic change; challenges to freedom of speech and creative expression; rising inequality and social division; disparities between rural and metropolitan areas. The norms that we know and understand are changing. Culture is changing.

Possibilities are changing. Our understanding of the world, and our place within it, is changing.

One role of culture in any environment is to ask questions—to explore, to probe, to stimulate and to reflect. Culture makes us look at our society, at our world, and drill down on what it is, how it is, why it is, and what it could be. Culture asks us to consider what we think and feel about what is going on in our world. It stimulates new thoughts, new ways of being and seeing. Developing creative minds is, therefore, fundamental to any society.

In the UK, the provision of creative education is diminishing in schools, higher education is expensive, and opportunities for creative and diverse interaction may well diminish as access to cultural education reaches a narrower cadre of society.

In other parts of Europe, where cultural education appears more embedded, different ranges of issues play out. The rise of nationalistic-focussed political parties, failed integration of new migrants, economic challenge and cultural regeneration all play their part in creating a complex and dynamic melee informing cultural understanding and enhancing cultural appreciation.

An international awareness and outlook are key, and there is much to gain from the healthy exchange of experiences and approaches. In the European context, the potential for intercultural learning is strong. Both migration and the internet bring the realities of diverse cultures right to our doorsteps. But are we taking this opportunity to learn and absorb or merely to watch and regard? Are we exchanging or simply affirming existing cultural norms?

Reflective Approach/An Outsider on the Inside

With over 30 years' experience as an arts and cultural practitioner, my experience of working within academia since the 1990s, has largely been that of the outsider on the inside—working with but not 'of' the institution. That combination of creative practice and academic consolidation for the learning environment is one that has both fed my own curiosities and dynamically supported a nomadic cycle of action and reflection.

I have been a Visiting Professor, an External Lecturer, a Visiting Research Fellow—I smile at my 'visits' into this academic world, where the particularities of culture, the standards, the norms and regulations, can make even the most confident of consultants feel out of place. I may have learnt the trade of comfortable exchange in the lecture theatre, where the dialogue is with students, usually keen to learn. However, traversing the campuses, navigating the corridors, pushing through the bureaucracies can be doubly daunting when your 'curve ball' is a very obvious cultural distinctiveness.

Certainly, in the UK, someone from my cultural background is not the norm in academia—the Higher Education Statistics Agency (HESA) figures show black academic staff make up just 0.01% of academic staff (HESA, 2019). There are no statistics for those of us who 'visit', but if anecdote and observation might be allowed, it would seem clear that, breaking into the world of academia in the Western world, understandably tough for everyone, has proven supremely challenging for those from non-Western cultures.

Whether in the UK, or in wider Europe, I have most often faced a room full of faces that are not like mine, both intrigued by the other with curiosities and anticipations—not always aligned. Whenever you are not the norm, it is easy to stand out. And in this case, that standing out can bring added challenge—the challenge to excel—to be not just good, but 'outstanding' /not just informed and knowledgeable, but 'inspiring', 'engaging' and positively stimulating—every time… Is that pressure self-imposed? Is it just the commonly experienced imposter syndrome running on overdrive? Engaging the minds of future leaders is and should be a daunting prospect; so a little trepidation is entirely reasonable. But is there more? Might the stakes be stacked just a little higher?

When the lecturer from another culture stands before a class of students, they are often communicating much more than the fundamentals of their subject—they are providing a window into the cultural norms, experiences, belief systems and perspectives of diverse cultures also. Beyond the metropolitan mix-ups of our urban cities, for some students, this may often be the first sustained opportunity for a deeper level encounter with someone who is 'other'—from a different ethnicity or lived experience, so the questions can veer off-piste. In this exchange, the questions may well reveal an ethnographical curiosity, above and beyond the basic thirst for technical knowledge.

Here, academics from a different cultural origin can find themselves placed as 'expert' not solely on their area of academic learning and expertise, but also on race, geography, religion, customs and traditions. This can be an awkward encounter as you scan your own individual experience for relevant insights and learning that might be helpful, albeit not universal. The pressure to represent brings added complexity and treacherous challenge. Is it a pressure that must be appeased? Must I perform as your expert just because I am different? Is it acceptable to politely decline the invitation? For many professionals in today's multi-cultural environments, diversity is an experience—not a qualification, so might they be allowed to be just a subject specialist?

Generating Conversations

Over time and with both good and challenging experiences, I have worked to achieve an equilibrium that affords the confidence to use that lack of diversity 'expertise' to generate conversations; to explore rather than to tell; to question rather than to inform—working through cultural questions rather than cultural assumptions; and nurturing cultural empathy rather than race privilege, class privilege or gender privilege.

In the spaces where I do choose to explore diversity, I seek to release the often inherent pressure value by creating an open space for dialogue and probing—a space where all might loosen some inhibitions and ask the sometimes awkward questions that enable us, over time, to be at ease with difference. Critically, I too am on that journey—and the mutuality of the learning experience is an important feature.

In the lecture theatre, my approach is to be as open as possible—to bring core facilitation skills into the room, so students feel encouraged to probe and to be curious. Not all learning environments embrace this approach and cultural collision can occur, so situational observation and the judicious balance of teaching and sharing has to be determined.

This drive for openness was tested back in November 2015 when teaching a module on Intercultural Leadership to a class of mainly Central-European students. We had explored issues of diversity—we had exchanged experiences, reviewed the literature and were grappling with some of the visible and tangible societal outcomes when, overnight the attacks on the Bataclan Theatre and other areas in Paris hit our TV screens. The so-called Islamic State claimed responsibility for the terrorist attack that had killed 130 people and injured many more. My class the next morning could not stay in the realms of literature, theory and hypotheses—there was no option but to open up to a fully wide-ranging discourse on the issues of diversity within Europe. Collectively, we explored the range of opinion felt by my students—from dismay and incredulity, to anger and resentment. We considered third world politics, the impact of globalisation on different societies and turned, with piercing insights, to the dynamics of intercultural interaction.

It was a challenging discussion, emotionally charged by experiences rather too close to home. For my part, I felt it critical to be both vigilant to and respectful of a wide range of views and maintain the room as a space of learning and reflection. Conversations and dialogue, whilst sometimes uncomfortable, are valuable in achieving understanding. The moment called for calm reflection, encouraging intercultural tolerance in the face of intercultural conflict. The students were impressive and engaging in embracing this most challenging of discussions with intelligent probing and a genuine desire to understand. The Paris attack had moved the intercultural debate from the abstract to the visceral. It demanded 'real' perspectives in this real-world scenario.

Creating Genuine Exchange

My particular relationship with academia means that my perspectives are not from within the institution, but from between—between academia and the cultural sector, academia and communities, academia and the outside world. In many ways it is like a bridge—connecting two entities, uniting two perspectives, creating channels for interaction and shared understanding.

And from that space in between, I have witnessed a notable expansion in the practice and encouragement of intercultural dialogue. It is now commonplace to witness a clear academic acknowledgement of the benefits of awareness, fresh perspectives and interaction with other cultures as enhancing the discourse and the understanding of cultural policy. Many university programmes now encourage and facilitate intercultural experience as an extension to the learning in the lecture theatre.

On a visit to an Austrian university, I had the pleasure of seeing students who were heading off to experience life in parts of the world as diverse as the USA, South America and Seoul, adding to my previous experience of supporting a student writing her dissertation in Sub-Saharan Africa, and who encountered first-hand the challenges faced by cultural organisations working under a strict political regime.

So, I am hopeful, that the critical life-skills, adaptability and resilience that those students will gain, will stay with them. I am hopeful that their encounters with different and unexpected cultural norms will broaden their understanding and make real the dichotomies of North and South, homogeneous and non-homogeneous, tolerant and non-tolerant societies. I am hopeful that these experiences will help them to build their cultural intelligence as well as their personal resilience.

What I see less often, however, is genuine 'exchange'—these visits mainly seem to go one way.

And it seems somewhat unfortunate that the narratives of the visiting students, shared on return, are not always convincing of gaining more than a superficial impression of these cities and cultures. Safety is, understandably, paramount, but what evidence is there that cultural exchange is genuinely taking place? Or are we more commonly facilitating cultural 'tourism' rather than intercultural 'exchange'? What and how are we exchanging?

The issue is not an easy one to resolve because the simple economics of contemporary societies usually mean that those relatively highly financed institutions in Europe and the Western hemisphere can afford to support international travel, but the regions they visit cannot always, or very easily, repay the compliment. The return visit is costly—but should it not be a critical part of the deal? It is axiomatic that the financial resources in the North exceed those in the South at the current time. But if we do not take steps to improve the mutuality—are we really facilitating 'inter' cultural dialogue (between cultures)? Or are we satisfying ourselves with extra-cultural dialogue—dialogue that is, and will always be, external to our own? Extra—Other—Outside—Peripheral—to be examined, analysed, critiqued and compared—but not actually exchanged? Is this not then a form of sophisticated cultural observation? Twenty-first century ethnographic studies of the intellectual kind?

Affirming the Environment for Learning

I have witnessed, first-hand, the impact of international students within a classroom. In cities such as London, the potential for intercultural exchange is common and regular, as the universities reflect, and even exceed the multi-cultural environments now common to urban locations. But, beyond the metropolitan centres, whether in middle Germany, Southern Austria or in rural UK—the opportunity for intercultural interaction is not so readily acquired by the student population. Yet it is so informative and valuable on 'home turf' as much as on a study visit. For example, when exploring the international impact of the Creative Industries, examples from Europe and America provide immediate recognition for everyone. Then references to K-Pop, Nollywood or the Creative Hubs in Brazil, provide (what seems like) a rare moment for any 'foreign' student in the class to shine, as they proudly respond to the acknowledgement of their cultural developments, and share insights from their history, highlights and nuances with their European classmates. Such instances provide opportunities for cultural vocalisation and projection that places the international/foreign student on equal terms.

So, I would advocate the strong benefits of making possible the second half of the 'exchange'—for bringing the intercultural dialogue home—and making it part of everyday learning rather than an isolated experience, in another land. Making normal the practice of intercultural dialogue is particularly important when one considers the mixture of cultures many of us are now seeing on our doorsteps. The current waves of migration and the high numbers of refugees across Europe mean that those 'other' cultures are very much within the mix. Within the European mix.

All the more reason to normalise the experience—not in 'special projects' that place these communities under a microscope—but in genuine, long-term interactions—mutually beneficial connections that build relationships, facilitate regular interaction and make genuinely possible the 'exchange' we are pursuing:

- Exchange at home as well as abroad.
- Exchange in the classroom, as well as in intellectual reflection.
- Exchange as core curriculum, as well as extra-curricular experience.

Our educational establishments can provide dynamic spaces for learning. Spaces to review, to question and to explore. To legitimately and conspicuously navigate differences of experience and differences of opinion, in order to expand, enrich and inform our lives and benefit from the diversity of opinion which stimulates, challenges and provokes credible responses to contemporary issues. Placing genuine opportunities for intercultural learning within this rich environment would surely be a priority for a society and a faculty seeking to stimulate fresh thinking and generate transferable knowledge?

Conclusion

In this text, I have tried to explore the situation and some of the challenges faced by individuals who are themselves from culturally diverse backgrounds engaging with intercultural exchange in the academic context. Through personal observation, reflection and insight, the role and contribution of the academic (including the sometimes-unwitting contribution of cultural difference) has been examined, probing what added elements they might bring to the discourse and to intercultural awareness.

The issues of mutuality and exchange have been reviewed, with particular reference to the purpose and impact of exchanges within an unequal North-South relationship and whether we can genuinely hope to achieve sufficient breadth and depth of intercultural experience with existing, significantly one-way programmes of interaction. Finally, I have explored the role of universities as centres of education and the long-term aspirations for cultural exchange to which we might aspire.

I am turning to the view that, to genuinely broaden our perspectives, we need to foster intercultural engagement—not just dialogue or cultural observation. I am hopeful that, if we can encourage and facilitate a move towards intercultural 'engagement' we will stir a passion in the next generation—so that they are not passive participants in the world as it is. So that they are less satisfied with accepting current imbalances and feel passionate enough to act for change. The students in these universities are, or will be, the enlightened ones. These are, or will be, the converted. Might we strive to encourage them to move from passive enlightenment to active evolution?

That is what I would really want to see happen—to achieve some tangible outcomes from our academic inputs—action for intercultural change. Outcomes/Action—not purely academic—but then neither am I. So, my work in cultural management will continue to promote these tangible outcomes, using my experience in between academia and communities to encourage the next generation of curious minds to create new possibilities for intercultural engagement—and make them happen!

Reference

HESA. (2019). Table 4—HE academic staff by ethnicity and academic employment function 2014/15 to 2017/18. Retrieved from https://www.hesa.ac.uk/data-and-analysis/staff/table-4

Part IV

Future Directions

12

Navigating Between Arts Management and Cultural Agency: Latin America's Contribution to a New Approach for the Field

Javier J. Hernández-Acosta

Introduction

Discourse on the creative economy has aroused a greater interest from higher education institutions on the importance of culture as an engine of economic and social development (UNCTAD, 2010; UNESCO, 2004). Since the 1960s, academic programmes and certifications in arts management started to emerge in the United States. Many of these programmes had a focus on adapting contents and disciplines based on functional areas of traditional business management, such as marketing, finance, operations and human resources, among others. However, for the Ibero-American context, this approach seemed very limited considering the social, cultural and political factors that surround arts and cultural production (Martinell, 1999; Quintero, 2013). Culture began to be conceived as a tool for social intervention to transform the condition of these countries, often being framed in scenarios of dictatorship, civil

J. J. Hernández-Acosta (✉)
Business Department, Universidad del Sagrado Corazón,
San Juan, Puerto Rico
e-mail: Javierj.hernandez@sagrado.edu

© The Author(s) 2020   271
V. Durrer, R. Henze (eds.), *Managing Culture*, Sociology of the Arts,
https://doi.org/10.1007/978-3-030-24646-4_12

wars, inequality and marginalisation. This new role was described by Doris Sommer (2006) as Cultural Agency.

For this reason, many universities in Latin America began to adopt cultural agency programmes, hosted mostly at social sciences and humanities departments with a great influence from cultural studies. Based on this, cultural agency has developed as a separate field from arts management and in some cases as a complementary field that defines a new alumni profile. More recently, specifically with the publication of the *Orange Economy Report* by the International Development Bank (IDB) in 2013, which promotes the opportunities of cultural and creative industries for Latin America, concepts such as arts management, cultural agency and entrepreneurship have ended up being used interchangeably (Buitrago & Duque, 2013). In this context, the chapter argues that this new focus on cultural enterprises could serve as an opportunity for a better integration from arts management practices in Latin America and the rest of the World.

Europe and United States share great challenges in terms of the impact of globalisation and migration flows. In the case of the United States, the Latino population represents one the fastest growing-segments of the population, representing at least 16% (50.5 million) (Hernández, 2013). Also, recent debates regarding the policies the Federal Government should develop in addressing the need to understand the role of immigrant communities and their cultural contexts. Arts and culture represent one of the main ways in which these communities communicate their identities. For this reason, it is important to understand differences in arts management and cultural agency practices in order to address diversity in the arts and cultural sector. This chapter discusses the theoretical, practical and training aspects that differentiate cultural agency as a complementary approach to arts management. Based on the experiences and practices of cultural agents from Latin America and Puerto Rico, a new model of incorporating cultural policy as a driver of cultural agency is proposed, integrating a cultural mission with local development and sustainable development goals.

Internationally, the arts management discipline (referred to in some instances as arts and cultural management or administration, depending upon the national context) has continued to evolve in recent decades through the increase in professionalisation through academic programmes and through constant changes in the external environment of arts organisations. Intersections with topics such as cultural policies, cultural value, creative economy, business startups and sustainable development continue to evolve. In many countries, economic crises have provoked a change in the structures of public funding for arts and culture, and with it a greater pressure has fallen on the role of cultural organisations to advance the human rights of access and participation in the cultural life of the territories. At the same time, other transformations, such as the acceleration of migration flows, place the issue of diversity as a central axis of cultural production.

This chapter is based on an important premise regarding the way in which this theoretical framework on arts management has been developed. We argue that a large part of this theoretical framework, in spite of its international dissemination, comes from countries in the Global North. Although this development has been important and useful for professionals, organisations and public policies related to arts and culture, there are multiple contributions based on the concept and practices of cultural agency, as developed in Latin American countries as a complementary field to arts management, and as based on the social, economic and political context, that are not fully recognised beyond this region. This notion of a theoretical construction bias as stemming mostly from North countries is not new, since there is a great discussion about the importance of countries in the Global South developing their own theoretical frameworks based on their context (Connell, 2007).

The main objective of the chapter is to highlight cultural agency practices, as well as their complementary standing to arts management practices in Europe and the United States. First, the evolution of arts management and cultural agency disciplines will be discussed. Based on this theoretical framework, we present some practical scenarios of cultural agency. Finally, some scenarios will be proposed by which a much more holistic discipline can contribute to social, political, economic and cultural changes. This chapter is based on a reflection on both disciplines as a starting point for a research agenda for the evolution of arts and cultural management and how practices from other geographical contexts could enrich the discipline. The chapter starts by reviewing literature on arts management and cultural agency. After discussing a case study from Puerto Rico, an approach integrating both practices will be proposed. Finally, by considering the importance of creative entrepreneurship as a new dimension of cultural work, some recommendations for the development of these professionals will be presented. Matters related to how art, creativity and culture are defined in different contexts will be clarified as the discussion evolves.

Arts Management

Although it is difficult to establish a starting point for the discipline, it is close to half a century ago when the first academic programmes on arts management began to be established, a process that happened more or less in parallel in countries such as the United Kingdom, the United States and Australia (Ebewo & Sirayi, 2009). Since then, multiple approaches have been developed whilst being dependent upon different national contexts, influences and theoretical frameworks from other disciplines. For example, Aleksandar Brkić (2009) establishes four main approaches, which he argues require some type of harmonisation for the development of the discipline. First, he picks out the focus of some programmes that directly copy and apply management processes and practices from traditional businesses to the arts. In these cases, the management approach maintains a focus on efficiency and effectiveness, both of which are much debated concepts within the arts. A second approach emphasises the production processes of artistic manifestations, something that can be adapted to theatre, film, music and visual arts, among others. Thirdly, he proposes another approach that is very pertinent to the practice of cultural management, which consists of an interconnection between arts administration and cultural policies. Brkić emphasises that an awareness of how arts and cultural managers advance public policy objectives has been much more present in Europe than in the United States. Finally, a fourth approach oriented towards entrepreneurship stands out. This last approach establishes a greater connection with creativity and innovation and risk-taking as part of a new management scenario.

According to Jung (2017), the main theories that started the arts management discipline are influenced by approaches within art, legal, sociology, psychology, public policy, marketing, organisational studies, management, political science and economics. Jung proposes the importance of a greater integration of these theories to advance the interdisciplinarity that is required to solve problems in arts management. In this connection, Evrard and Colbert (2000) discuss the development of arts management as a new discipline. An interesting argument developed by these authors relates to the influences that arts management have made to several areas of management theories, including strategic management, finance, human resources management and marketing/consumer behaviour. For example, in strategic management, the authors use examples such as discontinuity in operations and prototyping in traditional businesses, both of which are very present in arts organisations, which can consist of mostly project-based work. In human resources, they propose dual management; in finance, the non-economic value; and in consumer behaviour, the concept of product-oriented vs. market-oriented product development, all of which are other influences or practices very present in arts management (Evrard & Colbert, 2000).

Recently, Henze (2017) has broadened the discussion of arts management to address its international dimension. Her comparative study presents the importance of a geographic scope, languages, mobility and the diversity of the audiences that organisations address. Despite the increase in the internationalisation of arts administration, there is still a long way to go in terms of developing the soft skills managers need to ensure greater interaction rather than the integration of minority groups into the hegemonic culture.

In terms of the convergences and differences in the curricular structures of the academic programmes in arts management, Varela (2013) made an empirical analysis with 46 academic programmes in the United States out of a total group of 82. It is interesting to note that 65.2% of the programmes were hosted by arts faculties (visual and performing arts), while the remaining belonged to the humanities, public administration, education and business departments, among others. The courses or thematic areas that are most repeated in the programmes were marketing (88.6%), internships (86.4%), introductory courses on arts management

(79.5%), public policies (75%) and fundraising and development (68.2%). In general, the author highlights the importance of economic sustainability through private financing and audience development as critical factors to be developed through academic programmes in the United States. While this focus represents an important aspect of arts management, it also seems to undermine the importance of a better balance between economic and cultural value. This profile highlights some differences with the profile and role of the cultural agent, as will be discussed in the next section.

Cultural Agency

Although the concept of *"gestión"* is often translated as management, the truth is that in Latin America a complementary and different practice has been developed around arts and cultural production. For the purposes of this chapter, we propose translating the concept by the term 'cultural agency', as proposed by Doris Sommer (2006), who states that cultural agency consists of a practice that integrates a range of social interventions through the arts. This locates, in a certain way, the cultural agent as a political actor that generates transformation in his or her territory. According to Martinell (2009), the evolution of cultural agency began in Spain and Latin America in the mid-1990s. However, Martinell (2009) points out that the concern about cultural agency began to emerge since the 1980s with Spain's transition to democracy and the role that culture would play in social development.

According to Martinell (2009), culture was a fundamental part of democratic construction:

Recovering public space, denying local collective memory, recapturing buildings and equipment stolen from social groups, dignifying the role of creators and opening the doors to a new cultural life in freedom were the objectives of a mistreated cultural society. (p. 98)

According to this author, the contents and theoretical framework of the training programmes that were developed in the United States and

Europe were not adapted to the political and social reality of Latin American countries and Spain. Although it was not a structured process of professionalisation, the cultural action of the new Spanish political context led to the emergence of these programmes during the 1990s to supply the professional profile required by the sector.

While Spain was experiencing a transition to democracy and the cultural changes it entailed, Latin America sought its own space in arts and cultural management debates by exploring a focus much more oriented to cultural studies. It is necessary to remember that Latin America also experienced processes of transition from dictatorships, development issues and major social challenges. Disciplines such as anthropology, communications and artistic education began to play a fundamental role in cultural policies (Martinell, 2009). Latin America represents a very diverse region. Although the Spanish language represents a common ground for most of the countries, diversity of indigenous ancestry and tribes represents a challenge for governments in guaranteeing that diversity. Also, the twentieth century left dozens of countries under the political control of dictatorships. In the cases of Argentina, Uruguay, Brazil, Chile, Paraguay and Perú, to mention a few, military governments were present until the mid and end of the 1980s. At the same time, because most of those dictatorships emerged during the evolution of social and revolutionary movements, the United States played a key role in supporting the governments that took power (Galeano, 1973; Rabe, 2012). Another key aspect of social and economic development in Latin America has been a lack of understanding regarding the region's context, as in the case of international entities' policies, such as the World Bank and the International Monetary Fund, for developing countries, a thesis that has been most thoroughly developed by Arturo Escobar (1995).

In this context, the cultural manager was positioned as a cultural policy agent. As a result of this work, aspects related to creative freedom, access and participation and cultural diversity and democratisation are directly integrated. In addition to the elements directly related to artistic work, such as creativity, aesthetics and symbolic content, the cultural agent acts as a mediator in the cultural scenario, always bearing in mind aspects such as education, community, equity and quality of life. Likewise, it is a *political* actor that seeks social transformation through culture, a

key need in the Latin American social and political context. The importance of this role relies mostly on a bottom-up approach, where cultural
agents assume the responsibility of advancing cultural policy objectives in
a context of dictatorships or governments transitioning to democracy.
Even with the creation of ministries of culture in most Latin American
countries after the 1990s, the role of cultural agents has remained the same.

Doris Sommer (2006) describes different practices of cultural agency
in Latin America, processes that involve scenarios of violence, exclusion
of indigenous communities, urban and city development, public space,
migration and political action. The cases of pursuing equity in indigenous communities in Chile, Guatemala and Brazil, the use of the media
as a form of connection with the diaspora as in the case of Radio Martí in
Cuba, and gender issues in Afro-Brazilian cultures are just some of the
scenarios where cultural agency assumes a role of direct social intervention. However, one of the cases of greater recognition and impact has
been the work of Antanas Mockus, a former mayor of the city of Bogotá,
where the arts played a central role in improving the conditions of the
city. Mockus' work focused on strengthening citizenship regarding issues
related to violence reduction, compliance with norms and cooperation.

A Case Study: Cultural Agency in Puerto Rico

To understand more deeply some experiences of cultural agency in a territory, the case of Puerto Rico will be explored. This Caribbean island
with a population of 3.4 million represents a balance between being an
American cultural policy, but within a cultural environment of great
Latin American influence. Puerto Rico has been under the political control of the United States since 1898. In this complex political and economic environment, culture has represented a scenario of political
resistance and social transformation. Since the military invasion in 1898
and the first decades of cultural assimilation, Torres (2009) highlights the
role of writers in combating that process, especially from the imposition
of English as a teaching language in 1907. For that same time, the
University of Puerto Rico and the Ateneo Puertorriqueño became key
institutions in highlighting Puerto Rican identity as a form of resistance.

Cultural Agency through Creative and Artistic Practice

Since the end of the 1960s, music played a fundamental role in the processes of political resistance, a trend that is similar to what happened in the rest of Latin America. Many singer-songwriters, focusing on *protest song*, which, thanks to Cuban influence, acquired the name of the *nueva trova*, and thereby became an example of cultural agency, where the songs functioned not only as a resource of denunciation on social and political conditions, but also as a form of direct cultural action through their being sung in festivals and protest activities. Although there are multiple experiences of protest song beyond Latin America, such as Bob Dylan and Joan Baez in the United States and Joan Manuel Serrat in Spain, Latin America experienced a boom through figures such as Silvio Rodríguez in Cuba, Mercedes Soca in Argentina and Alí Primera in Venezuela. As an example of the level of repression experienced in Latin America, it is important to note that it was not until 2018 that Chilean military personnel were found guilty of the torture and murder of singer-songwriter Victor Jara, a direct action of the *coup d'etat* by General Augusto Pinochet.

One interesting aspect of the Puerto Rican case is that the role of the musical activity had such an important dimension of political action that the Puerto Rican Socialist Party (PSP) assumed the protest song as part of its cultural arm. This included the creation of a record label, *Disco Libre*, producing 18 records in six years (Ramírez, 2007). In a very interesting way, six decades later, the protest song continues to be a key resource of cultural agency in the multiple demands of social change in the country.

The cultural agency component also crosses multiple artistic manifestations such as theatre, visual arts and dance, among others. A very interesting and recent case has been the role of cultural agency in response to some form of natural disaster. After the impact of Hurricane María in September 2017, which caused the most complex catastrophe for the country in the last 100 years, the cultural response emerged as a complement to the immediate response support in issues of live rescues, health, safety and infrastructure, among others. In a multisectoral effort promoted by the Institute of Puerto Rican Culture (ICP) through the *Cultura*

Rodante (Culture on the road) programme, dozens of individual artists, collectives, non-profit organisations and cultural enterprises toured the island to bring art to the communities. Similarly, the role historically played by artists and cultural agents in the communities served to facilitate forms of self-sustained community organisation efforts to counteract the absence of government in many instances.

In this same experience, art and cultural agency once again served as a backdrop for denunciation, as is shown in the case of an artistic installation created in front of the local Capitol Hill. The action came after a study revealed that there could have been an estimated 4645 deaths directly or indirectly associated with the hurricane in subsequent months, even though the government presented an official total of 64 deaths. Three Puerto Rican writers proposed the idea of people delivering a pair of shoes representing each of these deaths. After 48 hours, citizens had carried over 2000 pairs of shoes, sometimes along with messages alluding to relatives or friends who had died. Again, cultural agency appears as a driver of social processes, from the ephemeral to recurrent and sustainable actions (Fig. 12.1).

As well as these examples, there are multiple experiences where cultural agency assumes the role of social intervention through creative practices, either through education, community development, economic participation, political action or solidarity. In this case, these components do not represent a mere complement to social responsibility but the main purpose of creative work. This experience represents an important opportunity for advancing the discussion regarding the instrumental vs intrinsic value of arts and culture. Cultural agency represents an opportunity for funding agencies in the United States to understand the broader scope of cultural work beyond traditional economic and social indicators that sometimes force organisations to adopt new discourses that could distract them from their role in society.

Fig. 12.1 Art installation to honour Hurricane María deaths. (Credit: Alfredo Nieves Moreno)

The Complementarity Between the Two Approaches

The description presented for these two approaches, related to artistic and cultural work, serve as a starting point to identify areas where both practices complement one another. Accordingly, it is recognised how complex it is to reach conclusions with the diversity of professional practices and content of the related academic programmes across countries. However, at least three main trends can be observed as a basis: the scope of the concept of art and culture, the field of action of professionals, and the disciplines or theoretical framework of training programmes.

Puerto Rico represents an interesting case to illustrate some contrasts between approaches to culture in the United States and Latin America. Puerto Rico, as a colony of the United States since 1898, seems to be trapped between a US legal and trade framework and a Spanish-speaking country that shares a Latin American culture. While neoliberal practices in financing for the arts seems to have an impact worldwide, the lack of public support in Puerto Rico for arts and cultural projects has perpetuated its precariousness and invisibility. Understanding similarities and differences could help address the needs of cultural projects, not just in Puerto Rico, but for Latino communities in the United States, which now represent over 16% of the total population.

Differences between the United States and Puerto Rico are evident in the scope of cultural work and in the role of public policy for the arts. It is interesting to note that, in the United States, for public policy purposes, the cultural field is often defined as a synonym for the arts, while in Latin America, 'culture' refers to all activities that define 'ways of life' (Williams, 1989). In terms of the role of the government, for reasons that could be tied to the constitutional system and scope of the federal government, the intervention of the State is presented in a very limited way, which justifies the absence of entities such as a Ministry of Culture. It is this public policy approach that defines the National Endowment for the Arts (NEA) as an entity that is limited, primarily, to the financing of artistic activity. However, in most Latin American countries, when considering the broader scope of culture as 'ways of life', including local identities, media and other activities, the role of the government requires a different approach (Hernández, 2013). This difference is exemplified in the scope of the ministries of culture in countries such as Colombia, Bolivia and Chile. In many of these cases, the multiple indigenous and black populations have managed to emphasise the importance of cultural and ethnic diversity in cultural policies for the public agenda.

Another key contrastive aspect between both approaches is the scope of cultural policies. Regarding the United States, Mulcahy (2006), based on a review of multiple definitions of cultural policy, states that cultural policy consists of all the activities of the state to support the creation, production and dissemination of heritage, entertainment and cultural infrastructure, with a great focus on the arts. However, in the Latin American context, it is possible that the most widely used definition was presented by García Canclini (1987; Coelho, 2000, cited in Ochoa-Gautier, 2003). Canclini describes cultural policies as the role of all actors involved in the development of symbolic content to meet cultural needs and promote social transformation. By not limiting actions to the role of government, the cultural manager is positioned as a cultural policy agent rather than an administrator or follower of cultural policy.

A third-key contrastive element could be the disciplines of influence for each of the approaches. The field of arts management naturally is greatly influenced by business management sciences, something that is evidenced in content related to the functional areas of an organisation, including marketing, finances and legal aspects. Similarly, there is influence from public administration, not only in order to understand the role of government and public policy, but also with regard to the applicability of many managerial styles that are closer to non-profit entities than to traditional companies. In some cases, influence from arts education and community development are also observed. In Latin America, cultural agency, which in many of the programmes also serves as the administrative component, curricula mostly respond to disciplines and content that allow us to understand many of the complexities of cultural and social diversity mentioned above. For this reason, a presence of cultural studies, anthropology, sociology and political science is observed. As also discussed above, this gives a deep level of theoretical reflection that defines the field of action for cultural agents.

The differences presented in the above paragraphs represent challenges and opportunities that serve a common interest: arts and culture as an integral part of human and community development. It could be suggested that cultural agents face a big challenge in the development of management skills that could support the execution of projects of social and cultural impact, especially when some cultural agency programmes are centred on the theoretical framework more than on those managerial skills required for community-based projects. On the other hand, arts management also runs the risk of a greater inclination to the administrative component, without getting professionals to understand the social, polit-

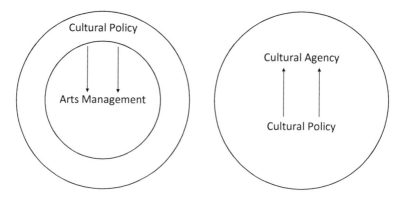

Fig. 12.2   Cultural policy/arts management relationship models

ical, economic and cultural complexities that surround the increasingly more diverse audiences they serve.

To identify a point of convergence between both practices, referring mainly to the United States and Latin America, it can be suggested that in the first case cultural policies are a factor that affect arts management. According to Durrer (2018) in her research on the relationship between cultural policy and arts management, for many arts managers, cultural policy functions as the framework or context to arts management. However, her study also indicates that there may be alignment between the two, with arts management potentially influencing cultural policies.

Based on this analysis, we can state that, in the context of cultural agency, the relationship is different. Beyond a relationship of influence, cultural policies are immersed in cultural agency and are precisely the driver of creative interventions. The following diagram seeks to illustrate this phenomenon. The arrows suggest the direction of the main influence between the components (Fig. 12.2).

Cultural Entrepreneurship as a New Creative Force

To address the major strengths of experiences from arts management in United States and Latin America, it is important to consider the new context in which cultural work has been developing. In recent years, cultural entrepreneurship has gained strength as a new engine of cultural activity. This could be related to the impact that neoliberal practices have over public funding for arts and culture. Similarly, it has emerged as a new field of academic research, although its conceptual framework still seems to be at a very preliminary stage (Hausmann & Heinze, 2016). Its development is closely related to the new discourse of the creative economy and the relationship with the experience of start-up development in traditional sectors. The influence of the creative economy discourse includes a greater focus on free market dynamics, a design of user-centred experiences and products, and a profile of new ventures based on high-risk tolerance, innovation and a certain approach to scalability.

While it is true that this new approach to entrepreneurship complements the dimension of the non-profit sector that predominates in the arts sector, there are also strong criticisms and debates about the neoliberal discourse that surrounds it and the possible disguise of precariousness in cultural work (Rowan, 2010; Banks, 2017). Nevertheless, entrepreneurship is gaining strength in universities and private sector training programmes, whether as a new field or as an approach within existing programmes. Issues such as trends in the different sectors of the cultural and creative industries, the identification of opportunities, the design of business models, innovation in the development of cultural products, and growth strategies, especially at the global level, represents a large proportion in the curricular sequence of the programmes.

In the case of Puerto Rico, as in other Latin American countries, multiple training initiatives have been developed for cultural entrepreneurship both within and outside universities, including cultural incubators such as *Inversión Cultural*, creative accelerators such as *Nuestro Barrio* (at Universidad del Sagrado Corazón) and undergraduate courses at Universidad del Sagrado Corazón (private) and Universidad de Puerto Rico (public). Similarly to the culture of startups, these training programmes include incubation, acceleration and mentoring processes. Increasingly universities incorporate innovation and entrepreneurship centres to support their students and entrepreneurs in nearby communities. This new stream of support tools presents a great opportunity to find greater integration of arts management and cultural agency experiences. Although these cultural ventures differ from the non-profit sector, it represents a growing sector, with the opportunity of also becoming cultural policy agents. As a result, the recommendations proposed within this chapter focus mostly on this new sector of cultural and creative enterprises.

An Integrated Approach

How can the new context of cultural entrepreneurship be used to ensure a form of training that integrates the role of cultural policies in arts management as a field of work and study practised in other nations? This section proposes a preliminary model based on the analysis of cultural agency as a complementary approach to arts management in the Puerto Rican context and its importance in the academic training of cultural professionals beyond that region.

The following diagram seeks to represent four areas of focus in the field of action of cultural agency: a cultural mission, focusing on a territory, cultural policies and United Nations' Sustainable Development Goals (SDGs). A model of concentric circles illustrates that it develops inside out, and that only the clear definition of a component can allow for the addition of the next component. These are described in greater detail below (Fig. 12.3).

- *The cultural mission*: The instrumentalisation of culture is one of the great debates around artistic work (Yúdice, 2003). Wyszomirski (2013) proposes that cultural organisations should work on a triple helix approach, by which it may be possible to balance financial sustainability, artistic vitality and elements of public value. Rather than thinking about these three elements in a parallel way, it is suggested that cultural initiatives should start from a cultural mission that responds to the aesthetic or creative concerns of the entrepreneurs beyond an economic mission. Defining a mission beyond its instrumentalisation is important to facilitate a dynamic that weighs it against the rest of the components for which entrepreneurs must analyse to what extent the mission is sustained.
- *Focusing on a territory*: An important practice within cultural agency is the importance of the political, social, economic and cultural context in which projects are developed. One of the great criticisms in arts

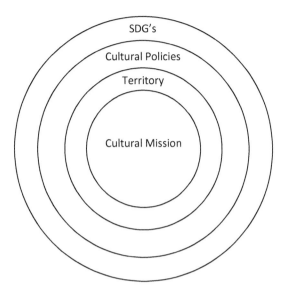

Fig. 12.3 Concentric circles model for cultural agency

entrepreneurship and management training is the focus on the applied components of management (marketing, finance, human resources, etc.), which often indirectly promotes a certain distance from the local context. Research by Henze (2017) on the international dimension of arts management practice demonstrates the great importance that the context has over managers, suggesting that any cultural action must start from the reality of the territory. Regardless of the international or global scope that a cultural practice may have, the original design must start by being based on a local impact unit, being a community, a city or a country. This responsibility and sensitivity to location and place will facilitate sustainable growth.

- *Cultural policies*: Once the geographic field of action has been identified, it is necessary to incorporate a component that regards cultural policy objectives. Although in many contexts it is difficult to understand these objectives from the context of an organisation, this represents one of the main added values of the practice of cultural agency. For example, the economist David Throsby (2012) proposes a list of economic objectives and cultural objectives. In the first category, it includes efficiency, equity, growth, employment, stability in prices and trade balance. In the case of cultural objectives, it includes artistic excellence, innovation, access, cultural identity, diversity and sustainability, both through education and heritage. All cultural ventures or enterprises must incorporate an assessment of how the project advances some of these objectives into their management model, something that has been called the 'cultural return model' (Hernández, 2016).

- *UN Sustainable Development Goals*: The broader scope of cultural management and agency has a direct impact on major global challenges, including poverty, quality education, sustainable cities, decent work and gender equality, just to mention some related to culture and creative economy. Although this component is usually present in the discussions and planning of many organisations, it is difficult to define specifically the area of impact. The Sustainable Development Goals developed by the United Nations represent a robust and well-founded framework that serves as a basis for policy decision-making (*United Nations*, 2017). These 17 goals incorporate most of the social, political, economic, environmental and educational dimensions that countries need to advance. Identifying alignments of organisational performance and the advancement of some of these objectives should be a good practice for cultural professionals.

Conclusions

This chapter brings to the fore of ongoing discussion the practices of cultural agency as an example of the importance of exploring diversity of practice within the discipline of arts management. The different levels of development, the historical, political and economic context, cultural diversity and the profile of communities are all aspects that in some way define the role of arts and cultural managers. In an exploratory way, some examples of this approach have been presented. It is especially worth noting that it is very likely that there are similar or different practices in Asian or African countries, which it would be important to collect in order to have a broad map of practices and to look for more diverse theoretical frameworks.

In the case of Latin America, cultural agency has important social and political dimensions that public policy entities need to understand and address with direct support, in order to overcome the complex reality that affects its communities. Artistic practices turn out to be a vital tool for social transformation, something that implies the challenge of sustainability due to the difficulty of accessing funds, developing stable organisational structures, operational continuity and growth. Understanding the basis of this approach allows the development of international cooperation projects that could support the development of arts and cultural entities and collectives in Latin America.

In terms of college education, the experience of cultural agency that exists in Latin America can provide lessons for the way programmes across national contexts may achieve a better balance between economic and cultural value. To achieve this, a new impact model based on four key components is proposed. Starting from a cultural mission, anchoring impact on a territory, aligning it with the main cultural policy objectives across territories, and, finally, aligning it within wider sustainable development goals, supposes a sequence of levels of impact that reflects the work of cultural agency. Many large arts organisations, such as museums and main cultural centres, are already addressing these components. However, in light of the boom that cultural and creative entrepreneurship has had, there is an opportunity to have these components at the micro level of small arts and cultural ventures. Artists, creatives and cultural entrepreneurs should be aligned with the cultural policy efforts of arts managers and agents. The broader the theoretical framework of arts management, the more holistic the form of training which could be developed. In this way, its full impact in society will be understood and realised.

References

Banks, M. (2017). *Creative justice: Cultural industries, work and inequality.* London: Rowman & Littlefield.

Brkić, A. (2009). Teaching arts management: Where did we lose the core? *The Journal of Arts Management, Law and Society, 38*(4), 270–280.

Buitrago, F., & Duque, I. (2013). *The orange economy: An infinite opportunity.* Washington, DC: International Development Bank.

Connell, R. (2007). *Southern theory: Social science and the global dynamics of knowledge.* Cambridge: Polity.

Durrer, V. (2018). The relationship between cultural policy and arts management. In V. Durrer, O. O'Brien, & T. Miller (Eds.), *The Routledge handbook of global cultural policy* (pp. 430–448). Abingdon: Routledge..

Ebewo, P., & Sirayi, M. (2009). The concept of arts/cultural management: A critical reflection. *The Journal of Arts Management, Law, and Society, 38*(4), 281–295.

Escobar, A. (1995). *Encountering development: The making and unmaking of the third world.* Princeton, NJ: Princeton University Press.

Evrard, Y., & Colbert, F. (2000). Arts management: A new discipline entering the millennium? *International Journal of Arts Management, 2*(2), 4–13.

Galeano, E. (1973). *Open veins of Latin America: Five centuries of the pillage of a continent.* New York: Monthly Review Press.

García Canclini, N. (1987). *Políticas Culturales en América Latina.* Mexico City: Grijaldo.

Hausmann, A., & Heinze, A. (2016). Entrepreneurship in the cultural and creative industries: Insights from an emerging field. *Artivate: A Journal of Entrepreneurship in the Arts, 5*(2), 7–22.

Henze, R. (2017). *Introduction to international arts management.* Wiesbaden: VS Springer Verlag.

Hernández, J. (2013). Differences in cultural policy and its implications to arts management: Case of Puerto Rico. *The Journal of Arts Management, Law and Society, 43*(3), 125–138.

Hernández, J. (2016). The role of arts organisations in cultural policy: The "cultural return" analysis. *International Journal of Arts Management,* Special Edition, Latin America, 56–69.

Jung, Y. (2017). Threading and mapping theories in the field of arts administration: Thematic discussion of theories and their interdisciplinarity. *The Journal of Arts Management, Law and Society, 47*(1), 3–16.

Martinell, A. (1999). Los Agentes Culturales ante los Nuevos Retos de la Gestión Cultural. *Revista Iberoamericana, 20*, 201–215.

Martinell, A. (2009). Las interacciones en la profesionalización en gestión cultural. *Cuadernos del CLAEH, 2*(32), 97–115.

Mulcahy, K. (2006). Cultural policy: Definitions and theoretical approaches. *The Journal of Arts Management, Law, and Society, 35*(4), 319–330.

Ochoa-Gautier, A. M. (2003). *Entre los Deseos y los Derechos: Un Ensayo Crítico sobre Políticas Culturales.* Bogota: La Silueta Ediciones.

Quintero, M. (2013). Cartografías cultural del entre siglos: arte y política en las décadas de 1990 y 2000. In *Historia de las Antillas Vol. 4.* Coord. by C. Naranjo. Series edited by: L. González & M. Luque. Madrid: Editorial Doce Calles.

Rabe, S. G. (2012). *The killing zone: The United States wages Cold War in Latin America.* New York: Oxford University Press.

Ramírez, J. (2007). *Dislocaciones para un disco libre. Política cultural y alternativa socialista en Puerto Rico.* Master thesis, University of Puerto Rico, Río Piedras Campus. Retrieved September 15, 2018, from https://www.academia.edu/6260880/DISLOCACIONES_PARA_UN_DISCO_LIBRE._POL%C3%8DTICA_CULTURAL_Y_ALTERNATIVA_SOCIALISTA_EN_PUERTO_RICO

Rowan, J. (2010). *Emprendizajes en cultura. Discursos, instituciones y contradicciones de la empresarialidad cultural.* Madrid: Traficantes de Sueños.

Sommer, D. (2006). *Cultural agency in the Americas.* Durham, NC: Duke University.

Throsby, D. (2012). *The economics of cultural policy.* Cambridge: Cambridge University Press.

Torres, C. (2009). *La religiosidad popular y la justicia social en los cuentos de Emilio S. Belaval.* Thesis (MA), Centro de Estudios Avanzados de Puerto Rico y el Caribe.

UNCTAD (2010). *Creative Economy Report 2010: Creative economy: A feasible development option* (No. UNCTAD/DITC/TAB/2010/3). Geneva: United Nations.

UNESCO. (2004). Formación en gestión cultural y políticas culturales: *Directorio Iberoamericano de Centros de Formación.* Red Iberformat: España.

United Nations. (2017). *The Sustainable Development Goals report.* New York: United Nations.

Varela, X. (2013). Core consensus, strategic variations: Mapping arts management graduate education in the United States. *The Journal of Arts Management, Law and Society, 43*(2), 74–87.

Williams, R. (1989). *Resources of hope: Culture, democracy, socialism.* London: Verso.

Wyszomirski, M. J. (2013). Shaping a triple-bottom line for nonprofit arts organizations: Micro-, macro-, and meta-policy influences. *Cultural Trends, 22*(3–4), 156–166.

Yúdice, G. (2003). *The expediency of culture: Uses of culture in the global era.* Durham, NC: Duke University Press.

13

Managing Cultural Rights: The Project of the 2017 Taiwan National Cultural Congress and Culture White Paper

Shu-Shiun Ku and Jerry C. Y. Liu

Introduction

Over the past two decades, the main concerns and core values associated with cultural policy have changed dramatically around the world. The importance of citizens' participation and cultural rights has been recognised widely in cultural policy-making (Baltà Portolés & Dragićevic-Šešić, 2017; Miller, 2007; Stevenson, 1997, 2003; Wang, 2014). These changes have extended the civil discourse of cultural policy on cultural rights and induced various practices in local contexts with diverse strategies and debates.

In Taiwan, civil rights and political rights have evolved substantially since the lifting of Martial Law in 1987. With the emerging social and

S.-S. Ku (✉)
Department of Cultural and Creative Industries, National Pingtung University, Pingtung City, Taiwan

J. C. Y. Liu
Graduate School of Arts Management and Cultural Policy, National Taiwan University of Arts, New Taipei City, Taiwan
e-mail: jerryliu@ntua.edu.tw

© The Author(s) 2020
V. Durrer, R. Henze (eds.), *Managing Culture*, Sociology of the Arts,
https://doi.org/10.1007/978-3-030-24646-4_13

cultural movements, the government was pushed to consider the issues of decentralisation, democratisation, and cultural rights in the late 1990s. Two examples of this push are the initiation of the *Community Empowerment Project* in 1994 and the *Declaration of Cultural Citizenship* in 2004 (Wang, 2013). Since then, 'cultural citizenship' and 'democratisation of culture' (civil cultural engagement) have become the essential discourses of cultural rights in Taiwan's cultural policy.

In response to public demands for cultural rights, the new Minister of Culture, in 2016, pledged to strengthen both cultural citizenship and the democratisation of culture by adopting a bottom-up approach to cultural policy—one that would solicit input from a fully participatory public. The Ministry of Culture (MOC) decided to commission the *2017 National Cultural Congress and Culture White Paper* (2017 NCCWP) to the third sector for the first time. With a mixed top-down and bottom-up approach (or a co-governance approach), the National Taiwan University of Arts (NTUA) and the Taiwan Association of Cultural Policy Studies (TACPS) worked together with researchers, artists, and cultural practitioners to co-organise and co-manage the 2017 NCCWP project with government officials in the MOC in order to promote citizens' cultural rights. Consequently, between March and July 2017, 16 cities and counties around Taiwan hosted 15 regional cultural forums and 4 thematic forums that were open to the public and that included the *National Cultural Youth Forum*, the *Forum on the Cultures of New Immigrants*, the *Forum on Cultural Heritage*, and the *Forum on Culture and Technology*.

Beyond the public in-person forums that took place island-wide and collected 731 public comments, government and social-media websites (National Cultural Congress, 2017a, 2017b) facilitated further discussions on cultural rights that eventually yielded 34 online petitions. Then, a preparatory conference was held in mid-August and was followed by a two-day national congress on 2–3 September 2017 in response to the aforementioned public comments and petitions. After analysing these public discussions, the MOC published the *Culture White Paper* in October 2018 as policy directives for future cultural policy.

In the current study, we use this co-governance case to explore the historical context of cultural rights in Taiwan, and to analyse specifically how artists, cultural practitioners, and the public have taken part in the managing, mismanaging, and upward-managing of the 2017 NCCWP project. This analysis also allows us to test the potentials and limits of cultural rights through the co-governing and co-managing process of a cultural project, which simultaneously involves the state, academics, artists, cultural practitioners, and the public.

In our study, we first conduct a historical-context analysis of the past and present cultural projects regarding community empowerment, cultural citizenship, and the cultural public sphere from various sources, including government documents, statements of politicians, and transcripts of debates. Our aim is to cast light on the development and influence of the cultural rights discourse in Taiwan. As the key members of the 2017 NCCWP's executive team, we employed the participatory-observation method to collect all the data. On the basis of these literature review and data, we investigate the project-related management and organisation between the MOC and the 2017 NCCWP executive team in order to further analyse the management of cultural rights and civil cultural engagement. We critically examine and reflexively interpret the management of cultural rights from the initial planning of the project in November 2016 to the end of the project in March 2018. Finally, in this chapter, we explore the implications of the 2017 NCCWP case and the challenges of cultural rights in Taiwan.

Context

The Historical Background of Cultural Rights in Taiwan

Taiwan is located in East Asia. As a small island in the Pacific Ocean, it is geographically surrounded by Japan, the Korean Peninsula, China, Vietnam, and the Philippines. The ancient inhabitants of Taiwan are Taiwanese aborigines, composed of at least 16 groups with their own languages, distinct cultures, lifestyles, and social systems.

Before the Second World War, Taiwan experienced a long process of colonisations by the Dutch (1624–1662), the Spanish (1626–1642), the Zheng family of the Ming Empire (1662–1683), the Manchus of the Qing Empire (1683–1895), and the Japanese (1895–1945). With Japan's defeat at the end of the Second World War, Taiwan claimed its independence and sovereignty. However, according to the agreement made by the Allies at the Cairo Conference in 1945, the ruling power of Taiwan was transferred from Japan to the Republic of China (ROC), which had been founded in 1912 upon the collapse of the Qing Empire and which was controlled by the Kuomintang (KMT) in 1945. In 1949, after suffering military defeats in the civil war with China's communist forces, the KMT-led government retreated to Taiwan. Soon, the Communist Party of China established the People's Republic of China (PRC) in Mainland China while the ROC was relegated to its island refuge. There has been continued hostility and ethnic tension between the ROC in Taiwan and the PRC in Mainland China ever since.

After occupying and declaring its legal right to govern Taiwan, the KMT regime promulgated martial law, which suspended citizens' rights of assembly, association, and political participation. From 1949 to 1987, Taiwan experienced a one-party authoritarian regime whose cultural policy consolidated the KMT's cultural hegemony on the island. This consolidation took place through the KMT's 'Chinese Cultural Renaissance Movements', which functioned to conserve traditional Chinese cultural roots in Taiwan and to counter the ideological principles of the PRC's communist regime (Liu, 2014). The 1970s and 1980s constituted a period of deregulation. The Council for Cultural Affairs (CCA), the highest central cultural administrative institution in Taiwan, was established in 1981 and started to bring about concrete measures for cultural development in preserving and promoting local cultural heritages, some of which were quite vulnerable to Taiwan's dominant KMT-aligned culture.

The abolishment of martial law in 1987 and the subsequent lifting of restrictions on political parties and mass media ushered in a wave of pro-democratisation and pro-localisation projects, which brought about significant transitions throughout Taiwan's political system, economy, society, and culture. These structural changes and policy practices shaped new relations between the government and the people: policymakers started to consult with the wider public and to replace rigid centralisation with a degree of local orientation (Ku, 2015). Moreover, the indigenous ethnic and 'New Taiwanese' consciousness, together with the emerging cultural demands of the population, pushed the government to fundamentally re-evaluate its cultural policy (Liu, 2014). In 1990, the CCA convened the first National Cultural Congress after collecting opinions from 40 small seminars on 10 topics (literature, drama, arts, music, dance, cultural communication, cultural heritage, publishing, cultural administration, and cultural exchange) in 3 main cities including Taipei, Taichung, and Kaohsiung (Council for Cultural Affairs, 1991).

It is worth noting that limits were placed on who could participate in the first *National Cultural Congress*. The CCA invited only select cultural professionals, scholars, association representatives, legislators, and local civil servants. This elite-dominated gathering collected 305 comments from participants; meanwhile, some media criticised the low attendance and the stifling formalism of the event, arguing that cultural development must base itself on local demands (Council for Cultural Affairs, 1991, pp. 211–213).

The Community Empowerment Project and the Emergence of Cultural Citizenship

Prompted largely by the emergence of democratisation in Taiwan after 1987, the CCA started to initiate local cultural projects and, specifically, launched the *Community Empowerment Project* (CEP) in 1994. The purpose of the CEP was to build residents' local consciousness and empower residents to participate in cultural affairs (Council for Cultural Affairs, 1998).

Although the term 'community' emphasised the idea of local perspectives, which quickly appealed to grassroots organisations, early on the CEP encountered many conceptual and practical difficulties. Most people were still worried about being involved in public affairs and had little or no familiarity with the idea of empowerment or with strategies designed to stoke local community participation (Tseng, 2007). Furthermore, the initial projects were rooted in the previous top-down model and focused on the improvement of infrastructure such as the establishment of local cultural centres. This focus reveals that, in Taiwan, the practice of community empowerment still exhibited its path dependency on previous authoritarian structures and struggled to find a reliable new path for the development of the CEP.

In this condition, many professionals and organisations played an intermediate role in developing participatory discourses and strategies. These actors organised civil education and training to mobilise community residents for participation in community public affairs. For example, the movement 'We Write the History of Our Village' encouraged local people to discover their community histories and discuss potential local industrial strategies (Council for Cultural Affairs, 1998). Moreover, community universities, which amount to institutions of lifelong learning for local residents, were set up around Taiwan and offered workshops and classes on public affairs with the aim of helping to strengthen the residents' citizenship consciousness (Council for Cultural Affairs, 2010). Furthermore, a number of groups organised the Association of Community Empowerment in 1997, for the purpose of promoting community empowerment research and policy suggestions that would be both reflective of local perspectives and useful to the government. In this context, the CCA hosted the second National Cultural Congress the same year. The event included six regional seminars and one television symposium entitled *Cross-Century Cultural Construction*. Although the CCA exercised strict control over who could participate in the second Congress, a central issue was cultural rights, which emphasised the sub-issues of minority rights and community empowerment. On the basis of these discussions, the CCA published the first-ever *Culture White Paper* in 1998 with a focus on five points: community empowerment, cultural heritage, publishing and media industries, cultural exchange, and resource integration (Council for Cultural Affairs, 1998).

Within these dynamic processes, the term 'community empowerment' entered the vernacular at the end of the 1990s and was often used in reference to the ongoing development of civil identity through engagement in public and cultural affairs. These community activities, workshops, community universities, and sundry associations have all helped construct the cultural public sphere at the community level, where community residents and cultural workers could actively discuss and develop participatory discourses and strategies.

At the start of the new millennium, Taiwan's cultural policy underwent a significant transformation. The Democratic Progressive Party (DPP), the first opposition party with a focus on Taiwanese identity and subjectivity, gained power in 2000 and applied Taiwan's cultural policy to the task of fostering a 'renaissance of Taiwanese culture' (Liu, 2014, p. 128). The CCA convened the third National Cultural Congress between 2001 and 2002. It featured seven regional forums including the first-ever cultural forum on the outlying islands of Kinmen and Mazu, and was attended by relevant officials, legislators, artists, and representatives of various cultural and local groups, all at the invitation of the CCA. This Congress was distinct from its predecessors insofar as it set up the CCA's first-ever consultant mechanism. Moreover, the CCA organised four keynote speeches (*The Impact of Joining the WTO on Cultural Development, Community Empowerment and National Development, City Visions and Simulations,* and *The Development of the World Heritage Preservation*). Together, the speeches reflected currently trending issues and international challenges. The CCA also arranged for three policy reports to discuss its future plans with participants. These discussions emphasised the establishment of a Ministry of Culture and the promotion of cultural empowerment.

Meanwhile, the CCA initiated the *New Hometown Community Empowerment Project* (New Hometown CEP) in 2002 to strengthen people's cultural identity and cultural rights through programmes that would advocate for participation in cultural activities, improvement of local cultural facilities, preservation of indigenous heritages, and artistic expression within indigenous tribes. These practices of the CEP and community movements laid the foundation for the emerging discourse of cultural citizenship in cultural policy (Wang, 2013). Chen Chi-Nan, the chairperson of the CCA, advocated the concept of 'cultural citizenship' in 2004 and framed it as the core value of the CEP. Then the CCA issued its 'Declaration of Cultural Citizenship', which outlined six key points:

1. Gaining basic human rights, political rights, and socioeconomic rights is not sufficient for the Taiwanese people. We need a new claim on cultural rights.
2. We believe that both central and local governments have a responsibility to organise cultural and art events through which people can practice their cultural rights.

3. We also believe that society as a whole should share in the development and maintenance of cultural and art activities and resources.
4. We believe that citizens should improve their knowledge of local culture and arts as the basis of cultural citizenship.
5. We advocate an identity forged through the arts and culture rather than through blood heritage, region, or ethnicity.
6. Our final purpose is to establish a common society based on culture and aesthetics.

This elaboration of 'cultural citizenship' operates at two levels. The first level of meaning concerns government's responsibility to guarantee everyone's access to cultural resources. The second level concerns people's responsibility to participate in cultural activities (Chen, 2004). In this vein, arts and culture are viewed as the foundation for empowering people. In other words, cultural citizenship encourages citizens to publicly practice their cultural rights. The discourse of cultural citizenship soon grew popular and encompassed a set of ideas that the CCA invoked to justify 'access to' and 'participation in' cultural policy, especially in the relevant projects of the New Hometown CEP.

It has been well noted that the CCA's six-point declaration formed a new approach to the practice of cultural citizenship by encouraging citizens to nurture not only their competence in culture, but also their citizenship and sense of place, all in association with the notion of cultural rights. However, Wang (2013) points out that the CCA still dominated the concept of cultural citizenship and that the government still developed most cultural policy—two patterns that might have weakened the autonomy of communities and their citizens (p. 104).

The Rise of the Cultural Public Sphere and Cultural Rights

The 2010s in Taiwan have witnessed the rise of a cultural public sphere and the promotion of cultural rights. Inspired by the central proposal of the second National Cultural Congress, the CCA in 2011 promoted the Cultural Basic Law, which would restructure the overall cultural architecture in Taiwan. What is even more striking, however, is the development of the cultural public sphere (cultural forums and cultural movements), which has reflected to a great extent the dispute around the *Dreamers* event. This grand-scale stage musical, costing 5 million Euro, was designed for the ROC's centennial celebration and resulted in a controversy over state cultural governance. Many artists and cultural workers criticised the event as a stunning example of the misallocation of state funds (Chi, 2011; Hung, 2011; Lin, 2011; Tseng, 2011). The public criticism surrounding *Dreamers* grew into a cultural movement. A group of cultural activists and arts workers established the Preparatory Office for the Cultural Renewal Foundation (Cultural Renewal) and organised a public petition calling for autonomy and diversity in Taiwan's arts-and-culture scene.

Under the pressure of both the public petition and intense media coverage, for the first time in Taiwanese history, candidates for the office of the presidency, including the then incumbent President Ma Yin-Jeou (2008–2016), participated, in November 2011, in an open debate focusing solely on the issues of cultural policy. During the debate, renowned artists and cultural workers asked the candidates several major questions ranging from the state cultural budget to cultural rights. The three-hour cultural policy debate was broadcast live to the general public on air and online by the Taiwan Public Television Service.

On 20 May 2012, the MOC replaced the former CCA and became the highest administrative body responsible for cultural policy. It expanded its competences from museums, heritage sites, and the arts to radio, TV, film, popular music, publications, and creative and cultural industries. The establishment of the MOC marked a new era for Taiwanese cultural governance. The new Culture Minister, Long Ying-Tai (2012–2014), claimed that cultural citizenship was one of the main goals of the MOC. In line with this assertion, the MOC held a series of Cultural Forums from June to August 2012. The events constituted a response to the *Dreamers* controversy and explored the newly designated role of the Ministry.

Another essential dispute that stimulated the expansion of the cultural public sphere was the cultural protests against the *Cross-Strait Service Trade Agreement* (CSSTA). Signed on 21 June 2013, the CSSTA is a follow-up trade pact within the Economic Cooperation Framework Agreement between China and Taiwan and took shape according to a highly undemocratic process. For this reason, the pact aroused widespread discontent among Taiwanese. Many cultural groups worried that the pact might profoundly damage Taiwan's national security and freedom of the press, especially in the publishing industry (How, 2013). For instance, the Taiwan Cultural Law Association held a citizen's forum on 24 June 2013 and called for a thorough cultural re-evaluation of the agreement based on cultural diversity and cultural citizenship (Liu, 2013). Later, Cultural Renewal held six *Crisis Decryption* fora to examine the MOC's cultural policy. The topics included (1) an overall examination of the role of the MOC; (2) the issue of cultural investment versus cultural subsidy; (3) the mission of the Taiwan Broadcasting System; (4) art's urban dynamic, urban gentrification, cultural governance, and heritage preservation; (5) the ecological thinking of industries and culture; and (6) the effect of the Cross-Strait Agreement on Trade in Services in the publishing industry (Tu, 2013).

The Sunflower Movement, which started with student-led protesters occupying the Legislative Yuan for 24 days to protest against the CSSTA, gave rise to unprecedented discussion and debate in March 2014. The movement not only postponed the agreement, but also led to a new discursive condition of cultural rights in cultural policy. In addition to cultural citizenship, cultural workers and groups acknowledged the importance of 'cultural diversity' and 'cultural exception'. These individuals not only asked the MOC to adopt these principles in all trade agreements and other free-trade protocols, but also proposed a 'cultural impact assessment' in response to the controversy between free trade and cultural values (Liu, 2015).

It is significant that the organisers of cultural forums have shifted from government servants to members of civil society and cultural groups. It is also important that people are increasingly concerned about their cultural rights and would like to play more active roles in policy-making. The TACPS, for instance, was founded in 2015 and started a series of public forums calling for citizens' active engagement in cultural governance. The organisation's aim was to develop a cultural public sphere through various forums and workshops that would both raise people's awareness of cultural policy and foster the cultural monitoring power of civil society.

In short, these various cultural forums, by serving as a cultural public sphere (McGuigan, 2005) organised by civil society for public discussions of cultural policy, have amounted to a contemporary bottom-up cultural movement in which the public openly pursues the kind of culture they want and need, rather than the kind of culture offered to them by the government. Moreover, the forums have expanded the scope of cultural rights from a focus on participation and accessibility to a focus on such policy proposals as those related to cultural diversity and cultural exception. This expansion in scope paved the way for a paradigm shift in cultural governance, as exemplified by the 2017 NCCWP.

The 2017 National Cultural Congress and the Culture White Paper

In 2016, the Democratic Progressive Party regained power, and the new Minister of Culture, Cheng Li-Chun (2016–present), proposed the core concept of 'Taiwanese cultural empowerment' as the basis for a national cultural policy that, in a bottom-up approach, would strengthen cultural democracy and enhance cultural citizenship (Talk to Taiwan, 2016). Moreover, inspired by previous cultural forums and cultural movements, Cheng pledged to convene a National Cultural Congress and edit a *Culture White Paper* that would help map out a blueprint for Taiwan's cultural policy. Therefore, the MOC commissioned a project entitled the 2017 National Cultural Congress and Culture White Paper (2017 NCCWP). Responsible for commissioning the project were two parties: the NTUA and the TACPS. For the first time, the MOC has worked together with NPOs (non-profit organisations) in co-organising and co-managing a National Cultural Congress that would incorporate people's comments into a state-issued white paper about culture.

NTUA and TACPS served on the executive team of the 2017 NCCWP, and, in constant coordination with the MOC, identified five core values: cultural citizen, public participation, diversity and equality, deliberative thinking, and collaborative governance. In addition, the executive team members emphasised the NCCWP's connection to the Cultural Basic Law and, thus, to Taiwanese cultural empowerment. In other words, the 2017 National Cultural Congress is the foundation of both the Culture White Paper and the passage of the Cultural Basic Law, all with an eye towards promoting people's cultural rights. The aim of this three-in-one project is to form a network of co-governance among citizens, civil society, the NPOs, and government to facilitate public participation through deliberative democracy in cultural affairs (Liu, 2018).

In the initial stage of the NCCWP, the executive team reviewed 634 cultural opinions that had been expressed in media between 2015 and 2016 and analysed 105 research projects undertaken at some point between 2010 and 2016 to recognise the main issues that are most concerning to people affiliated with cultural policy. Drawing on this analysis, the NTUA and TACPS negotiated with the MOC and reorganised its five policy planks (rebuild cultural governance and construct a support system for artistic freedom, preserve the historical memories of the land and its people, empower communities and advocate regional cultures, improve culture-driven economic development, and usher in a new chapter of cultural development) into the following six topics presented in Fig. 13.1.

Six central topics for the NCCWP

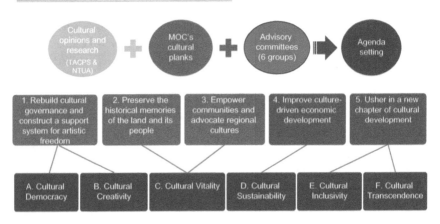

Fig. 13.1 The genesis of the six central topics for the 2017 NCCWP

The six topics (and their sub-agendas) for the 2017 NCCWP are elaborated on below:

A. *Cultural Democracy*: Promoting changes and organisational transformations in the nation's cultural governance. This topic's sub-agendas include cultural values, Executive Yuan Culture Conferences, the Cultural Basic Law, cultural public forums, cultural administrators, intermediary cultural organisations, cultural budgets, and cultural impact assessments.

B. *Cultural Creativity*: Supporting artistic and cultural freedom and enhancing the perception and the quality of aesthetics. This topic's sub-agendas include support systems for creative endeavours, talent cultivation, cultural workers' occupational safety, labour rights, art history, festival and cultural participation, cultural-experience education, aesthetic education, and cultural facilities.

C. *Cultural Vitality*: Preserving the shared memories of people and conserving heritages within their original contexts and historical landscapes. This topic's sub-agendas include participatory mechanisms for heritage preservation and regeneration, mechanisms for the promotion of museum-library-archive cooperation, local studies, community empowerment, national cultural memory, and the regeneration of historical sites.

D. *Cultural Sustainability*: Developing the cultural economy via the construction of a sustainable and culturally ecological system. This topic's sub-agendas include art markets, media and music industries, public media systems, the Cultural Content Agency, publishing, cultural trade and cultural exception, and animation, comics, and games.

E. *Cultural Inclusivity*: Fostering diversity in culture and embracing exchanges. This topic's sub-agendas include cultural diversity, cultural equality and accessibility, multiculturalism, cultural centres in foreign countries, international cooperation, and cultural exchange.

F. *Cultural Transcendence*: Supporting interdisciplinary projects and cultural applications of technology and science. This topic's sub-agendas include cultural laboratories, guidelines for culture and technology policies, cultural databases, civil cultural infrastructure, and smart cities.

Later, the executive team invited six groups of advisory committees to participate in the NCCWP. On the committees were people of many ages representing academics, industries, cultural groups, and civil groups. Every group consisted of some ten committee members. A convener was appointed by the Minister of Culture to chair the committee. As a result, the executive team, the MOC, and the six groups of advisory committees constituted the engine of the deliberative working meetings for the 2017 NCCWP, and all participants co-governed the overall progress of the National Cultural Congress, the Culture White Paper, and the Cultural Basic Law (see Fig. 13.2).

The 2017 National Cultural Congress comprised three levels of gatherings: regional forums, thematic forums, and the National Congress. Each of these three levels has its own specific set of purposes. First, the regional forums offer the general public opportunities to engage in and exercise their cultural rights. From March to June 2017, 12 regional forums took place in 4 regions (Northern Taiwan, Central Taiwan, Southern Taiwan, and Eastern Taiwan) and 3 offshore islands. In regional forums, every participant has 5 min to share opinions or advocate proposals and can register again to elaborate an idea. During the last 30 min

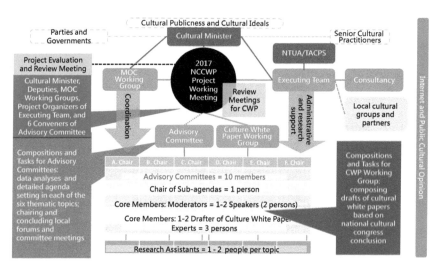

Fig. 13.2 The co-governing mechanism of the 2017 NCCWP

of every forum, local and MOC officials would respond to participants' initial statements or questions.

Held in June and July 2017, four distinct thematic forums, each incorporating ideas from the regional forums, constituted the second type of gathering. The four thematic forums focused respectively on youth culture, new immigrants' cultural participation, controversies surrounding cultural heritages, and the collaboration between culture and technology. Among them, the executive team organised the first-ever *Youth Culture Forum*, which took place in Taipei on 17 June. Bolstered by travel grants and an accessible environment (e.g. sign-language services), about 140 mostly young people participated in the forum by the participatory approaches of 'World Café' (Brown, Isaacs, & World Cafe Community, 2005), exploring the effects of cultural policy on youth culture and seeking feasible solutions to various problems. More specifically, the Forum on Cultures of New Immigrants, which was held in Taoyuan City on 18 June, pertained to Taiwan's approximately one million immigrants, many of whom are foreign spouses, migrant workers, and students. This particular forum discussed ways of improving the cultural participation and cultural rights of immigrants in Taiwan. Supported by translators in the English, Vietnamese, Thai, and Indonesian languages, the one-time event attracted more than 200 immigrants, many of whom expressed concerns and offered suggestions. All the comments and proposals were analysed with the conclusions of the previous regional forums, as the discussion basis for the third level.

The third level of gathering at the 2017 National Cultural Congress was also its peak: the National Congress. Held in Taipei on 2 and 3 September, the National Congress presented ideas hashed out in six groups of advisory committees, all working with the executive team and the MOC to analyse people's opinions from the regional and thematic forums. Before that, hosted by six conveners on 19 August, a preparatory meeting brought together roughly 300 people—encompassing advisory-committee members, scholars, and representatives of civic groups and government agencies—to discuss issues raised at the previous forums. In addition to the public forums that took place island-wide, social-media communications via website and Facebook were used to facilitate the discussions online as well. It is worth noting that the members of the preparatory meeting also considered comments and online petitions that people had submitted to the website ('Citizen Think Tank') operated by the executive team.

Indeed, the two aforementioned types of gatherings, coupled with the online comments and questions, served as the foundation for the two-day National Congress, which addressed six topics, and which held two focus forums. One focus forum was on cultural governance and was hosted by the director of TACPS. At this forum, the Minister of Economics and the Deputy Minister of Education, the Mayors of the special municipality Taoyuan and the small city of Keelung, and the Chair of the National Culture and Arts Foundation discussed—from various perspectives—such cultural governance issues as the controversies over cultural trade and cultural exception, cultural education, heritage preservation, and cultural subsidies. The other focus forum was about the Cultural Basic Law, on which the executive team, in concert with the Taiwan Cultural Law Association, worked to cover such issues as cultural budgets, cultural procurements, cultural impact evaluations, and cultural exceptions. At the end of the National Congress, the Minister of Culture promised the participants that the government would carefully evaluate their advice, would convene a National Cultural Heritage Congress within a year, and would soon pass a Cultural Basic Law.

Overall, there were 4796 participants in the 2017 NCCWP including 20 forums and the National Congress, which, together, accounted for 1763 public comments and 34 online petitions. In attendance at the National Congress were 711 officials from local governments and the MOC, listening to, recording, and replying to the public. Furthermore, the entire process yielded both 46 introduction papers written by advisory committees and forum transcripts consisting of 1.65 million words, all open to the public (see Fig. 13.3). These texts came to constitute the analytical foundation for the *Culture White Paper*.

The advisory committees, the MOC, and the executive team continued to work together in the months following the National Congress in order to analyse and clarify the issues raised in the public comments. In October 2018, the MOC finally published the *Culture White Paper*. By late 2018, the Taiwanese government has put into practice some of the civil proposals from the Culture White Paper, such as the passage of the

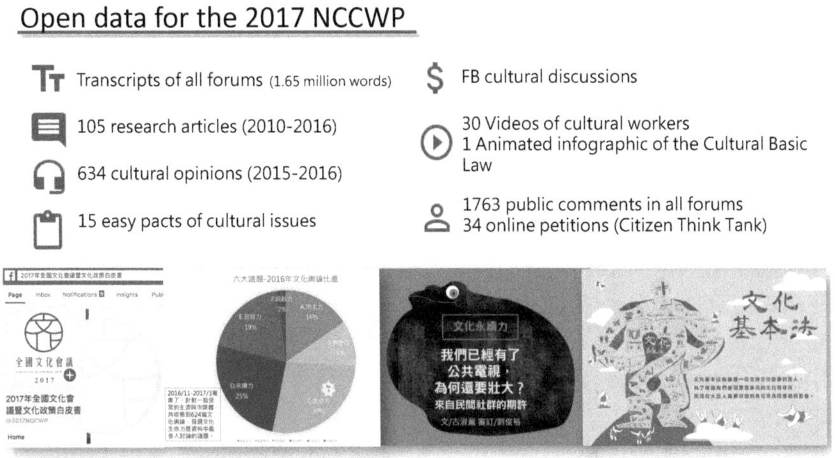

Open data for the 2017 NCCWP

T⊤ Transcripts of all forums (1.65 million words)　　$ FB cultural discussions

💬 105 research articles (2010-2016)

🎧 634 cultural opinions (2015-2016)

▶ 30 Videos of cultural workers
1 Animated infographic of the Cultural Basic Law

📋 15 easy pacts of cultural issues

👤 1763 public comments in all forums
34 online petitions (Citizen Think Tank)

Fig. 13.3　Open Data for the 2017 NCCWP

Cultural Basic Law and the National Languages Development Act, the drafting of the *Public Media Act*, and the launch of the Cultural Content Institute in mid-2019.

Reflective Approach

Cultural rights in Taiwan have improved significantly in the past three decades. After the lifting of martial law, it was obvious that the state was gradually involving citizens in cultural policy. Although the three previous National Cultural Congresses (in 1990, 1997, and 2002) were still very much dominated by the CCA in the process of agenda-setting and participant selection, Taiwanese civil society has managed to insert itself in governmental policy-making by discussing cultural rights—whether in terms of the CEP, the *Declaration of Cultural Citizenship*, or some other topic. It is clear that the 2017 NCCWP reflected an awareness that citizens generally, and cultural movements and civil forums specifically, had developed cultural citizenship after 2012.

The 2017 NCCWP is a case of experimental co-governance between the executive team (NTUA and TACPS), the advisory committees of six topics, and the MOC, with the aim of promoting public participation in the discussion and management of cultural rights and cultural policy.

Discussion

Recent studies on culture and governance indicate that self-governing, decentralisation, or diverse forms of collaboration, participation, and networking among governments and other agents are key features in the promotion of people's cultural rights (Liu, 2018). The case of the 2017 NCCWP presents a similar trend, one in which the executive mechanism has shifted from a top-down process to a co-governance process embracing the state, academics, cultural practitioners, artists, and the public. In addition, the 2017 NCCWP has created a dynamic cultural public sphere where Taiwanese can exercise their cultural rights and express their concerns with, and expectations of, cultural policy. People's growing preoccupation with the 'substantial right' to access and participate in cultural life is evident around the world. As Baltà Portolés and Dragićevic-Šešić (2017) stressed,

> not only the decentralisation of cultural resources or the identification of obstacles and factors which hinder participation in cultural life [are required], but [also] a set of instrumental measures, including the existence of forums or spaces for participation in decision-making and management. (p. 170)

Regarding the 2017 NCCWP, several over-arching points and implications can be drawn from this instance of co-management, co-governance, and cooperation.

In recent years, academic institutions, professional associations, and non-governmental organisations have been enthusiastic about developing cultural policy and cultural participation in Taiwan. In order to facilitate ordinary Taiwanese people's grasp of the 2017 NCCWP's six topics and sub-issues, the executive team (the NTUA and the TACPS) created visual explanations of such ideas as cultural intermediaries, cultural impact assessments, national cultural databases, cultural exceptions, cultural diversity, unreasonable work conditions of cultural workers, and pertinent media factors. The NTUA and the TACPS also produced an animated infographic about the Cultural Basic Law to promote its importance. Through the team's promotion of a government website (National Cultural Congress, 2017a) and a social-media webpage (National Cultural Congress, 2017b), these visual aids spread widely and stoked discussion of the issues. Moreover, the executive team invited actors, actresses, directors, and cultural workers from diverse areas of the social landscape to make 30 videos promoting people's participation in the 2017 NCCWP.

Another important aspect of the 2017 NCCWP is in its implementation mechanism, which rested on collaboration between the MOC, advisory committees, and the executive team. The 2017 NCCWP's operations adhered to a bottom-up model and spurred the MOC to negotiate with the participants of the National Cultural Congress. Through this co-governance mechanism, the three aforementioned players were able to co-manage the agenda-setting and co-plan the 2017 NCCWP and co-analyse the public input from comments of the forums via the deliberative working meeting. In fact, the MOC had initially hesitated to accept the setting of the six groups of advisory committees and the deliberative working meetings but gradually found their importance to the commissioned relationship between the MOC and the executive team. The conveners and advisory committees not only assisted in introducing the issues and responding to people's questions in the forums and the National Congress; in the drafting of the *Culture White Paper*, but also worked with the MOC's officials to develop feasible strategies and improvements. These players were central to the forums, and they worked with MOC officials to draft the Culture White Paper.

It is noteworthy that, shortly before the 2017 NCCWP, the MOC had made a preliminary draft of the Culture White Paper, identifying five project-oriented policy planks and several corresponding projects, all organised by the MOC's seven departments in charge of cultural affairs. However, the final draft of the 2017 NCCWP's white paper rests on widespread public input, which shaped both the forums and the content of the National Congress. The process was bottom-up, deliberative, consensual, and feasible. The result was a values-oriented white paper.

In contrast to the MOC's preliminary draft, the NCCWP version identifies three core values: those of cultural democracy, cultural diversity, and cultural autonomy (Ministry of Culture, 2017). On the basis of these core values, the NCCWP version set 10 primary goals for every major topic (Ministry of Culture, 2017), including the establishment of legislative mechanisms for cultural governance (Cultural Democracy), the examination of grant mechanisms (Cultural Creativity), transparent and equal participation in cultural heritage preservation (Cultural Vitality), interdisciplinary collaboration on the cultural content and the formulation of a *Public Media Act* (Cultural Sustainability), the promotion of cultural equality and accessibility (Cultural Inclusivity), and the implementation of cultural laboratory projects for facilitating cultural technology (Cultural Transcendence).

In October 2018, approximately one year after the 2017 National Cultural Congress, the Culture White Paper was finally published. The MOC had solved several issues raised in the regional forums. For example, in February 2018, the Act for the Recruitment and Employment of Foreign Professionals went into effect, enabling foreign artists and cultural workers to apply for a work permit directly from the government rather than through an employer. In addition, the MOC oversaw the 2018 National Cultural Heritage Congress, at which the sitting minister promised to resolve controversies over heritage preservation. In late 2018, the MOC held seminars about the Culture and Arts Reward Act and the revision of the *Public Television Act* into the *Public Media Act*, both of which were two main goals outlined in the 2018 *Culture White Paper* (Ministry of Culture, 2018).

Taiwan's experience of the 2017 NCCWP shows that the general public, researchers, associations, artists, and other cultural practitioners can work in concert with the MOC and the executive team of the 2017 NCCWP (specifically, the NTUA and the TACPS), to promote cultural rights. One advisory-committee member commented that the most important outcome of this collaboration was the reorientation of government officials away from their ordinary paperwork and towards peoples' core demand of cultural affairs (Wu, 2017).

However, the public's engagement in cultural affairs remains distressingly limited. On the one hand, the 2017 NCCWP was a temporary project. After all, let us be honest with ourselves: the civil servants working in the MOC are still confronted with bureaucratic structures and administrative procedures. Furthermore, the average Taiwanese person remains indifferent to cultural affairs and unaware of the important link between culture and life. As Liu (2018) noted, this project has failed to significantly enlist Taiwan's formidable industrial and business sectors in the essential debate over cultural values' relevant to economic development.

In short, the co-governing and co-managing project of the 2017 NCCWP, while unable to fully resolve cultural problems, encouraged a sizable swathe of the general public to participate in cultural discussions.

Conclusion

This chapter has investigated the evolution of cultural rights in terms of cultural citizenship in Taiwan, and it has explored the case of the 2017 NCCWP to reveal the co-governing and co-managing processes of its cultural policy-making, which involved the MOC, the NTUA and TACPS (the executive team), and advisory committees. The 2017 NCCWP followed a bottom-up strategy to collect the general public's opinions about cultural citizenship and recent cultural movements in civil society. At the same time, the NTUA and TACPS commissioned the 2017 NCCWP as a practice field—as an opportunity to empower people regarding their cultural rights, which include participation in cultural affairs. The 2017 NCCWP can, thus, be viewed as an experimental case of cultural rights practices insofar as the project plugged government officials, academics, artists, other cultural practitioners, and civil society into a collaborative public conversation about Taiwan's cultural policy.

The 2017 NCCWP yielded its fair share of challenges. First, the co-governing executing mechanism between the Ministry of Culture, advisory committees, and the executive team of the 2017 NCCWP set up an operational bottom-up model for future National Cultural Congresses. However, this model depended mostly on the MOC minister's insistence on cultural citizenship and a deliberative strategy rather than on a legally binding requirement of co-governance. Dependence on figureheads rather than on universally binding rules creates an inherently unstable system of cultural governance and, consequently, weakens people's cultural rights. Thus, the Taiwanese government should regulate National Cultural Congresses, requiring that they be held regularly and that they reflect people's views on past, current, and future cultural policy.

The second major challenge arising from the 2017 NCCWP is the management and practice of cultural rights in Taiwan. How can Taiwanese society create and preserve continuity between academics, artists, other cultural workers, the public, and the government? During the 2017 NCCWP, both the NTUA and the TACPS closely collaborated with six groups of advisory committees in investigating challenges that were afflicting Taiwanese cultural policy. With the completion of the 2017 NCCWP, the connection between the executive team and the six advisory-committee groups seems to have significantly diminished, in turn weakening the cultural rights of Taiwanese citizens in policy-making and monitoring.

The case of Taiwan's 2017 NCCWP sheds significant light on the promotion of cultural rights. This case study should be of equally significant value to other countries possessing similar democratic development. The Taiwanese case indicates that a combination of democratic mechanisms, empowering strategies, and co-governing/co-management strategies adopted by the state, NPOs, and fence-straddling entities (e.g. advisory committees) can facilitate cultural rights. Furthermore, everyday cultural links between various cultural groups will benefit public participation in cultural affairs and strengthen peoples' cultural rights.

Regarding further research, it would be fruitful to analyse the development and implications of cultural rights after the 2017 NCCWP. Since 2017, the MOC has subsidised local governments and cultural groups in an effort to conduct annual civil cultural forums that are based on deliberative democracy and that are supportive of cultural citizenship. Taiwan had 9 groups in 2017 and 12 groups in 2018—including 1 local government entity—hosting various cultural forums in which citizens freely discussed cultural policy. The civil cultural forums were people-dominated and local-oriented. Moreover, cultural groups that are unaffiliated with government continue to hold forums and workshops assessing the implications of government cultural policy. For example, on 30 January 2019, the TACPS organised a public forum possessing the rather complex name

Post-Culture White Paper Era: New Civil Actions and Movements. With the Culture Minister been held accountable again to questions about the implementation of Culture White Paper, this forum is a reasonable gauge of the NCCWP's effectiveness. These latest developments and participatory approaches merit exploration in future research on the dynamic practice of cultural rights.

References

Baltà Portolés, J., & Dragićevic-Šešić, M. (2017). Cultural rights and their contribution to sustainable development: Implications for cultural policy. *International Journal of Cultural Policy, 23*(2), 159–173. https://doi.org/10.1 080/10286632.2017.1280787

Brown, J., Isaacs, D., & World Cafe Community. (2005). *The world café: Shaping our futures through conversations that matter.* Berrett-Koehler Publishers.

Chen, C.-N. (2004). Towards a civil society with aesthetics. *Traditional Arts, 44,* 4–5.

Chi, W.-J. (2011, October 17). The country without Dreams. *China Times,* np.

Council for Cultural Affairs. (1991). *The record of National Cultural Congress.* Taipei: Council for Cultural Affairs.

Council for Cultural Affairs. (1998). *1998 Culture White Paper.* Taipei: Council for Cultural Affairs.

Council for Cultural Affairs. (2010). *The record of community empowerment (1994–2010).* Taipei: Council for Cultural Affairs.

How, R. (2013). We only have less than 24 hours. Retrieved October 9, 2018, from https://www.facebook.com/rexhow.dna/posts/609379339096275

Hung, H. (2011). There is no art but politics, no Taiwan but ROC. *Performance Critics Platform.* Retrieved October 9, 2018, from http://pareviews.ncafroc. org.tw/?p=776

Ku, S.-S. (2015). *The trajectory of industrialisation of cultural policy in Taiwan (1994–2012).* PhD thesis, University of Leeds, Leeds.

Lin, T.-Y. (2011). Without quality production, how to make the dreams come true. *Performance Critics Platform.* Retrieved October 9, 2018, from http:// pareviews.ncafroc.org.tw/?p=716

Liu, J. (2013). From "Cross-Strait Service Trade Agreement" to see Taiwan's position on 'national discourse of cultural economy'. Retrieved October 9, 2018, from https://ppt.cc/fx

Liu, J. (2014). ReOrienting cultural policy: Cultural statecraft and cultural governance in Taiwan and China. In H. K. Lee & L. Lim (Eds.), *Cultural policies in East Asia* (pp. 120–138). London: Palgrave Macmillan.

Liu, J. (2015). Cultural governance and the cultural public sphere in Taiwan: Can aesthetic values, social impacts, political power, and economic benefits ever be in harmony? *Arts Management Network, 121*, 18–21.

Liu, J. (2018). *ReOrient: An East Asian approach to cultural policy and cultural governance*. Kaohsiung: Chuliu.

McGuigan, J. (2005). The cultural public sphere. *European Journal of Cultural Studies, 8*(4), 427–443.

Miller, T. (2007). *Cultural citizenship: Cosmopolitanism, consumerism, and television in a neoliberal age*. Philadelphia: Temple University Press.

Ministry of Culture. (2017). *The first draft of Culture White Paper (2018)*. New Taipei City, Taiwan: Ministry of Culture.

Ministry of Culture. (2018). *The Culture White Paper (2018)*. New Taipei City, Taiwan: Ministry of Culture.

National Cultural Congress. (2017a). About. Retrieved February 22, 2018, from https://nccwp.moc.gov.tw/about_front

National Cultural Congress. (2017b). Facebook Group Page. Retrieved February 22, 2019, from https://www.facebook.com/2017NCCWP

Stevenson, N. (1997). Globalisation, national cultures and cultural citizenship. *The Sociological Quarterly, 38*(1), 41–66.

Stevenson, N. (2003). *Cultural citizenship: Cosmopolitan questions*. Maidenhead, Berkshire: Open University Press.

Talk to Taiwan. (Producer). (2016). From heritage preservation to cultural and creative industries: What is the new government's cultural vision? Retrieved October 9, 2018, from http://talkto.tw/talk/13

Tseng, D.-H. (2011, November 3). Making our cultural affairs more accountable. *Taipei Times*, p. 8. Retrieved October 9, 2018, from http://www.taipeitimes.com/News/editorials/archives/2011/11/03/2003517326

Tseng, S.-C. (2007). *Community empowerment in Taiwan*. Taipei: Walkers Cultural Publisher.

Tu, T.-M. (2013). Ministry of Culture will publish the cultural impact assessments within one month. Retrieved October 9, 2018, from http://newtalk.tw/news/view/2013-07-16/38222

Wang, L.-J. (2013). Towards cultural citizenship? Cultural rights and cultural policy in Taiwan. *Citizenship Studies, 17*(1), 92–110.

Wang, L.-J. (2014). Cultural rights and citizenship in cultural policy: Taiwan and China. *International Journal of Cultural Policy, 20*(1), 21–39. https://doi.org/10.1080/10286632.2012.729823

Wu, C.-H. (2017). Further reflection needed for the National Cultural Congress. *ARTCO Monthly* (299), 100–103.

14

Rethinking Cultural Relations and Exchange in the Critical Zone

Carla Figueira and Aimee Fullman

Introduction

Humanity is the cause of fundamental changes to Nature which affect our life on Earth and its sustainability. Our evolution has not been inclusive; on the contrary, its progress has been built on the exclusion, expulsion and destruction of individuals, groups, and physical spaces, as documented by Sassen (2014). But the state of emergency in which we live is also a state of emergences. We borrow this key idea from Homi Bhabha's 1986 foreword to Frantz Fanon's *Black Skin, White Masks*, but prefer to reinforce the plurality of emergences than to use the original notion of 'state of emergence'. The worlds in which we live do feel to be more than ever before in a state of crisis, and we need to encourage

C. Figueira (✉)
Institute for Creative and Cultural Entrepreneurship, Goldsmiths, University of London, London, UK
e-mail: c.figueira@gold.ac.uk

A. Fullman
George Mason University, Fairfax, VA, USA

© The Author(s) 2020
V. Durrer, R. Henze (eds.), *Managing Culture*, Sociology of the Arts,
https://doi.org/10.1007/978-3-030-24646-4_14

approaches and solutions that consider an inclusive future for humanity (Figueira, 2018). The authors of this chapter argue that higher education is key in the pursuit of solutions for our future. We feel there is a need to re-orient arts and cultural management education to meet the demands of our time and this involves a reflection about 'the way we think and are trained; in the subjects and approaches our discipline values and rewards' (Burke, Fishel, Mitchell, & Levine, 2016, p. 501)—which, in our case, includes international relations (IR), arts and cultural management, and cultural policy. We argue in this paper that emerging thinking and action, guided by these disciplines, can support leverage point interventions to tackle the ecological crisis and change the system so that we can become a sustainable cosmopolitan and inclusive human society.

The 'emergence', we are focusing on, is an understanding of cultural relations and exchange as cultural engagement, stressing contextual meaning and commitment. In the following section, we present our views on the state of crisis in which we live, describing the impact humanity has had on Earth and introducing the Critical Zone as an interdisciplinary framework for the study of the impact and the identification of solutions. Then, we argue for the need to rethink cultural relations and exchange as part of the solution to the ecological crisis. In two further sections, we engage with the disciplines across which the authors of this chapter situate themselves—International Relations, Arts and Cultural Management, and Cultural Policy—to explore how these areas of study engage with societal change in connection with the ecological crisis. This discussion allows us to understand how thinking from both these areas can contribute to an emerging new paradigm of cultural relations and exchange, conceptualised as cultural engagement. The concept is finally applied to a discussion of the work of arts and cultural organisations in that area, and to higher education in arts and cultural management.

The Critical Zone

Climate change is demonstrated by severe weather, rising sea levels, increasing CO_2 levels, diminishing Artic sea ice and rising temperatures. It is the single most species altering—and thus life as we know it—critical challenge facing the world and each individual today. The latest Intergovernmental Panel on Climate Change report (IPCC, 2018) warns that there are only a dozen years left to make the needed changes to limit global warming to a maximum of 1.5 °C; the point beyond which the necessary techniques to reduce global temperature are potentially less effective and the impacts on ecosystems, human health and well-being are greater. Negative repercussions on human health will continue to be affected by air pollution, changes in ecology, increasing allergens, changes in water and food quality and supply, environmental degradation and extreme heat. As Scranton (2015, p. 16) puts it: 'We're fucked. The only questions are how soon and how badly'. If you are not a climate change denier—although we all are to an extent (Hamilton, 2010)—you know what we are talking about. Humanity has grown so impactful on the earth system processes that geologists have classified it as a major geological force and named Earth's most recent geologic time period the Anthropocene. This impact is felt in the Earth's Critical Zone, which is the permeable surface layer from the tops of the trees to the bottom of the groundwater, where rock, soil, water, air and living organisms interact (Banwart et al., 2013). The Critical Zone concept provides an interdisciplinary framework for the different sciences to work together to study the consequences of the impact and the interventions that can deal with the changes. To date, the focus has been on leverage point interventions by the natural sciences that can produce big changes in our complex biosphere system. However, the arts, humanities and social sciences have an underutilised and significant contribution to make through their approaches to cultural and societal engagement and (ex)change that contribute both awareness to and knowledge co-creation across societies and disciplines (Galafassi et al., 2018).

The global ecological crisis resulting from the impact humanity collectively has on the planet's Critical Zone is an escapable context any academic field has an obligation to consider in its educational content and pedagogy. We, the authors of this paper, both teach, research and practice in international cultural relations, arts and cultural management and cultural policy, and we are concerned about how thought and practice within our disciplinary systems of knowledge can face this crisis. We are further compelled by the specific environmental and societal contexts we are experiencing first hand in our daily lives: the UK is pushing ahead with fracking and is engaged in withdrawing from its largest international and regional relationship with the EU—the Brexit process; meanwhile, the USA is shifting to become a 'majority-minority' (i.e. a 'minority white') country by 2045 (Frey, 2018), and finds itself afflicted by regular flooding in the largest Naval port in the world, threatening life, property and strategic military interests; all the while governed by a federal administration that is not prioritising climate change and includes key administrators who do not recognise it as a human-effected situation. The political leaderships of both countries are focusing on tightening their borders and keeping migrants and refugees out, echoing concerns of large sections of their populations. Moving beyond nationalism (Harari, 2018) in these countries and elsewhere is imperative, since only embracing a view of humanity as one community, as in the universalist and cosmopolitan understanding, will enable us to tackle the issues affecting our complex biosphere complex, which do not stop at national borders.

Rethinking Cultural Relations and Exchange: Critical Contributions to Solving the Ecological Crisis

The Anthropocene points to humanity as the collective responsible for the biosphere crisis (a devastation that has taken place throughout human history and which is well illustrated by Diamond, 1997), while alternative geological 'cenes' (Capitalocene, Plantatiocene) try to precisely point to who in humanity, and what practices, are to blame. All highlight how many human cultures see the Earth as a given, something to possess and explore. This attitude indicates a separation between nature and culture, and an ideology of the domination of the human being. However, humanity exists diversely in both culture and nature (see e.g. Descola, 2013) and has never really separated from the non-human world (Latour, 1993). Human beings, as individuals and members of groups, form networks. Thus, the authors agree with Latour's (2011, p. 6) observation that the global is generated locally: things are ordered by connectedness as if they were nodes connected to other nodes. Through this connective tissue, humanity lives, creating, changing, and destructing. The current destruction of nature affects the links that humanity builds with it at a deep level: 'climate change can directly challenge traditional or established identities' (Adger, Barnett, Brown, Marshall, & O'Brien, 2013, p. 114), since it can disrupt place attachment. Climate change can have paradoxical effects by simultaneously resulting in: cognitive dissonance between community (often felt as local) change, and perception of climate change as a global-scale problem which enables the formation of new links and forms of action across transnational communities (Adger et al., 2013).

A redefinition of (trans/inter/cross/multi/intra-*national*) cultural relations and exchange is thus required in the same sense that Latour (2016, p. 311) challenges the Empire of the Globe, as the knot tying together

> a certain definition of nature and questions what it means to inhabit a territory, the shape of our common abode, and what it means to be a calculating subject.

We need inclusive human relations, in the cosmopolitan sense of humanity, as one community with shared moral values as enshrined in the *UN Declaration of Human Rights* made possible by *cultural relations*, defined here as experiencing individual trans/inter/cross/multi/intra-*national* opportunities to create mutual trust. As Appiah (2018) notes, we have moral obligations not to screw up the world for everyone, because everyone matters: the cosmopolitan impulse of a shared common humanity where we are socially linked as citizens of the world is necessary. We do not wish to avoid the difficult question of how to deal with those states, groups and individuals, who do not share understandings compatible with cosmopolitan ideals, but this discussion is far too complex to be included in this chapter. Metaphysics of morality are also beyond our discussion scope; thus, we assume our subscription to a certain degree of normative moral relativism, which accepts that we ought to tolerate the behaviour of others even when we disagree—however, we do believe in a universal ethic, which we prefer to attach to transcendent rationality although it may not be totally compatible with some belief systems.

In our contemporary world, when we talk about cultural relations and exchange, often we focus on culture and cultural groups along the dimension of nationality, particularly when we depart from the lenses of IR and also from the point of view of culture as a public policy for arts and heritage. Similarly, anthropological lenses (culture as a way of life) may also reinforce the identification of particular features of material and non-material culture with specific groups. These views may, at times, overshadow what we see as facts: that humanity is one, that no one owns culture, that culture changes over time, that there are many ways in which to be part of a cultural group—identity is multiple and is further complexified by factors such as class, religion, race, or gender (see e.g. Appiah, 2018). Being aware of these different factors is not an invitation to essentialism—we do not believe that one single identity factor speaks for the whole person or for a whole social group; both dimensions encapsulate diversity. Cultural relations and exchange need to be fundamentally inclusive human relations and be conceived as meaningful cultural engagement, stressing contextual meaning and commitment—which we see as crucial elements in the connectedness implied from being part of the cultural nodes on the Earth's Critical Zone.

Trying to find a solution for the biosphere crisis that saves humanity is a difficult task—well, if you think we are worth saving (unlike Gray, 2002). Like other humanists, Haraway (2015, p. 160) has a hopeful attitude to which we subscribe:

> I think our job is to make the Anthropocene as short/thin as possible and to cultivate with each other in every way imaginable epochs to come that can replenish refuge. Right now, the earth is full of refugees, human and not, without refuge.

We often characterise and acknowledge human refugees, those seeking safe shelter, based on their past point of origin, rather than honouring their commitment towards adapting and their ability to survive and thrive in an unknown future. In this sense, we are all refugees and we need to work forward on being an inclusive humanity, considering each other and Nature. Thus, we argue that openness to, and investment in, cultural relations and exchange can facilitate change, as this enables the dissemination and discussion of new ideas, approaches and solutions that can be beneficial to all. Supporting this line of thinking, Adger et al. (2013, p. 114) stress that

> changes in individuals and collective identities can open up possibilities for forming symbolic identities with distant others and 'elective communities' and facilitate new forms of collective action.

Forms of action in which people come together to celebrate common and binding cultural forms that make them act as a group, and which are interrelated, strengthen the nodes that locally make up the global.

Haraway (2015) calls this job of intense commitment and collaborative work and play, the Chthulucene. This is not an easy task, since paradigmatic assumptions of our different socio-political-economic-cultural systems are difficult to transform. Meadows (1999), reflecting on the difficulties of changing systems, notes that in an individual, change can happen in a millisecond, but whole societies resist harder. Individuals are key to a systems change approach (Abercrombie, Harris, & Wharton, 2015; Eisenhardt, 1989), and this point is why we focus on education in a later section of this chapter. However, at the same time, the coming together of individuals in groups through the forging of diverse bonds, which form a diversity of defined systems of thinking and action, is a crucial level of action to enable more systemic change.

Academic disciplines, as systems of thinking and guides of action, are one important level to take into account in the task of changing systems. We now reflect on how our academic disciplines—IR, arts and cultural management and cultural policy—as systems of knowledge and institutional practices that traditionally maintain a separation between society and nature are responding to the biosphere crisis and engaging with societal change. Each discipline encapsulates diverse understandings of humanity and how cultural relations and exchange happen, which are important to support leverage point interventions to tackle the global ecosystem crisis.

International Relations, Societal Change and the Ecological Crisis

IR, as an academic discipline, emerged in the period between the two world wars, driven by a quest for peace. Its main concerns were and are with modern sovereign states and their relations. The nation-state is still posited as the moral and ontological foundation of world order (Burke, 2013, p. 65). The discipline is thus in a unique situation to analyse the rules of the international political system and understand who has power over them. This is an important entry point for change, considering the scale and nature of the crisis.

However, many argue that established IR practices, such as (traditional) diplomacy, can do little for the ecology of the Earth. Criticism on IR's focus on the nation-state and its limitations has forced the discipline to develop into other (marginal) areas, such as critical geography, posthuman IR, global governance, and ecological politics. However, even with these efforts to make IR become a truly international and reflexive discipline (Tickner, 2011), IR seems to have failed humanity because it has been unable to escape the interests of the nation-state, even in universalist and cosmopolitan (we are all one human community) approaches for the realisation of the global common good. Bull (1977, p. 82 in Burke, 2013, p. 67) noted, and it is still mostly true,

> universal ideologies that are espoused by states are notoriously subservient to their special interests, and agreements reached among states are notoriously the product of bargaining and compromise rather than any consideration of the interests of mankind as a whole.

Reflecting on how to move forward, Burke (2013, p. 72) notes that while the state remains important, as a system of democratic representation, governance, resources allocation and international legality, the ontological figure of the state should be replaced by humanity. This humanity is conceptualised by both an historical event of unification of life and death and a global community of interdependence, in which an embodied vulnerability is shared with each other, the earth and the cosmos (Burke, 2013, p. 73). The replacement of the ontological figure of the state by that of humanity is not an easy and quick process to undertake. We assert that education (very much in line with Freire's 1970 thinking), at different levels, and particularly using the arts, can enable formative and transformational cognitive processes for individuals, which will in the long term enable the required change of individual and communitarian archetypes for the re-orientation of humanity. Burke (2013, p. 75) further suggests that

> State responsibilities to their own citizens and the global community of humans must now be discharged together through a web of cooperative action, management, norms and critique that would express our common interest in a more just, secure and environmentally sustainable world.

That web of cooperation oriented by common interests and underpinned by environmental and social justice can be fostered partially by cultural relations and exchange as these are conducive to knowledge and understanding of diverse ways in which to be human and in Nature. Being Earth-worldly, that is 'responsive to, and grounded in, the Earth', embracing the condition of being entangled (meaning being-with or being singular plural, not being truly autonomous or separate, be it at the scale of international politics of quantum physics) is proposed by Burke et al. (2016, p. 518). This proposition comes from the realisation that human activity and nature are bound in a singular 'social nature' (Dalby, 2009). In our view, culture(s) and the arts are diverse projections of that singularity. The knowledge of and engagement with this diversity needs to be developed in each individual and group to develop empathy and humility. This point reinforces our argument about the importance of teaching and learning about cultural relations and exchange, as we discuss later.

Cultural Policy, Societal Change and the Ecological Crisis

If one can, to an extent, regard IR as the public policies of the international sphere, cultural policy can be simply defined as the branch of public policy that deals with the administration of culture (Bell & Oakley,

2015). For cultural policy, the nation is a pervasive level for its development and application, although it operates in a range of scales from and across the international to the local (e.g. from UNESCO, to the Francophonie, to a country or a city). Nation-states encourage the development of culture in an anthropological sense, as their particular way of life (in Anderson's 1983 'imagined community' sense), of which are also part artistic practices and products that they use in their cultural relations and exchanges with other actors. These relations and exchanges have globalised and increasingly diversified. This causes a dynamic tension between cultural homogenisation and cultural heterogenisation that is seen by many as the central problem of globalisation (Appadurai, 1990). The global cultural relations and flows are thus composed of complex, overlapping and disjunctive orders, made up of a diversity that harbours in itself homogeneity and hegemonic processes (Appadurai, 1990). After all, culture is dynamic and typically hybrid. Cultural relations and exchange thus serve as catalyst for the creation of new synthetic cultural expressions (Cowan, 2002).

At an individual level, the important category of national cultural identity is embodied along with many other identities each of us holds. Individual cultural identity has multiple expressions made complex by factors (some legally recognised within cultural rights and diversity policies) such as class, religion, race, gender, generation, sexuality and education. These multiple dimensions of cultural diversity, at a time when individual and social identity is often accepted/highlighted as an unidimensional category, offers paradoxically potential nodes of networking and relationship that can transcend borders and narrow views of individual and group identity and belonging, which can enable a change of minds and hearts towards the building of an inclusive nature-aware humanity. Individuals themselves gain from cross-cultural exchange, via a 'gains from trade' model, as Cowan (2002, p. 12) puts it, since those transactions make them better off by expanding their menu of choice, and we would say, of being.

Culture and the arts are key for societal change and for adapting to the biosphere crisis as, in addition to their worldly quality, they have a dyadic connection with climate (Hulme, 2015). Culture in both its material and non-material aspects is affected by the ecological crisis and at the same time, it mediates every dimension of societal response to the perceived crisis (Adger et al., 2013). We agree with Latour (2018) that art can help us to deal with our current challenges: we need new attitudes and feelings, and artists, writers will be able to provide that through their imagination. Leiserowitz reinforces this idea, noting that art 'provides us with a vicarious experience of something we can't experience directly and so helps us imagine and learn' (Frasz, 2016, p. 3). Furthermore, art is (arguably) more inclusive in not being constrained by standard scientific methods, it can allow the involvement of artists, scientists, citizens and different types of change agents to challenge the status quo (Stockholm Resilience Center, 2018). This is why, we advocate that culture, in a wide sense meaning the arts and heritage, the cultural and creative industries, but also education, sports and leisure, and those who produce it, support it and engage with it, are fundamental in contributing to thinking and action around the ecological crisis and societal change and it is also the responsibility of arts and cultural management education to prepare their faculty, staff and students to be up to the task of developing thinking and action conducive to cosmopolitan conceptions of humanity.

Beyond agency of cultural communities, links between the relatively young fields of cultural policy and arts and cultural management and the area of ecology and climate change are recent, and often emerge through the murky guise of sustainability or in complex association with the words 'culture', 'sustainable' and 'development' (Isar, 2017). Isar (2017, p. 154) finds the engagement of cultural policy and arts management in 'ecological' sustainability to be problematic, because of the conflation of the meaning of culture as the arts and heritage and as a way of life, which is not operationally translatable in terms of public policy, since cultural policy is arts and heritage. However, Isar (2017, p. 157) notes that promoting the transformation and (re)imagination of ways of life 'that can bring us closer to true sustainability' should be at the heart of cultural policy—we agree. A good example of cultural policy research focusing on the popular 'culture and sustainable development' strand of research is that of Kangas, Duxbury, and De Beaukelaer (2017). They propose four roles for culture in sustainable development: safeguarding cultural practices and rights; greening the cultural sector's operations and impacts; raising awareness and catalyse actions about sustainability and climate change; and fostering 'ecological citizenship'. Focusing on the last strand, the authors (Kangas et al., p. 131) allude to the role of cultural policy 'as a tool for creating "imagined communities" (Anderson, 1983)' as a way to foster global citizenship (in a cosmopolitan sense) 'to help identify and tackle sustainability as a global issue'. However, they acknowledge the elusive role of this type of cultural policy, since '[p]ublic policy is, by definition, defined and articulated within the framework of a state that has the political legitimacy to enforce it' (Duxbury, Kangas, & De Beukelaer, 2017, p. 224). Duxbury et al. (2017, p. 225) go on to say that 'To date—and to the best of our knowledge—this principle has not found its place in actual policy strategies'. Perhaps, not a surprising find, as Maxwell and Miller (2017) note that there is a key vulnerability in sustainable development when economic self-interest in the satisfaction of human needs tilts the balance of the relationship between human and non-human beings. They remind us of the need to reflect on changes about cultural activities that are ecologically dangerous or destructive in ways that account for intra- and inter-generational equity, allow for the participation of the affected communities (if not directly, through representatives), and are recognised in international agreements ensuring some inter-territorial equity.

Therefore, it is in practice and at the local level, where it is crucial for policy officials and funders, arts organisations, artists, and cultural professionals to work in eco-cultural policy, informed both by ecological elements and cosmopolitan cultural elements, and also including the development of meaningful cultural engagement (more later on this). Underpinning this stance, is the understanding of the global as local—already discussed and which is for us so important. The level of local impact and awareness within communities is where a systems' change needs to start working urgently, as the most affected by global climate change are often marginalised.

Although there is a long way to go, the arts and cultural sector is increasingly engaging with the ecological crisis. *Raising the temperature: the arts on a warming planet* reported 199 climate artworks and 102 climate art projects between 2000 and 2016 based on a literature review (Galafassi et al., 2018). 'Like a kaleidoscope, the idea of climate is now refracted through photography, cartoons, poetry, music, literature, theatre, dance religious practice, and educational curricula' (Hulme, 2015, p. 9) as well as specific programmes and experiences linking arts, nature, and well-being including eco-arts therapy programmes. *Twelve ways the arts can encourage climate action* offers that the arts can encourage climate action by: 'showing it's more fun to be a creator than a consumer...highlighting the downside of car culture...encouraging human empathy', addressing the 'hope gap', and using stories to 'stand out from the noise' (Leach, 2016, np). Leading by example, the arts and cultural sector can further contribute to the development of sustainable arts and cultural infrastructure by considering: the way they themselves operate in regards to physical implantation in ecologically sensitive areas, sources of energy and control of temperature, light and humidity; the wider impact they may have (movement of people, transportation—including international travel); their own collections and archives for sources of non-traditional knowledge and problem-solving towards today's eco-challenges. Naming as a tool for investment in physical infrastructure is a well-established global practice in development and it behoves us to consider partnering with individuals who are forward thinking and to stress articulation and measurement of environmental and cultural impacts when bidding out new projects. A substantial number of studies is already available in this area of arts/culture and ecology, but this framework of discussion needs to become a more mainstream topic both theoretically and in practice.

Cultural Engagement as a Leverage Point Intervention

Human cultures and their behaviour repertoires are one of the causes and part of the solution for the global ecological crisis. Unfortunately, as Meadows (1999, p. 16) notes in her study of leverage points,

> people appreciate the precious evolutionary potential of cultures even less than they understand the preciousness of every genetic variation,

and she adds:

> I guess that's because one aspect of almost every culture is the belief in the utter superiority of that culture. Insistence on a single culture shuts down learning. Cuts back resilience.

In order for humanity to be able to survive as part of Gaia (Lovelock, 1979), our planetary ecosystem, human cultures need to work together and learn from each other how to sustain (bio)cultural diversity and socio-cultural exchange. The practice of cultural exchange, and the dialogue and cooperation inherent in successful cultural relations in the best of conditions, allows the creation of deep working relationships, exposure to other diverse world views and thus the ability for reflective development and collaborative problem-solving that transcends borders and communities.

The inherent connectedness derived from the cultural nodes on the Earth's Critical Zone, leads us to consider (trans/inter/cross/multi/intra-*national*) cultural engagement, with an emphasis on meaning produced in context, through connectedness and exchange, to be a crucial leverage point intervention that can produce significant change in our complex biosphere system. In this section, we draw from our experience and knowledge as educators, in higher education, cultural policy, arts management and international cultural relations programmes, as well as our experience as, and of, arts/cultural managers and organisations, to examine one of the ways in which this leverage point intervention via cultural engagement can take place.

First it is important to establish why and how organisations operating in arts and culture engage with cultural relations and exchange as an activity. Research presented at the Association of Arts Administrator Educators in 2017, undertaken by the authors of this chapter, built off the 2009 *Art of Engagement: Trends in U.S. Cultural Exchange and International Programming* baseline survey of 134 respondents originally conducted by Fullman (2009). The 2017 *Trends in International Cultural Exchange* survey captured information from 29 arts, cultural and, to some extent, educational organisations, engaged in international cultural engagement and exchange in 140 countries, and yielded that motivations for engagement are predominantly mission related (89.5%), linked to objectives of increased cultural or mutual understanding (78.9%), focused on the development of art and or artists/participants (68.4%), and in support of or to raise awareness of specific social justice or policy issues (42.1%). Respondents indicated that the majority of exchanges include educational workshops (79%) often combined with a visit abroad of international guest artists (Figueira & Fullman, 2017). The overall 10-year trend continues towards embedding capacity building into international exchanges both from an arts management skill set, as well as to build out infrastructure and to support development of artists. The additional management implication is that those in the arts and cultural sector continue to be defeated by international cultural engagement because it is perceived and experienced as being 'too difficult to coordinate'. As a result, 90% of these experienced international cultural engagement participants in 2017 still indicated a need for specific training to support international cultural engagement and exchange. Areas of increased capacity building requirements include: implementing educational workshops, social network outreach, managing partnerships, government funding mechanisms and grant writing and evaluation. For the survey participants that did not take part in international cultural engagement, the most common barriers remain lack of funding, opportunities and staff resources. Evaluation of engagement has been strengthened since the original 2009 benchmark survey, but there is still a notable proportion of organisations that do not evaluate the value of their cultural exchanges, including higher education programmes. However, the emergence of funders requiring additional data over the past 10 years has positively contributed to this trend with 77.8% of participants indicating that their funders or governance structure requires them to evaluate their international cultural engagement/exchanges. Meaningful measurement noted include: achievement of artistic goals, anecdotes and testimonials, audience and visitor metrics, establishment of goodwill, repeat partnerships, partner feedback, programme evaluations, and reviews and experience of the participants. Funding trends lead us back to the importance of local interventions and training; of the 2017 surveyed participants, 92% were funded in some way by their local level/municipal or county government, while only 85% were funded by their own national/federal level government body.

The above confirms how the global is generated locally. Participants are locally contextualised in particular city/region/national cultural ecologies which inform their thinking and structurally enable/disable their international cultural engagement (e.g. funding or visas). It is thus important that those able to influence and determine cultural policy, at different levels of governance, are able to understand the importance of facilitating the means for cultural engagement. How this facilitation is structured connects with conceptions of the individual and of the nation-state—in terms of IR understandings of the working of the international system, swaying more towards nationalism or cosmopolitanism, will have an effect in, for example, releasing funds for nation branding or the fostering of national cultural identity, instead of no-strings attached co-creation. For cultural engagement to work as a leverage point of intervention, policymakers and funders, as well arts organisations and cultural professionals, need to be aware of the potential impact of their engagements, and understand how specific objectives can be achieved. Thus, it is important to note that increased focus on meaningful evaluation, inclusive of eco-impacts, which needs to be embedded from the planning stage—so that those involved understand at what intervention points change is being aimed.

Education is an important guide for action further evidenced by the data above and key to prepare leverage point interventions due to its fundamental role in the development of the cognition of the individual and in creating maps of value and meaning for individual and collective orientation. Focusing specifically on higher education, it should be noted that this level of education is recognised as a public good and has 'the social responsibility to advance our understanding of multifaceted issues' (including climate change and intercultural dialogue) and 'our ability to respond to them' (UNESCO, 2009, p. 2). This role of leading society in generating global knowledge to address global challenges is of great importance and those engaging in higher education as administrators, academics and students should be aware of it and prepared for it. Again, here it is important that not just students are offered education in cultural engagement, but that faculty and staff too are trained and supported—which is not always the case.

Evolutions in higher education are creating an environment where, for both of us working in public universities located in the London, UK and the Washington, DC metropolitan regions, we see the myriad of possibilities for cultural exchange and cultural relations within our own classrooms and local communities. Our 'gateway' cities, defined by their demographically diverse and somewhat cosmopolitan environments, have strong cultural infrastructures that have attracted proportionally large numbers of international arts and cultural management students predominantly representing Americans, UK and broader European citizens and the Chinese. Our students, by their enrolment in a postgraduate education, have made an active commitment to learning and thus to change. They find themselves in multicultural environments that stretch and stress their own identities, values and assumptions as they themselves become translators between their community of origin, their new professional community and their response to the new environment. Everyday exchanges and group work with their peers provide the ground for the development of personal and professional relationships, exposure to diverse world views and engagement in collaborative problem-solving while challenging a student's contextual cultural assumptions, and hopefully developing cultural, social and emotional learning to include: responsibility, respect, compromise, empathy, understanding, compassion, tolerance and humility.

The classroom, as a site of experiential and transformational learning and cultural exchange, is an under-recognised and under-utilised early leverage point intervention of emerging cultural engagement for future arts and cultural practitioners and thought leaders to prepare to fully participate in and contribute to humanity's adaptations to climate change. With the internationalisation of higher education, the classrooms have become a unique site of cultural engagement, the positive results of which we will for sure be able to reap in the long term if the terms of engagement are clearly and positively laid out to reinforce conceptions of humanity as inclusive and ecologically aware through processes that embrace cultural engagement.

*Un*disciplined Food for Thought

The cosmopolitan impulse that draws on our common humanity is no longer a luxury; it has become a necessity. (Appiah, 2016)

Politics, the media and academia each play a powerful role in defining identities, empowering individuals and motivating communities to proactively plan or reactively respond to change. At a time when the future of humanity on Earth is being questioned and while confusion around the blurring analytical boundaries of domestic and external affairs has been reactively focused around migration and security in order to protect the status quo, more needs to be done to consider ways in which we can think about how individuals and groups can act as mediators and translators between their national, civil and cultural national/group identities and cosmopolitanism. These issues affect our complex biosphere, which do not stop at (national) borders. Thus, we fully embrace the potential of arts and cultural leaders trained as interdisciplinary and cross-cultural facilitators through cultural exchange to address the 'hope gap' and contribute meaningfully to problem-solving processes.

As undisciplined academics and practitioners straddling IR, arts and cultural management and cultural policy, we believe that theory and practice should guide humans to being better citizens of the world, working for a common good. Furthermore, we believe that there are critical leverage points of intervention with the ability to assemble alternative world and discipline views between IR, arts and cultural management and cultural policy, as these disciplines share a commitment to exploring relationships, building infrastructure and capacity and addressing how we can meaningfully and inclusively live together at the highest level of human development and quality of life.

Working as educators, researchers, and practitioners of international cultural relations within the framework of the Critical Zone, prompts us to consider the higher education classroom, as a key site for cultural learning and encounters, an early leverage point of intervention in the biosphere system that is able to inform thinking and guide action for individuals and collective action. The cultural engagement produced there can change societies by bringing diverse individuals and groups together and enabling the dissemination, discussion and implementation of new ideas, approaches and solutions needed to combat the current and future impacts of climate change on macro and micro levels.

References

Abercrombie, R., Harris, E., & Wharton, R. (2015). *Systems change: A guide to what it is and how to do it.* London: Lankelly Chase Foundation.
Adger, W. N., Barnett, J., Brown, K., Marshall, N., & O'Brien, K. (2013). Cultural dimensions of climate change impacts and adaptation. *Nature Climate Change.* https://doi.org/10.1038/NCLIMATE1666

Anderson, B. (1983). *Imagined communities: Reflection on the origins and spread of nationalism*. London: Verso.

Appadurai, A. (1990). Disjuncture and difference in the global culture economy. *Theory, Culture, and Society, 7*, 295–310.

Appiah, K. A. (2016, November 9). There is no such thing as Western civilisation. *The Guardian*. Retrieved October 6, 2018, from https://www.theguardian.com/world/2016/nov/09/western-civilisation-appiah-reith-lecture

Appiah, K. A. (2018). *The lies that bind: Rethinking identity*. New York and London: Liveright Publishing Corporation.

Banwart, S. A., Chorover, J., Gaillardet, J., Sparks, D., White, T., Anderson, S., et al. (2013). *Sustaining Earth's critical zone: Basic science and interdisciplinary solutions for global challenges*. The University of Sheffield. Retrieved October 6, 2018, from https://www.czen.org/sites/default/files/Sustaining-Earths-Critical-Zone_FINAL-290713.pdf

Bell, D., & Oakley, K. (2015). *Cultural policy*. London: Routledge.

Burke, A. (2013). The good state, from a cosmic point of view. *International Politics, 50*(1), 57–76. https://doi.org/10.1057/ip.2012.28

Burke, A., Fishel, S., Mitchell, A., & Levine, D. J. (2016). Planet politics: A manifesto from the end of IR. Conference article. *Millennium: Journal of International Studies, 44*(3), 499–523. https://doi.org/10.1177/0305829816636674

Cowan, T. (2002). *Creative destruction: How globalization is changing the world's cultures*. Princeton, NJ: Princeton University Press.

Dalby, S. (2009). *Security and environmental change*. Cambridge: Polity Press.

Descola, P. (2013). *Beyond nature and culture*. Chicago: Chicago University Press.

Diamond, J. (1997). *Guns, germs, and steel*. London: Vintage.

Duxbury, N., Kangas, A., & De Beukelaer, C. (2017). Cultural policies for sustainable development: Four strategic paths. *International Journal of Cultural Policy, 23*(2), 214–230. https://doi.org/10.1080/10286632.2017.1280789

Eisenhardt, K. M. (1989). Agency theory: An assessment and review. *Academy of Management Review, 14*(1), 57–74.

Figueira, C. (2018). *Strengthening global cultural relations*. Thought paper for IFA. Retrieved October 6, 2018, from http://research.gold.ac.uk/24776/

Figueira, C., & Fullman, A. (2017). *Trends in international cultural exchange*. Presented to the Association of Arts Administrator Educators, Edinburgh, UK, June 2, 2017.

Frasz, A. (2016, Fall). Can art change how we think about climate change? *GIA Reader, 27*(3). Retrieved January 10, 2019, from https://www.giarts.org/article/can-art-change-how-we-think-about-climate-change

Freire, P. (1970). *Pedagogy of the oppressed*. London: Penguin.

Frey, W. H. (2018). The US will become 'minority white' in 2045, Census projects: Youthful minorities are the engine of future growth. Retrieved January 10, 2019, from https://www.brookings.edu/blog/the-avenue/2018/03/14/the-us-will-become-minority-white-in-2045-census-projects/

Fullman, A. (2009). *The art of engagement: Trends in US cultural exchange and international programming.* New York: Robert Sterling Clark Foundation.

Galafassi, D., Kagan, S., Milkoreit, M., Heras, M., Bilodeau, C., Bourke, S. J., et al. (2018). 'Raising the temperature': The arts on a warming planet. *Current Opinion in Environmental Sustainability, 31,* 71–79. https://doi.org/10.1016/j.cosust.2017.12.010

Gray, J. (2002). *Straw dogs: Thoughts on humans and other animals.* London: Granta Books.

Hamilton, C. (2010). *Requiem for a species.* London: Earthscan.

Harari, Y. N. (2018). Moving beyond nationalism. *The Economist: The World in 2019,* pp. 79–80.

Haraway, D. (2015). Anthropocene, capitalocene, plantationocene, chthulucene: Making kin. *Environmental Humanities, 6,* 159–165.

Hulme, M. (2015). Climate and its changes: A cultural appraisal. *Geo: Geography and Environment, 2,* 1–11. https://doi.org/10.1002/geo2.5

IPCC. (2018). Summary for policymakers. In V. Masson-Delmotte, P. Zhai, H. O. Pörtner, D. Roberts, J. Skea, et al. (Eds.), *Global warming of 1.5 °C. An IPCC Special Report on the impacts of global warming of 1.5 °C above pre-industrial levels and related global greenhouse gas emission pathways, in the context of strengthening the global response to the threat of climate change, sustainable development, and efforts to eradicate poverty.* Geneva: World Meteorological Organization.

Isar, Y. R. (2017). 'Culture', 'sustainable development' and cultural policy: A contrarian view. *International Journal of Cultural Policy, 23*(2), 148–158. https://doi.org/10.1080/10286632.2017.1280785

Kangas, A., Duxbury, N., & De Beukelaer, C. (2017). Introduction: Cultural policies for sustainable development. *International Journal of Cultural Policy, 23*(2), 129–132. https://doi.org/10.1080/10286632.2017.1280790

Latour, B. (1993). *We have never been modern.* Cambridge, MA: Harvard University Press.

Latour, B. (2011). *Waiting for Gaia. Composing the common world through arts and politics.* A lecture at the French Institute, London, November 2011. Retrieved October 3, 2018, from http://www.bruno-latour.fr/sites/default/files/124-GAIA-LONDON-SPEAP_0.pdf

Latour, B. (2016). *Onus Orbis Terrarum*: About a possible shift in the definition of sovereignty. *Millennium: Journal of International Studies, 44*(3), 305–320. https://doi.org/10.1177/0305829816640608

Latour, B. (2018). *The critical zone of science and politics: An interview with Bruno Latour.* Steve Paulson interviews Bruno Latour, February 23, 2018. Retrieved October 3, 2018, from https://lareviewofbooks.org/article/the-critical-zone-of-science-and-politics-an-interview-with-bruno-latour/

Leach, A. (2016, April 25). 12 ways the arts can encourage climate action. *The Guardian.* Retrieved December 15, 2018, from https://www.theguardian.com/global-development-professionals-network/2016/apr/25/12-ways-the-arts-can-encourage-climate-action

Lovelock, J. (1979). *Gaia: A new look at life on earth.* Oxford: Oxford University Press.

Maxwell, R., & Miller, T. (2017). Greening cultural policy. *International Journal of Cultural Policy, 23*(2), 174–185. https://doi.org/10.1080/10286632.2017.1280786

Meadows, D. (1999). *Leverage points: Places to intervene in a system.* Hartland, VT: The Sustainability Institute.

Sassen, S. (2014). *Expulsions. Brutality and complexity in the global economy.* Cambridge, MA: Harvard University Press.

Scranton, R. (2015). *Learning to die in the Anthropocene.* San Francisco: City Lights Books.

Stockholm Resilience Center. (2018). *The art of transformation.* Retrieved December 15, 2018, from https://www.stockholmresilience.org/research/research-news/2018-02-19-the-art-of-transformation.html

Tickner, J. A. (2011). Dealing with difference: Problems and possibilities for dialogue in international relations. *Millennium: Journal of International Studies, 39*(3), 607–618. https://doi.org/10.1177/0305829811400655

UNESCO. (2009). *World conference on higher education: The new dynamics of higher education and research for societal change and development,* UNESCO, Paris, July 5–8, 2009. Retrieved January 10, 2019, from http://unesdoc.unesco.org/images/0018/001832/183277e.pdf

Index[1]

[1] Note: Page numbers followed by 'n' refer to notes.

© The Author(s) 2020
V. Durrer, R. Henze (eds.), *Managing Culture*, Sociology of the Arts,
https://doi.org/10.1007/978-3-030-24646-4

341